M000286210

Arts Evaluation and Assessment

Rekha S. Rajan • Ivonne Chand O'Neal
Editors

Arts Evaluation and Assessment

Measuring Impact in Schools and Communities

palgrave
macmillan

Editors
Rekha S. Rajan
PANCH Research, LLC
Chicago
IL, USA

Ivonne Chand O'Neal
MUSE Research, LLC
Kensington
MD, USA

ISBN 978-3-319-64115-7   ISBN 978-3-319-64116-4   (eBook)
https://doi.org/10.1007/978-3-319-64116-4

Library of Congress Control Number: 2017955047

Cover illustration: © zhazhin_sergey/ iStock / Getty Images Plus

Printed on acid-free paper

This Palgrave Macmillan imprint is published by Springer Nature
The registered company is Springer International Publishing AG
The registered company address is: Gewerbestrasse 11, 6330 Cham, Switzerland

For our children,
Jagan, Madhavi, Arjun, Ishaan, and Asha,
The next generation of artists, innovators, scholars, and creative thinkers

As Editors of this collection, it is with deep respect and admiration that we pay tribute to Dr. James Catterall, who passed away during the publication of this book. Throughout his illustrious career, Dr. Catterall shared his love of the arts, his passion for creativity, and his intellectual curiosity. His numerous publications and contributions to the field included chapter contributions to the seminal work, Champions of Change: The Impact of the Arts on Learning (1999), which influenced a generation of arts researchers, educators, funding agencies, and students. His scholarship has changed the landscape of arts research, and we are profoundly honored to publish his last written work in these pages.

Rekha and Ivonne

FOREWORD BY MICHAEL QUINN PATTON

Evaluating music, theater, musical theater, dance, opera, and multimedia arts is a daunting and controversial challenge. The postulate that "beauty is in the eye of the beholder" has become axiomatic in modern society, a way of acknowledging that people have different tastes, value preferences, and responses to artistic creations of all kinds. Culture, education, religion, socioeconomic status, politics, and aesthetic sensibilities all come into play in valuing, interpreting, judging, and appreciating, or deprecating, artistic creations and endeavors. Now, add yet another layer of complexity by taking on the challenge of *evaluating arts programs*. This means evaluating the impacts of music, theater, musical theater, dance, opera, and multimedia arts on students, teachers, teaching artists, and administrators. That's the challenge this book takes on—and does so with methodological creativity, rigor, and savvy.

This book is important because the arts are important and cannot be taken for granted. Evaluating arts programs must be understood in the larger context of enduring debate about the role of arts in education specifically and art's contributions to society more generally. For another foundational aphorism is that *humans do not live by bread alone*. Art matters. Artistic expression and appreciation are at the core of what makes us human. The inclination, indeed, the compulsion and mandate to evaluate artistic expression, is also an essential trait of our shared humanity.

An Ancient Framework for Evaluation of the Arts

The chapters in this book offer exemplary evaluation case studies of specific arts programs. The cases report on the goals of the program, identify key stakeholders for the evaluation, and present the primary evaluation questions, methods used, data collected, and key findings. The cases also report on how the findings were used by educators, policy makers, and funders. But how are you, the reader, to judge these evaluations of arts programs? Let me offer an ancient framework that emphasizes inspirational artistic criteria.

Greek philosopher Plato (428 B.C.E.–348 B.C.E.), student of Socrates and teacher of Aristotle, offered three noble and majestic evaluation criteria that still resonate today: truth, beauty, and justice. Ernest House, one of the field of evaluation's pioneering thought leaders, has articulated how these criteria are still relevant today and can be applied to assess the validity of any evaluation:

> Truth is the *attainment* of arguments soundly made, beauty is the *attainment* of coherence well wrought, and justice is the *attainment* of politics fairly done. (House, 2014, p. 31)

House argued that if an evaluation is untrue, or incoherent, or unjust, it is invalid. So an evaluation, any evaluation, must be true, coherent, and just. All three criteria are necessary, he insisted. Jane Davidson, one of the profession's emergent thought leaders, has added her own provocative and inspirational twist to House's criteria:

> True "beauty" in evaluation is a clearly reasoned, well-crafted, coherent evaluation story that weaves all three of these together to unlock both truth and justice with breathtaking clarity. ...I'd like to flip House's idea on its head. What if beauty wasn't merely about how well the evaluative story is told? What if the *process* of creating a clear, compelling, and coherent (beautiful) evaluative story was in fact the key to unlocking validity (truth) and fairness (justice)? (Davidson, 2014, p. 43)

Artistic Inspiration Through Valid Evaluation

Mastery of artistic technique is but one element of meaningful and inspiring art. Methodological rigor is but one dimension of evaluation excellence. Art is too important to be reduced to technique, and evaluation is too important to be reduced to method. Arts evaluation, then, must meet standards of evaluation excellence while offering inspiration for the value and meaningfulness of art to society. In my judgment, this book succeeds in fulfilling both aspirations. But judge for yourself, for beauty does, indeed, lie in the eye of the beholder, and both art and arts evaluation reveal truths and invite us to reflect on the meaning and manifestation of justice as experienced and portrayed through artistic creations and access to quality arts education.

Saint Paul, MNM   Michael Quinn Patton

References

Davidson, E. J. (2014). How "beauty" can bring truth and justice to life. *New Directions for Evaluation, 142* (Summer), 31–43.

House, E. R. (2014). Origins of the ideas in *evaluating with validity. New Directions for Evaluation, 142* (Summer), 9–16.

CONTENTS

NOTES ON CONTRIBUTORS

Hal Abeles is Director and Professor of Music and Music Education at Teachers College, Columbia University where he also serves as the Co-director of the Center for Arts Education Research. He has written numerous articles and books on music education. He is the co-author of the *Foundations of Music Education* and the co-editor of *Critical Issues in Music Education: Contemporary Theory and Practice*. His research has focused on the evaluation of community-based arts organizations, the assessment of instrumental instruction, the sex-stereotyping of musical instruments, and the evaluation of applied music instructors. Dr. Abeles has served as program evaluator for numerous arts partnerships, including Carnegie Hall, The Cleveland Orchestra, the MacArthur Foundation, Arts Centered Education—Detroit, The Baltimore Symphony, Lincoln Center Institute, The William Penn Foundation, The New Jersey Symphony, The Hartford Symphony, and Amp Up—New York City.

Ross Anderson serves as PI for a multi-year federally funded arts education model development, research, and dissemination project working with five local middle schools to increase creative teaching and learning opportunities through rigorous integration of the arts across content areas. Mr. Anderson's work aims to develop the creative engagement of teachers and school communities, at large, in the design and delivery of learning that taps the diversity of students' talents, cultures, and interests. From a constructivist perspective, Ross researches the growth trajectory of skills and dispositions, such as creativity, persistence, self-efficacy, and motivation in school during adolescence. As Prinicpal Researcher at

Inflexion, he serves as a strategic thought partner in support of responsive program development and evaluation, multimethod research, and cross-sector collaboration.

Johanna Blakley is the managing director at the Norman Lear Center, a think tank that explores the convergence of entertainment, commerce, and society. Based at the University of Southern California's Annenberg School for Communication and Journalism, she is co-principal investigator on the Media Impact Project, a hub for collecting, developing, and sharing approaches for measuring the impact of media. Blakley received her Ph.D. in English from the University of California, Santa Barbara, and she teaches courses on transmedia storytelling at USC.

James S. Catterall In July 2011, Dr. Catterall co-founded the Centers for Research on Creativity based in Los Angeles and London, UK. Dr. Catterall is Professor Emeritus and past Chair of the Faculty at the UCLA Graduate School of Education and Information Studies and an Affiliate Faculty member at the UCLA Center for Culture, Brain, and Development. The author of groundbreaking research and analysis in arts education, Dr. Catterall focused on measurement of children's cognitive and social development and motivation in the context of learning in the arts, before expanding his research into the burgeoning field of creativity and youth development. He is the author of *The Creativity Playbook* (2015) and *Doing Well and Doing Good by Doing Art*, a 12-year longitudinal study of the effects of learning in the arts on the achievements and values of young adults (2009). In 2012, Dr. Catterall and colleagues Prof. Susan Dumais (LSU) and Prof. Gillian Hampden-Thompson (York University, UK) published *The Arts and Achievement in At-risk Youth: Findings from Four Longitudinal Studies*, published by the National Endowment for the Arts. Professor Catterall holds degrees in economics (with honors) from Princeton University and Public Policy Analysis from the University of Minnesota; he holds a Ph.D. in Educational Policy Analysis/Learning Studies from Stanford University. He is an accomplished cellist and bassist and performs with the Topanga Symphony Orchestra. On page vii, please read the editors' tribute to Dr. James Catterall (1948–2017). May he rest in peace.

Kelly Fisher is the Director of Dissemination, Translation, and Education at the Johns Hopkins University Science of Learning Institute and an Assistant Professor of Education. Kelly's research draws upon multiple disciplines—developmental science, industrial-organizational psychology, implementation science, education, and public policy—to improve learning and development in children and adults. Kelly also works with community organizations, businesses, and government to translate the science of learning research into new educational programming and evaluate its effectiveness. Prior to her current position, Kelly was an Executive Branch Science and Technology Fellow in Washington, DC, a fellowship sponsored by the Society for Research and Child Development (SRCD) and the American Association for the Advancement in Science (AAAS), where she initiated and directed research aimed at improving the understanding of organizational capacity and data-driven decision making in early childhood programs. Kelly received a Ph.D. in Developmental Psychology from Temple University and a M.S. in Industrial-Organizational Psychology from Missouri State University.

Kristin Gagnier is the Outreach and Evaluation Specialist at the Science of Learning Institute and Assistant Research Scientist in the Department of Cognitive Science at Johns Hopkins University. Kristin oversees the institute's mission of connecting science to practice. She partners with schools, museums, government organizations, and policymakers to advance research and translate the science of learning research into evidence-informed practices. Kristin's work is motivated by her passion for improving learning outcomes by connecting research and practice and based on her interdisciplinary training in cognitive science, psychology, and education.

Don Glass Ph.D., is a visual artist, learning designer, and developmental evaluator based in Washington, DC area. His work focuses on the integration of *inclusive arts curriculum design* and *developmental evaluation* strategies into the ongoing professional development of educators in and outside of schools. Central to this work are clear, meaningful learning goals, systems of assessment and feedback, and supports and options to address learning variability and foster expert learning. Dr. Glass is currently the Research Manager for the Kennedy Center and has held positions at the National Commission on Teaching and America's Future and the Annenberg Institute for School Reform at Brown University. He was also a Universal Design for Learning Leadership Fellow at Boston College. As an independent consultant, he has done design and evaluation projects for a wide range of arts and cultural organizations.

Jeanette Goddard holds a Ph.D. in Comparative Literature from the University of Wisconsin, Madison. While her scholarly work focuses on comedies in early modern Europe, as an ACLS public fellow she curated education-focused public programming for the Chicago Humanities

Festival. She is currently an assistant professor of the Humanities and Communication Department at Trine University and a board member of the University's Humanities Institute.

Mary Hafeli is Director and Professor of Art and Art Education at Teachers College, Columbia University. She is the author of *Exploring Studio Materials: Teaching Creative Art Making to Children* and co-editor of *Conversations in Art: The Dialectics of Teaching and Learning*. She has also written numerous articles and book chapters on art education. Current research projects include a study of youth and adult perspectives on "good" teaching in art and visual and literary art forms and practices as methods in qualitative research. A recipient of the Manual Barkan Memorial Award, the Mary Rouse Award, and the Marilyn Zurmuehlen Award, all from the National Art Education Association for scholarly contributions to the field, she serves as chair of the National Art Education Association's Research Commission.

Jessica Hamlin is a Clinical Assistant Professor in the Art+Education program at the Steinhardt School for Culture, Education, and Human Development at New York University. She previously served as Art21's Director of Education facilitating professional development and programming as well as generating curriculum and resources for educators across disciplines. Her work is focused on the intersections between contemporary art, critical pedagogy, and public education.

Lois Hetland is Professor of Art Education at the Massachusetts College of Art and Design and a cognitive psychologist, researcher, and artist-teacher. She taught PK-12 students for 17 years before focusing on undergraduates, graduate students, and practicing educators. Her research addresses arts cognition and professional practice in education venues, and she consults frequently across the USA and internationally on arts education, arts-integration, and arts assessment. She is co-author of *Studio Thinking 2: The Real Benefits of Visual Arts Education* (2013, 2nd Edition) and is now co-authoring *Studio Thinking in the Elementary School*, due out in 2018.

Steven Holochwost is a developmental psychologist whose work examines the effects of poverty and its correlates on children's development and how programs and policies can mitigate those effects. Over the past ten years, he has worked in government, academia, and research firms as a researcher and program evaluator focusing on education, with an emphasis on early childhood education and access to high-quality arts education. His areas of specialization include the use of mixed quantitative and qualitative methods in program evaluation, the application of advanced analytics to longitudinal data, and the incorporation of physiological measurement into studies of child development. Dr. Holochwost is Senior Research Scientist and Associate Principal at WolfBrown. Before joining WolfBrown, Dr. Holochwost was Associate Director of Research at the Early Learning Center and, prior to that, Senior Assistant Child Advocate with the Office of the Child Advocate for the State of New Jersey.

Rob Horowitz is a consultant to arts organizations, school districts, and foundations. He is a contributing author to *Champions of Change: The Impact of the Arts on Learning*, published by the President's Committee on the Arts and Humanities and the Arts Education Partnership, and *Critical Links: Learning in the Arts and Student Academic and Social Development*, a compendium of 62 studies of arts learning and its connections to broader human development. As a consultant for Jazz at Lincoln Center, he wrote the instructional content of *Jazz in the Schools*, a National Endowment for the Arts curriculum that "explores jazz as an indigenous American art form and a means to understand American history." Dr. Horowitz helped develop numerous educational partnerships throughout the country and has conducted over 100 program evaluations for organizations, such as the Kennedy Center, National Endowment for the Arts, Jazz at Lincoln Center, Carnegie Hall, and ArtsConnection, and has served as researcher for numerous federal, state, and private grants.

Wendy A. Jones Former Director of Education, Minnesota Historical Society, has over 29 years' experience developing educational programs and exhibitions. She led numerous initiatives to transform MNHS's delivery of learning experiences to diverse audiences across varied platforms, including live interpretation, museum theater, static exhibits, interactive video conferencing, and mobile technology. She is a passionate proponent of free-choice learning, audience-centered design, and DIY evaluation, and she strives to be a "space maker" who gives her teams room for failure and growth. One of the best decisions she ever made was to hire Jennifer Sly to lead the *Play the Past* project.

Julie Kendig B.F.A., M.A., is pursuing a Ph.D. in education with a focus on social justice at Claremont Graduate University. She has served as a Research Associate at the Centers for Research on Creativity, where, in addition to working with The Wooden Floor, she was the lead researcher to the California Arts Council's arts for incarcerated youth programs and worked with the Alameda County Office of Education through a US Department of Education Arts in Education Model Development and Dissemination grant. Ms. Kendig is also the Education Director at a creative youth development organization called A.R.T.S. (A Reason to Survive) in National City, CA. Ms. Kendig volunteers for the San Diego Housing Commission's Homeless Division and Habitat for Humanity and stays active in a local reader's theatre group.

Brian Kisida is an Assistant Research Professor in the Department of Economics and the Truman School of Public Affairs at the University of Missouri. He has over a decade of experience in rigorous program evaluation and policy analysis. He has extensive experience conducting randomized controlled trials and has co-authored multiple experimental impact evaluation reports through the Institute of Education Sciences at the US Department of Education.

The dominant theme of his research focuses on identifying effective educational options and experiences for at-risk students that can close the achievement gap, the experience gap, and the attainment gap. Increasingly, his research agenda has evolved toward examining policy outcomes broader than student achievement on standardized tests, such as non-cognitive outcomes, cultural and social capital, student engagement, civic outcomes, and long-term educational attainment. His academic publications include articles in the *Journal of Policy Analysis and Management, Sociology of Education, Educational Researcher, Journal of Research on Educational Effectiveness, Economics of Education Review, Policy Studies Journal, School Effectiveness and School Improvement,* and *Education and Urban Society.* His work has been cited in congressional testimony before the US House and Senate, and it has appeared in numerous media outlets, including *The New York Times, USA Today, The Washington Post, The Wall Street Journal,* and *CNN.*

Serena Magrogan has been in the field of education for over 20 years. She transitioned from a biochemistry research setting to one of secondary science education, where she spent 15 years teaching in both urban and suburban high schools. Currently, Magrogan is a Senior Director for the College Board's AP Curriculum, Instruction, and Assessment division. She currently manages the AP Chemistry and AP Research courses worldwide. She works on preserving and improving the quality and validity of the AP Program's core deliverables of the curriculum, exam, and the professional development content for both courses and continues to create these deliverables by leading committees of subject-matter experts and practitioners.

Linda T. Mesesan brings over 30 years of experience in the nonprofit sector to her work as an independent consultant in program planning, organizational development, fundraising, and grant writing. She provides services to nonprofits in Los Angeles and Orange County, with special focus in the field of creative youth development. Prior to her consulting business, Linda worked in the field of public policy education as a program planner and fundraiser for Town Hall Los Angeles and the Los Angeles World Affairs Council. Linda received her Bachelor of Arts in Political Science from Loyola Marymount University.

Sheena Nahm is a cultural anthropologist who focuses on health, education, media and social change. Dr. Nahm is adjunct faculty in Anthropology and Sociology for The New School. She holds a Bachelor's degree in Biological Basis of Behavior and in Anthropology from the University of Pennsylvania, a Master's degree in Public Health from Drexel University, and an M.A. and Ph.D. in Socio-cultural Anthropology with a Critical Theory Emphasis from the University of California, Irvine.

Kylie Nicholas is a Senior Research Analyst for The Improve Group, an evaluation and research firm in Saint Paul, Minnesota. Ms. Nicholas has a strong background in conducting research on social justice programs, and she has conducted evaluations in the areas of museums and performing arts, public health, health disparity, and human services. She received her Master of Public Affairs from the School of Public and Environmental Affairs at Indiana University where she focused her studies on policy analysis and health policy.

Daren Nyquist currently serves as Research and Evaluation Director for The Improve Group, an evaluation and research firm in Saint Paul, Minnesota. With a background rooted in community engagement and evaluation, Mr. Nyquist understands that the best evaluations seek to be inclusive and make room for a wide variety of stakeholder perspectives. He has managed research projects for prominent public and private sector organizations with a focus on health care and the provision of services to seniors and people with disabilities. Mr. Nyquist obtained his Master of Public Policy from the University of Minnesota—Twin Cities.

Kerry O'Grady is a Research Fellow at WolfBrown and is currently pursuing a Ph.D. in Education at Johns Hopkins University, where her research involves an epistemological investigation of artistic processes and socioemotional dispositions. She has taught visual art at the high school and university levels and has engaged students in curatorial projects and collaborative art-making. In addition, she has directed university art galleries and a museum education department to engage diverse audiences in dialogue around visual arts. She has a B.A. in art and anthropology from Connecticut College, an M.A.T. in art education from Tufts University and the School of the Museum of Fine Arts, Boston, and an M.F.A. in studio art from UMass Amherst. Her artistic practice informs her research, writing, and teaching.

Ivonne Chand O'Neal Ph.D. is the Founder and Principal of MUSE Research, LLC, a creativity research think tank which provides arts assessment, research design, and arts evaluation services for multinational companies. She currently serves as Chief Research Strategist for Crayola, and is also Senior Research Fellow for Creativity Testing Services, a creativity assessment firm examining creativity with such organizations as Red Bull, Lego, and Disney.

Prior to her current position, Chand O'Neal served as founding Director of Research and Evaluation for the John F. Kennedy Center for the Performing Arts where she created the Center's first comprehensive research agenda of over 25 research studies designed to examine the impact of the arts on society on local, national, and international scales. Her work has been featured by the NEA, The Washington Post, and various news outlets. Preceding her tenure at the Kennedy Center, she held a joint appointment as Co-Investigator and Research Director at the David Geffen UCLA School of Medicine, where she examined the effects of acute cocaine administration on the creative process. Her work in applications of creativity research led to her term as Associate Curator for the Museum of Creativity.

Chand O'Neal earned her Ph.D. in Cognitive Psychology with emphasis on Creativity, Arts Integration, and Program Evaluation at Claremont Graduate University. She sits on the Editorial Board for the Creativity Research Journal, the Research Advisory Board for the University of Pennsylvania's Human Flourishing Initiative, the College Board's Development Committee for AP Research, and serves as Co-Chair for the Arts, Culture, and Audiences Topical Interest Group for the American

Evaluation Association. She has also worked actively with the entertainment industry (Disney Channel, NBC, TNBC) to increase the use of creative thinking skills in educational television programming for children and teens.

Lynnette Young Overby Ph.D. is Deputy Director of the University of Delaware Community Engagement Initiative and a Professor of Theatre and Dance. She is the author, coauthor, or coeditor of 40+ publications including 12 books and the 2016 Human Kinetics publication—*Public Scholarship in Dance*. Her honors include the 2004 Leadership Award from the National Dance Education Organization. Dr. Overby is currently collaborating with literary historian P. Gabrielle Foreman on a long-term "Performing African American History" research project. "Sketches: The Life of Harriet E. Wilson in Dance, Poetry and Music" is based on research by Foreman, who edited Wilson's 1859 book *Our Nig*. Their collaboration continued in 2014 with the premiere of "Dave the Potter" a multidisciplinary work designed to honor the history and creativity of an enslaved potter and poet, David Drake, through performance. The current project "Same Story Different Countries" extended the work to South Africa.

Christine Pitts is a research scientist from NWEA. She works on analyzing the efficacy of assessment systems and leadership practices in schools. Her work includes assessment design for social, emotional, and learning skills. Her research as a Ph.D. candidate in Educational Methodology, Policy, and Leadership at the University of Oregon focuses on education policy and longitudinal social networks.

Rekha S. Rajan is co-director for PANCH Research, LLC (Chicago, IL), an international consulting firm specializing in biomedical, health, education, arts research, and program evaluation. Her interdisciplinary team has led projects for several agencies, including the National Endowment for the Arts (NEA) and the National Institute of Aging.

Rajan is a nationally recognized arts education specialist and is Visiting Associate Professor of Research and Program Director for the Masters in Grant Writing, Management, and Evaluation at Concordia University Chicago. She is the author of over 50 evaluations, articles, and books, including *Integrating the Performing Arts in Grades K–5*, *Grant Writing*, *From Backpacks to Broadway*, and the forthcoming *Musical Theater in Schools* with Oxford University Press.

She serves as the editor for *General Music Today*, is on the editorial board for the *Music Educators Journal*, and is a co-program chair for the Teaching of Evaluation Topical Interest Group for the American Evaluation Association. Rajan sits on various appointed councils for the arts and education, including the Illinois Core Arts Standards Steering Committee with Arts Alliance Illinois and the Kindergarten Individual Development Survey (KIDS) Advisory Committee for the Illinois State Board of Education. Her research has been featured in *Education Week*, on *National Public Radio*, with the NEA and the National Head Start Association. Rajan is the recipient of numerous grants including a two-year research award from the NEA and a grant from the Chicago Community Trust to study audience response to musical theater performance. She is also a professional singer and actress with performances including Mabel in *The Pirates of Penzance*, Lili in *Carnival!*, and a guest role on *Chicago P.D.* on *NBC*. She received her doctorate in Music Education from Teachers College, Columbia University.

Dawn S. Reese is the Chief Executive Officer of The Wooden Floor. She has leveraged her years of business and nonprofit management experience to be a life-changer for low-income youth and help propel The Wooden Floor forward. Since 2009, Dawn's unique blend of talent and experience working in business, arts, education, and technology adds to the mission-driven, business-minded focus of The Wooden Floor. Dawn led the efforts to take The Wooden Floor's model national and signed their first licensed partner in Washington, DC, as well as heading their local expansion plans to add a second location in Santa Ana. Dawn received the 2016 *Center for Leadership Award for Innovation* from California State University Fullerton and the 2015 *Difference Makers Award for Small Nonprofit Person of the Year* from the Santa Ana Chamber of Commerce. Prior to The Wooden Floor, Dawn worked for Opera Pacific and was the Managing Director. Dawn serves on several Board of Directors and advisory committees for arts, education, and social sector issues. Dawn is a coach, mentor, consultant, and national conference presenter on the topics of strategic planning, board governance, creative youth development, as well as college access. Dawn received her Bachelor of Arts in Psychology from California State University Long Beach.

Patti Saraniero is principal of Moxie Research, a program evaluation and consulting practice that collaborates with arts, cultural, STEM, and education organizations. Dr. Saraniero works on large- and small-scale projects to identify and address questions leading to effective learning programs and experiences. Her work with clients frequently leads to multiple projects with them, creating deep and rich working relationships. Dr. Saraniero has worked in and with large and small arts organizations, including running the education programs at La Jolla Playhouse and the Old Globe Theatre. She is on faculty in the Non-Profit Leadership and Management graduate program at the University of San Diego and in the graduate theater program at the University of California, San Diego. She currently serves as board president of the San Diego Cooperative Charter Schools.

Jennifer Sly Manager of Digital Learning and Assessment, Minnesota Historical Society, has been working at the intersection of technology, community development, and youth empowerment for the past 20 years. She managed the development of the *Play the Past* project and leads other digital learning initiatives at MNHS. Over the years, she has had the most fun working in partnership with the Minnesota Historical Society, the Institute of Museums and Library Services, NASA, the United Nations, the MIT Media Lab, and the youth of Queensbridge and Swaziland. She loves using audience research and new technologies to design transformational digital experiences. The favorite part of her work is trying things out, and then trying them out again.

Laura Smyth Ph.D., has over two decades of experience in the arts and education field as a teacher, researcher, and program specialist. She is currently the Program Director for the California Alliance for Arts Education's Title I Initiative. She began her career as a third-grade teacher in Houston, TX, and later earned her Ph.D. from Stanford University, where she studied with Dr. Shirley Brice Heath. With Heath, she co-wrote the resource guide ArtShow: Youth and Community Development, and later helped design the nation's first master's degree in arts management with a focus on community and youth development at Columbia College Chicago. Laura also served for three years as Senior Associate for Communications and Partnerships at the Arts Education Partnership. Laura is interested in the intersection of in-school and out-of-school time, partnership between community and youth organizations, Title I and education equity, and making research and policy information accessible to a general audience.

Greg Taylor Ph.D. is Professor of Cinema Studies at Purchase College, SUNY, where he also served as the Director of the Conservatory of Theatre Arts from 2010–2016. He is the author of *Artists in the Audience:*

Cults, Camp, and American Film Criticism (Princeton University Press), along with numerous articles on criticism, cinema, modernism, and taste. He is currently completing his first novel.

Dennie Wolf Ph.D. is a principal at WolfBrown and brings over 40 years of experience in the fields of research and evaluation to the work of building equitable learning opportunities for children, youth, and families. She graduated from Harvard University where she trained in developmental psychology and served as a researcher at Harvard Project Zero for more than a decade, leading studies on the early development of artistic and symbolic capacities. While continuing her work as a researcher, Wolf has expanded her work to include planning and evaluating a number of collective impact projects designed to build municipal and regional systems that support equitable creative learning in and out of school time (e.g., Big Thought in Dallas, Right Brain in Portland, or the Arts Expansion Initiative in Boston, Arts Assessment Project in Seattle). Through this work, Wolf has published widely on issues of assessment, participatory evaluation, as well as artistic and imaginative development, consistently arguing that creative work is a human need and a human right.

Kim Zanti is the Assistant Director of the Centers for Research on Creativity, where she contributes to all aspects of the business, including evaluation plan design, field research, report writing and editing, project management, and business operations. Prior to joining CRoC, Kim enjoyed a 20-year career in the public benefit arts arena with such agencies and organizations as the Los Angeles County Arts Commission and Will Geer's Theatricum Botanicum in Topanga, CA. She has served as a development consultant to Arts for LA and the California State Summer School for the Arts Foundation, and currently, serves as a development consultant to Get Lit—Words Ignite and Pacific Resident Theatre. Kim is a published writer and founder of Transport Topanga Literary Festival. She holds a Bachelor's Degree in Psychology from Towson University in Baltimore, Maryland.

LIST OF FIGURES

LIST OF TABLES

CHAPTER 1

An Introduction to Arts Evaluation

Rekha S. Rajan and Ivonne Chand O'Neal

Arts evaluation is a term that is both innovative and daunting. The inception of any arts organization, program, performance, exhibition, or collection comes with the need for assessing the value of these experiences and understanding how people appreciate and interpret different art forms. When we attend the opening of a new gallery, we bring expectations for the visual art we will examine and analyze. When we attend the opening of a new concert, play, dance, or musical, we prepare to experience the performing arts in new and exciting ways. When we spend our weekends at the local movie theater, we expect to be entertained and transported by film. When students prepare for a visit from a teaching artist, they anticipate learning about the arts, engaging and participating, in addition to diving into their daily curriculum.

In that sense, as participants, audience members, and patrons of various arts forms, we are constantly evaluating what the arts mean in our lives (Rajan, 2015). These informal assessments help to shape our own understanding of the arts, help us to learn about the arts, and learn from the arts, even if we are not formally doing so. As such, the idea of evaluating the arts should seem simple and obvious, right?

R.S. Rajan (✉)
PANCH Research, LLC, Chicago, IL, USA

I.C. O'Neal
MUSE Research, LLC, Kensington, MD, USA

© The Author(s) 2018
R.S. Rajan, I.C. O'Neal (eds.), *Arts Evaluation and Assessment*,
https://doi.org/10.1007/978-3-319-64116-4_1

1

Probably not. The term evaluation itself has been known to challenge even the most experienced artist and educator. But why? Evaluation is a term simply defined as "judging the merit, worth, or value of something" (Scriven, 1967). Isn't that a component of what we are already doing with the arts? Why then, is evaluation, and evaluating the arts, such a difficult concept? And, one that is often relegated to the idea that the impact of the arts can't be measured?

This dichotomy is not necessarily new and certainly not a product of evaluation as a burgeoning field of study and practice. The arts themselves have been challenged in our schools, curriculum, and community (Chand O'Neal & Runco, 2016; Rajan, 2012a, 2012b). Our culture has to value the arts before our educational system can. It is only in recent years that the experience of music, theater, dance, visual, and multimedia arts has been given credibility and value in our school system (Chand O'Neal, 2014; Rajan, 2015). And, that change has been coming. The evidence is found in the development of an educational outreach program in nearly every arts organization across the United States—from national champions of the arts like the Lincoln Center and the John F. Kennedy Center for the Performing Arts, to smaller, regional organizations found in each state and city. Each of these development or outreach programs brings the necessity of evaluating and assessing the strength, challenges, benefits, and viability of each program.

The purpose of this chapter is twofold. First, we hope to present an overview of evaluation theories, models, and applications to readers who are unfamiliar with this field. Additionally, we hope that those who are reading this book with a strong understanding of evaluation practices will be challenged further to examine how evaluation is applied and aligned to meet the unique requirements inherent to the various artistic disciplines outlined in each chapter. We begin then with a brief description of program evaluation, both as a supplementary component to grants and as its own field of study, before applying these ideas to the arts.

Throughout this book, we encourage you to think about the following questions that are woven throughout each contributed chapter: How has program evaluation changed in the past decade? What are the challenges arts evaluators face that other disciplines avoid (and why)? How can we strengthen our own understanding of the arts, and capacity to experience the arts, through evaluation? How do our findings support, augment, or impede arts policy and practice?

So, What Is Evaluation?

Program evaluation as a field of study is relatively new. A theory-based practice, "the evaluation process identifies relevant values or standards that apply to what is being evaluated, performs empirical investigation using techniques from the social sciences, and then integrates conclusions with the standards into an overall evaluation or set of evaluations" (Scriven, 1991). Guskey (2000) added to this definition by stating that evaluation is a systematic process used to determine the merit or worth of a specific program, curriculum, or strategy in a specific context. One perspective views evaluation as originating as a counterpart to grant writing (Rajan & Tomal, 2015). Much of the challenge with defining evaluation is that the term is often used interchangeably with research, and they are not the same. While research is traditionally a hypothesis-based, systematic collection of data for analysis and generalizability, evaluation is the theory-driven, systematic collection of data focused on assessing a program's goals and viability. Though research and evaluation are both grounded in scientific inquiry, evaluation is often used to give focused information on a specific program. Evaluation is about finding ways to sustain an organization, maintain connections to the community, and utilize innovative methods for documenting the individual strengths and benefits of a program. An evaluator has to have the ability to "not only state preferences, but render judgments" (Eisner, 2007, p. 425). This is even more important when considering not just *what* we are evaluating, but *how* our evaluations can make an impact.

Program managers are now finding great value in the systematic documentation of organizations' goals and the development of measurable outcomes. Evaluation reports are proudly displayed as part of an organization's mission and outreach. Program managers want us to know that they are investing in evaluation. This, in turn, has also made evaluation more accessible for practicing professionals. Consider how there are now several universities that offer degrees, courses, and certificates in program evaluation. There are graduate programs dedicated to understanding evaluation theory, logic models, and methodology. And, ironically, these programs are often housed in a department or division of research. As the field of evaluation continues to grow (and gain validation) so too does the need for individuals to have an educational background that demonstrates their understanding of evaluation theory.

But, does that really matter? Do we need a degree in evaluation to be an evaluator? Sure, we wouldn't want a physician to treat us without a recognized medical degree, or teachers working with our children who didn't have the licensing to support their knowledge base. What makes evaluation different? And, how do we define this field (especially in the arts)—both for its programmatic value and practical application?

Evaluating the Arts

It is no secret that arts programs typically receive less funding than other disciplines (Rajan, 2015). Some of this is attributed to how the arts (and their value) need to be continuously justified (Cohen, 2009). But, the argument is deeper than how the arts support student achievement in the form of grades and standardized testing, or whether they generate more ticket sales. The larger issue is *how are we assessing the impact and value of the arts? Is it documenting the quantity or quality?* Consider how "a majority of funders require that quantitative data be included in the final report, something that is not always accounted for when planning an artistic performance" (Rajan, 2015, p. 32). It is important to capture not only what is happening and how it is being done in a program, but to maintain the integrity of each art form in the process.

Early efforts to address the relationship between student outcomes and arts programming began in 1982, the year the President's Committee on the Arts and the Humanities (PCAH) was established by Ronald Reagan's Presidential Executive Order. The dual purpose of this Committee was to embolden private sector support, and to increase public appreciation, understanding, and value of the arts through projects, publications, and meetings. In the late 1990s, the Arts Education Partnership and PCAH combined efforts to initiate the *Champions of Change: The Impact of the Arts on Learning* initiative which invited teams of leading educational researchers to explore why and how young people were changed through their arts experiences. These targeted studies utilizing data from national databases (e.g., NELS:88), schools across the United States, as well as community youth centers, yielded six key results: (1) the arts reach students who are not otherwise being reached, (2) the arts reach students in ways that they are not otherwise being reached, (3) the arts connect students to themselves and each other, (4) the arts transform the environment for learning, (5) the arts provide new challenges for those students already considered successful, and (6) the arts connect learning experiences to the world of real work (Fiske, 1999).

The six key findings from the 1999 PCAH report led the United States Department of Education (USDoE), to create the Arts Education Model Development and Dissemination (AEMDD) program which was established in 2002 (Ten Years of Arts Integration, 2012).

In FY 2012, the USDoE committed $11,497,000 to the implementation of arts learning and arts integrated programs throughout the United States (Department of Education Fiscal Year 2012 Congressional Action, 2013). Supporting the implementation of effective arts programming, a resurgence in the call for evidence of the benefits of this work has begun to emerge among educators, lobbyists, private equity firms, and the Federal government. With the recent emphasis on creativity as capital, the need to provide evidence linking arts programming with such outcomes as creative thinking skills and social emotional learning becomes increasingly urgent (Burton, Horowitz, & Abeles, 2000; Chand O'Neal, Paek, & Runco, 2015). These constructs are not only outcomes of arts programming, but are capacities that funders and larger entities are expecting to see in evaluation reports. It changes the dynamic of arts evaluation, forcing us, in many ways, to be more accountable.

A number of new initiatives have recently emerged highlighting the combination of the arts with other sectors of society to promote change. Take for example the National Endowment's (NEA) Creativity Connects Initiative, launched in celebration of the NEA's 50th anniversary. This new leadership initiative invites grantees to show how the arts contribute to the nation's creative ecosystem, specifically examining the ways in which the support system for artists are changing, and explores how the arts can connect with other sectors that want and utilize creativity. A grant competition released by the Institute of Educational Sciences in 2017 focused on how arts education may help students meet high standards with limited resources. The focus of this work is on exploring how factors such as type, duration, intensity, and quality of arts programming may affect student education outcomes. Additionally, the Arts Education Partnership provides a cornerstone of research and evaluation, encouraging appropriate practices, and influencing policy in the arts. These are just three examples of the current needs and trends on the national level that require and encourage the use of rigorous, innovative methods to evaluate arts programs that will ultimately change the creative ecosystem of the United States.

Executive decision-makers and stakeholders are eager to ensure that arts programs are accomplishing their intended purpose. Our goals are often to:

- Push boundaries and introduce audiences to new, provocative materials
- Respond to societal issues through spoken word showcases and curated conversations
- Provide young audiences with witty, relatable, immersive artistic experiences
- Transport audiences through live, culturally sensitive, artistic performances
- Give value to the concepts of self-expression, creativity, and individuality

In any case, the work of evaluation in the arts is rich with multiple methods of examining impact and assessing learning. Elliot Eisner discussed educational connoisseurship in that "experienced experts, like critics of the arts, bring their expertise to bear on evaluating the quality of programs" (Fitzpatrick, Sanders, & Worthen, 2004). Evaluators in the arts are often interested in assessing the effects of arts programs by asking questions like "What changes occurred?" "How did this performance/ exhibit/festival impact the individual or audience?" "What are the unique aspects of this program in bringing access to the arts to underserved populations?"

These questions frame the overall aim and scope of this volume, highlighting examples of how prominent evaluators have collaborated and designed effective program evaluations. To better understand the current state of the field of arts evaluation, we hope that this collection of chapters offers a clear path of increased emphasis on evidence-driven arts program evaluation over time.

ABOUT THE BOOK

The idea for this book began from a chapter in *The International Handbook of Research in Arts Education*, edited by Liora Bresler (2007), that briefly noted an absence of full-scale arts evaluations in the literature. It was an interesting concept and inquiry. We would be remiss if we didn't acknowledge the innovation of that handbook in its introduction of both research and evaluation as separate and important practices in the arts. However, beyond this project, program evaluations were simply not available to larger audiences, particularly for smaller organizations that might have utilized examples for their own purposes. This led us to examine larger questions when outlining this project. We questioned why is there a large absence of arts evaluations made available to the general public? We wondered if it was an issue of access or understanding—or both? Or, perhaps, it was simply due to the fact that there had never been a need to disseminate this information.

Another dilemma faced by the field is whether to document the outcomes of the arts for arts' sake, or in the interest of how the arts impact success in another domain. Is one of these pathways to evaluation really better? Or do we value both equally when assessing the impact of the arts? Although each perspective is of critical importance, they often come in conflict with one another as arts organizations reconcile how to market and create appetites for their works for both stakeholders and throughout the community. Eisner (2007) noted that "the challenge to those who wish to do assessment and evaluation in the arts is to be able to see the qualities that constitute virtue in an art form" (p. 426). His point, and one which many scholars have emphasized, is that any assessment of the arts needs to maintain the integrity of the art form itself. Would we evaluate a dance program the same way we would evaluate an exhibition? A concert the same as film? This is a challenge that artists, researchers, educators, and in more recent years, evaluators have had to grapple with in many different ways.

While this chapter introduced some general ideas about evaluation and its development as a field of study and practice, there is still much more to explore. The purpose of this chapter (and this book) is not to teach, outline, or dictate evaluation methods. Certainly, there are many resources available that describe and explore qualitative, quantitative, and mixed-methods for program evaluation. This book, from its inception, was never intended to be a scripted portfolio of how to evaluate the arts; instead we hope to present a varied collection of program evaluations that encompass nearly every art form, methodology, demographic, and timeline.

Each chapter presents a complete evaluation of an arts program, and collectively encompasses schools, communities, neighborhoods, performance halls and exhibitions. Our contributors present an array of evaluation approaches that deftly consider nuances of each artistic discipline (music, theater, dance, visual art, multimedia arts, arts integration, exhibits) and context (museums, community centers, schools, higher education, performing arts venues). Each individual or team of evaluators identifies their charge as a result of their initial stakeholder conversation, evaluation plan, iterative process, results, and interpretation with detailed commentary outlining the challenges, strengths, suggestions for improvements, and implications of their work. We have considered the importance of presenting evaluations that spanned only two months to those that explored the impact of learning and participating in the arts over several years.

As you read each chapter, we challenge and invite you to identify and analyze each evaluation, to recognize the qualities that make each program (and process) unique, and to define arts evaluation for yourself. In our concluding chapter, we discuss the thread that we have woven throughout this book and circle back to not only defining evaluation as field of study, but understanding the implications of evaluating the arts for policy and practice.

REFERENCES

Bresler, L. (Ed.). (2007). *International handbook of research in arts education.* Dordrecht, NL: Springer.

Burton, J. M., Horowitz, R., & Abeles, H. (2000). Learning in and through the arts: The question of transfer. *Studies in Art Education, 41*(3), 228–257.

Chand O'Neal, I. (2014). *Selected findings from the John F. Kennedy Center's Arts in Education Research Study: An impact evaluation of arts-integrated instruction through the Changing Education Through the Arts (CETA) program.* Washington, DC: The John F. Kennedy Center for the Performing Arts.

Chand O'Neal, I., Paek, S., & Runco, M. A. (2015). Comparison of competing theories about ideation and creativity. *Creativity: Theories-Research-Applications, 2*(2), 1–20. https://doi.org/10.1515/ctra-2015-0018

Chand O'Neal, I., & Runco, M. A. (2016). Uncover & unleash students' creative potential: Translating research into practice. *Principal,* National Association of Elementary School Principals and Crayola.

Cohen, P. (2009, February 24). In tough times, the humanities must justify their worth. *The New York Times,* p. C1.

Department of Education Fiscal Year 2012 Congressional Action. 2013. Retrieved from https://www2.ed.gov/about/overview/budget/budget12/12action.pdf

Eisner, E. (2007). Assessment and evaluation in education and the arts. In L. Bresler (Ed.), *International handbook of research in arts education.* Dordrecht, NL: Springer.

Fiske, E. (Ed.). (1999). *Champions of change: The impact of the arts on learning.* Washington, DC: Arts Education Partnership and President's Committee on the Arts and Humanities.

Fitzpatrick, J. L., Sanders, J. R., & Worthen, B. R. (2004). *Program evaluation: Alternative approaches and practical guidelines* (3rd ed.). Upper Saddle River, NJ: Pearson Education Inc.

Guskey, T. R. (2000). *Evaluating professional development*. Thousand Oaks, CA: Corwin Press.

Rajan, R. S. (2012a). *Integrating the performing arts in grades K-5*. Thousand Oaks, CA: SAGE, Corwin Press.

Rajan, R. S. (2012b). Who needs the arts? Focus on teacher education. *ACEI, 11*(4), 6–8.

Rajan, R. S. (2015). Artistic assessment: Strategies for documenting learning in the arts. *Journal of the Grant Professionals Association, 13*(1), 31–37.

Rajan, R. S., & Tomal, D. (2015). *Grant writing: Practical strategies for scholars and professionals*. Lanham, MD: Rowman & Littlefield Publishers.

Scriven, M. (1967). The methodology of evaluation. In R. Tyler, R. Gagne, & M. Scriven (Eds.), *Perspectives on curriculum evaluation. AERA monograph series on curriculum evaluation, No. 1* (pp. 39–83). Rand McNally: Skokie, IL.

Scriven, M. (1991). *Evaluation thesaurus* (4th ed.). Newbury Park, CA: SAGE.

Ten Years of Arts Integration. (2012). Retrieved November 1, 2013, from http://www.ed.gov/oii-news/ten-years-arts-integration

A Step in the Right Direction: Early Lessons from a Longitudinal Study of Dance Education as a Developmental Catalyst

James S. Catterall, Julie E. Kendig, Linda T. Mesesan,
Dawn S. Reese, and Kimberley G. Zanti

The Wooden Floor (TWF) and The Centers for Research on Creativity (CRoC), both based in Southern California, embarked on a longitudinal study in 2013 to assess the impacts of the organization's dance-centric model on students. One of the most compelling aspects of this collaboration is that it is unfolding over 10 years, mirroring the length of time a student might participate in TWF programs, between third and twelfth grade. Finding the right partners, on both sides of the relationship, is an intricate process that relies on different domains of expertise yet common goals, interests, and approach to collaborative work. In this chapter, we

J.S. Catterall (✉) • K.G. Zanti
Centers for Research on Creativity, Topanga, CA, USA

J.E. Kendig
Centers for Research on Creativity, San Diego, CA, USA

L.T. Mesesan • D.S. Reese
The Wooden Floor, Santa Ana, CA, USA

© The Author(s) 2018
R.S. Rajan, I.C. O'Neal (eds.), *Arts Evaluation and Assessment*,
https://doi.org/10.1007/978-3-319-64116-4_2

hope to shed light on the process of developing and planning a longitudinal study and the lessons learned in the early stages of implementation.

ORGANIZATIONAL CONTEXT

Founded in 1983, The Wooden Floor (TWF) is a prominent arts-for-youth, 501(c)3 public benefit organization. TWF's mission is to use dance as a creative youth development catalyst that empowers youth from diverse backgrounds to strengthen self-esteem, self-discipline, and their sense of accomplishment through dance, academic, and family programs. Serving the most economically disadvantaged youth, its vision is to break the cycle of poverty through generational change.

At TWF in Orange County, and through national licensed partners, the organization's formative approach uses exploratory dance education to foster the confidence and gifts within each child to innovate, communicate, and collaborate—skills believed necessary for success in school and in life. Since its inception, TWF has impacted the lives of over 85,000 young people through its year-round and community outreach programs.

STUDY BACKGROUND

The Wooden Floor has an enduring commitment to assessment and evaluation. Prior to the current study, TWF engaged in two independent studies first in 1993 and again in 1998. The 1993 commissioned study evaluated the organization's impact on students' self-esteem, self-discipline, and achievement. The 1998 study examined the impact of TWF on children's long- and short-term social and behavioral development. This study was based on the concept of the "resilient" child—a child with a set of developmental assets that support him or her in becoming a positive, healthy, and engaged adult.

Continuing the commitment to reflective, data-driven practice, TWF benefited from a two-phase (2006–2009 and 2009–2012) capacity-building grant from The James Irvine Foundation under the Arts Regional Initiative. Support from The Foundation allowed the organization to further its strategic vision and develop an evaluation plan that would measure outcomes informed by a theory of change. Due to the nature of its unique, holistic model, TWF sought a research firm willing to develop assessment tools specific to the organization's ecosystem.

The initial framework for the study was to measure achievement motivation, self-concept, student creativity, future orientation, and student engagement, with:

- New benchmarks to measure the impact of its exploratory dance curriculum, incorporating somatic studies (e.g. modern dance, contact improvisation)
- Longitudinal study data to substantiate progress toward TWF's ultimate goal of bringing about generational change to break the cycle of poverty
- Documentation of TWF outcomes to support advocacy of its theory of change through dance and its model of youth development and community-building
- A deeper understanding of how TWF's cultural participation practices affect life-long engagement with contemporary dance and the arts in general

Prior to developing a long-term evaluation tool, TWF first had to inventory the existing instruments and the data that it had collected annually over the years. This process revealed where shifts in data collection should occur in accordance with the newly developed theory of change. TWF began an internal review led by an independent evaluator. This work examined the organization's evaluation practices, assessed staff capacity for data collection and management, and provided a literature review of external research that contextualized the field.

Upon completing the internal review, The Wooden Floor distributed a request for proposals to firms and academic institutions to engage in a longitudinal study. TWF looked for a partner that met the following criteria: (1) national prominence for arts evaluation and assessment practices; (2) willingness to collaborate and adapt as partners; (3) ability to provide capacity-building to TWF on research methodologies; and (4) ability to shepherd a long-term evaluation study over 10 years.

During the selection process, TWF realized it was equally important to find a research firm that not only had expertise in arts evaluation and assessment but also had expertise in evaluating youth development outcomes. Together with an independent research firm that met these criteria, TWF would be poised to meet the challenges of conducting a successful, comprehensive assessment.

The Centers for Research on Creativity (CRoC) also considered the project from several perspectives. Founded in 2012 to investigate human creativity and the conditions that can promote imaginative approaches to learning, design, and problem solving, CRoC was interested in the potential of this study because the field of dance education is comparatively "under-studied" in contrast to the visual arts, music, and theatre education programs. CRoC was also keen to explore a long-term study design because most of its projects to date had ranged, typically, over 2 to 3 years. The 10-year time span offered an almost unprecedented look into a dance education program. And the work had the potential to inform other organizations about how they might consider shaping an extended multi-year evaluation of their programs. Also appealing was the idea of working with a management team that was creatively astute, assessment savvy, and had the capacity to carry out a study with consistent protocols and detailed attention to the study's logistics and administration.

After consideration of all candidates, TWF determined that CRoC met the criteria for an ideal research partner, which was a mutual estimation of the proposed relationship. In 2013, the organizations reached an agreement, and the partnership began.

ORGANIZATIONAL BACKGROUND

Since 2005, 100% of students who graduate from The Wooden Floor also graduate from high school and enroll in higher education. In this same time-frame, 52% of TWF alumni have graduated from college with a bachelor's or master's degree. Comparatively, the Pell Institute for the Study of Opportunity in Higher Education and the University of Pennsylvania's Alliance for Higher Education and Democracy (2016) reported that only 15% of people in the lowest income brackets nationwide earned a bachelor's degree. Evidence of TWF achieving its mission is found in alumni who attend colleges nationwide and graduate with degrees in business, engineering, education, medicine, and the arts. Many are the first in their families to attend college or university.

The Wooden Floor's program model uses dance education and "wrap-around services" in three areas: academics, college and career readiness, and family services. The properties of TWF's dance approach center upon innovation, creativity, teamwork, self-sufficiency, and courage. Courage is really important to building TWF students' sense of achievement when they strive for excellence or to attempt something new in the dance studio. When they succeed, those same feelings of accomplishment permeate their own academics and dreams for their futures. As the students master their dance class instruction and choreographic process over their 10-year journey with TWF, the students learn to apply those properties to their everyday lives. In pursuit of overcoming a challenge at home, or to tackle a school project, they follow the same process they learn through dance and art-making: ideation, exploration, collaboration, planning, execution, and reflection. Over and over, these are repeated in the dance studio and on stage, as well as their classrooms, for up to 10 years. Descriptions for each segment of TWF's model are provided below.

Dance Education

In TWF dance studios, 54 dance classes are held each week, 1–1.5 hours per class, 38 weeks per year. At the beginning of their studies, students attend classes twice a week and increase to 20 hours per week. A sequential curriculum is taught over a period of 10 years. Students progress in dance proficiency in ballet, modern dance, improvisation, and choreography. An annual concert is held in a prominent performing arts venue, premiering works co-created by students with leading guest choreographers who are shaping the genre of contemporary dance. Additional outside performances are presented, as invited.

Through their work in the studio, students develop self-knowledge, which evolves into self-assurance, leadership, collaborative learning, positive decision-making, and joy. Rehearsal and performances teach discipline, goal-setting, commitment, and achievement through hard work. The Wooden Floor's students transform their lives by learning to put forth their best effort and strive for excellence in all they do—in the studio, on stage, and in the classroom.

Academic Services

The Wooden Floor's academic services include year-round individualized one-to-one tutoring, summer learning workshops, year-round reading groups, and test-taking skills classes. These services are facilitated at an on-campus resource center/computer lab. TWF's case management approach also includes individual academic plans that help staff and parents focus their efforts on remedial and tutoring support to help students progress in areas most in need. Additionally, the organization strategically integrates family and emotional support opportunities via monthly check-ins with students and parents.

College and Career Readiness Programs

To prepare students for the world they will face beyond The Wooden Floor, curricula for students in grades 6–12 offer three components appropriate to each grade level. The college and career readiness program prepares first-generation college students for successful transition through academic, social and financial support. The program is designed to remove barriers to college access, prepare parents to support their student's path through college financially and emotionally, and support persistence in college through mentoring and web resources.

The program includes monthly individual student meetings, student and family group meetings organized by graduating class cohorts, and career nights to expose the TWF students to a variety of career opportunities outside their current awareness. Additional curriculum components include SAT/ACT preparation, goal-setting workshops, how to navigate college entrance, and where to find financial aid. TWF also coordinates guided tours to local college and university campuses and provides merit-based college scholarships.

Family Services Programs

The Family Services Program uses a case management approach to address the root causes of family issues that affect student well-being and academic performance. The family services component reaches the entire student body of 375 children and their parents through timely interventions and referrals to a local network of health and human services.

Services at TWF campus include counseling, crisis intervention, and referrals to additional social services at no cost and in a private setting. Families have access to these services 6 days per week over 38 weeks, Monday-Friday 4:00–8:30 P.M. and Saturdays 9:00 A.M–1:30 P.M. Small group workshops on topics of nutrition, parenting, adolescent development, communication skills, college planning, and financial literacy are held in TWF's Community Center. Nearly 300 adults and children receive free health screenings annually during an annual health fair.

Sequential parent workshops, organized by high school graduation year, over a 10-year period, strengthen families by improving relationships and fostering economic self-sufficiency through training in communication, parenting, goal-setting, college financing, health, and financial literacy. Small group workshops taught by TWF alumni or parent cohorts reinforce one-on-one mentoring to educate and build supportive communities among students and parents toward their higher education goals as a family.

THEORY OF CHANGE

In 2009, TWF embarked on a strategic planning process, resulting in a 10-year strategic vision to advance the program model, grow local impact, and increase visibility and advocacy. This vision set the course for scaling the organization's impact, both locally and nationally, through licensing of the programmatic model. A major initiative of the planning process was the development of a theory of change, which puts dance at the center of student transformation and strategically integrates academics, college and career readiness, and family support services, as discussed above. TWF's theory of change was copyrighted in 2014 and is being evaluated as part of the 10-year longitudinal study.

The theory states that students who learn collaboratively in the dance studio develop self-knowledge, confidence, leadership skills, and experience, and benefit from increased well-being and joy. To inspire and support the change process, TWF differentiates itself in its approach to creative youth development through the following:

- Close and positive long-term relationships over a 10-year mentoring commitment
- Rigorous, deep, long-term arts immersion
- High expectations for students
- Exposing students to new experiences and opportunities
- Focusing on the well-being of each youth in their individual family context
- Providing a safe and healthy environment
- Supporting successful high school graduation
- Increasing college access rates

Figure 2.1 illustrates the theory of change.

RESEARCH QUESTIONS

The major research questions driving the 2014–2024 longitudinal study by the Centers for Research on Creativity are below.

- Does long-term participation in TWF's holistic program model boost student achievement and socio-emotional development?

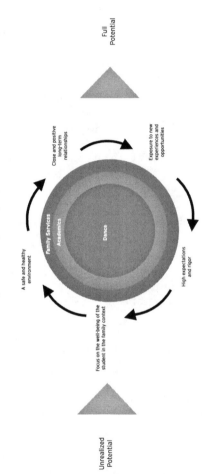

Fig. 2.1 Theory of change model for The Wooden Floor

The triangles represent the direction students progress as they participate in programming. The concentric circles are the program offerings, with dance being the central focus of the organization's work. The arrows show aspects and approaches to the program offerings as well as define the outcomes. Figure 2.1 is from the federal copyright for *The Wooden Floor: From here, you can step anywhere* by The Wooden Floor for Youth Movement, 2014, Santa Ana, CA. Reprinted with permission

- Does evidence support progress toward TWF's ultimate goal of breaking generational cycles of poverty?
- What are critical ages and domains in which students mature through programmatic interventions at TWF? Does gender matter?
- How can the longitudinal data help TWF continually refine, improve, and, if necessary, change programmatic designs and methods? How can the study provide insights to assist other programs to improve their methods and outcomes?
- Do TWF's programmatic outcomes substantiate advocacy of its dance-based theory of change and replication of its model to serve more youth in low-income communities?

SIGNIFICANCE

Few studies exist in arts education literature that examine the impacts of dance-centered arts programming on youth. Lacking these resources, our understanding and knowledge of the discipline continue to be limited. TWF research presents a rare opportunity to contribute to the body of knowledge and to do so over an unprecedented length of time. The researchers will continue to publish and present findings over the course of five data panels that will follow this first complete round of data collection.

From an organizational perspective, the study has deepened TWF's commitment to staff professional development to ensure sufficient capacity to effectively carry out a study over the course of a decade, despite potential staff changes and other unforeseen circumstances. Moreover, the study data informs strategic planning, decision-making, and the impact story the organization can share with its current and potential stakeholders.

EVALUATION METHOD

Custom Survey Development

TWF and CRoC collaboratively developed a custom assessment instrument to address core research questions and measure growth across 16 constructs and developed the plan to use the instrument over time and across cohorts. The study will ultimately generate data from the youngest students, age eight, to the oldest, age 18 (grades 3–12). Unlike many youth-serving organizations, TWF is able to maintain contact with its students even after high school graduation due to close relationships with students and families and through administration of college scholarships to 80% of its alumni.

TWF's theory of change embraces a number of motivation and self-belief concepts that are long-established in the developmental psychology literature as positive individual states. Using measures from validated studies as well as exploratory indicators, TWF and CRoC identified the following list of constructs and subscales for inclusion in the survey (example scale questions in parentheses):

- Achievement Motivation: Self-efficacy Beliefs (I am confident that I can solve problems), Collaboration Skills (I enjoy helping when another student is having difficulties), and Intrinsic Interest (I pursue things that are important to me—not just for grades or praise). (Ames, 1990; Stipek & Seal, 2004; Weiner, 2006)
- Self-Concept: Sense of Identity (I like pursuing opportunities in the community) and Self-attributions for Success (My success depends on my own efforts) (Graham & Taylor, 2002; Stipek & Seal, 2004)
- Social Self-Concept and Engagement: Interpersonal Skills, Pro-social Behaviors (Catterall, 2009; Johnson & Johnson, 1989)
- Empathy: Ties to Community, Self-Image as Student, and Academic Integrity (Catterall & Runco, 2013; Salkind, 2008)
- Dance Education: Self-Image as Artist, Creative Confidence in Dance, Interest and Engagement in Dance (Bradley, 2002)
- Creative Youth Development: Creative Problem-solving skills that include problem-finding, creative fluency, flexibility, and originality (Catterall & Runco, 2013)

Scales on the TWF pilot survey drew on the authors noted above (e.g. achievement motivation and its components: self-concept, cognitive engagement, collaboration, empathy). Other scales were drafted originally for the pilot (e.g. ties to community, academic integrity, sense of purpose, sense of possibilities). Scales for creative behavior and creative motivation are derived from a recent creativity assessment instrument (Catterall & Runco, 2013).

At the start of TWF's longitudinal work, CRoC had piloted the creativity instrument with 1106 students in 10 Art and Science programs in seven states. Most constructs are measured through multiple-item scales and have been tested for internal validity. Some items require written responses and problem solutions; these are scored and analyzed through human judgment, based on scoring rubrics.

Survey Administration

Survey administration occurs once a year, every other year, between 2014 and 2024. The survey was beta-tested in 2013 with students in grades 3–9. Studio teachers were trained by CRoC staff to administer the survey during a regularly scheduled class period (1 hour, 15 minutes). The training was repeated in 2014 and 2016. Each student was assigned an ID (letter/number). Absent students completed the survey on one of several makeup dates. Teachers collected surveys in envelopes marked with student names, IDs, dance level, teacher name, class date, and class time.

Collected surveys are shipped to CRoC in their class envelopes and data are recorded on an Excel spreadsheet designed for statistical analysis in Statistical Package for the Social Sciences (SPSS).

Participants

In December 2013, the TWF pilot survey was tested by 25 TWF students, ages 9 to 17, and then refined for institution-wide implementation with 375 students in February 2014. Students were invited to indicate their levels of agreement on Likert-type scales and provide written responses to open-ended questions designed to measure creative fluency. In 2014, the first year of survey administration, 347 students aged 9–17 completed the survey.

In 2016, TWF's year-round student body consisted of 375 children and their families who remained with TWF for up to 10 years. Furthermore, TWF plans to serve 100 more students and their families at a second location in the area by 2017 for a total student body of 475 students eligible for inclusion in the longitudinal study. The student body averages 73% girls, 27% boys; 97% are Latino; and 92% are considered low or extremely low-income by U.S. Department of Housing and Urban Development standards. The average earning of TWF's typical family of five is $37,470, which is 50% under the median household income for the area. TWF makes a long-term commitment to each student and their families to help them navigate socio-economic, educational, and emotional challenges that are encountered due to poverty.

EARLY RESULTS

2014 Baseline Data

Growth results suggested by scale averages at successively increasing ages from the first survey administration in 2014 were parsed by age and gender. Early findings showed older groups had higher scores on self-efficacy belief, collaboration skills and other pro-social behaviors, and sense of personal identity, such as following intrinsic interests compared to their younger peers. Areas of decline among older students appeared in certain areas. For boys aged 13–14, scores on the creative self-concept scale were lower than all other age groups. Likewise, there was an overall decline in self-confidence in dance among the girls according to age. For the girls, levels were high early in life (age 9–10) and then began to decrease consistently as they matured across ages 11–17.

Table 2.1 shows the 2014 baseline survey scale results for this project. Table 2.1 is a comprehensive scale chart for all constructs measured in the pilot survey and shows scores for each age grouping, along with standard deviations. Scores are based on a four-point scale. The two sample charts build on these data and show the general trends in scales by age and the overall magnitude of the scales for each age group. CRoC has produced displays of this type for all boys and girls who comprise the sample of 375 students (54 charts).

Table 2.2 displays sample scores by age on the pro-social behavior scale. We see in Table 2.2 that the pro-social behavior scores differ for girls than for boys. Girls start out high at ages 9 and 10 and remain relatively high as they grow older. Boys start fairly low at age nine and 10 and plateau at about a score of 3.0 for six years and peak at age 17 at nearly 3.8.

2016 Interval One Results

In 2016, the second year of data collection, 338 students completed the survey. One hundred eighty-seven students were returning cases from the first year of testing, and 151 new participants joined in the study. These new participants came from the incoming cohorts of third and fourth graders at The Wooden Floor.

The 2016 survey contained the same items as in the 2014 version. The constructs included are: student self-concept (general), student self-concept (dance), creative confidence, self-efficacy, collaboration, pro-social

Table 2.1 2014 Baseline scale scores, all students

Age (n)	9–10 (80)	11–12 (83)	13–14 (81)	15–16 (55)	17 (26)
Item/Scale	M (SD)	M (SD)	M (SD)	M (SD)	M (SD)
I am an artist as a dancer	2.81 (0.83)	2.99 (3.04)	2.65 (0.68)	2.55 (0.69)	2.77 (0.65)
I am a top student	1.91 (0.90)	2.06 (2.01)	2.41 (0.78)	2.49 (0.91)	2.50 (0.71)
Creative confidence in dance	3.20 (0.62)	3.12 (3.22)	3.03 (0.50)	3.02 (0.62)	3.03 (0.44)
General self-efficacy belief	3.34 (0.49)	3.37 (3.40)	3.28 (0.49)	3.16 (0.44)	3.37 (0.40)
Collaboration skills	3.15 (0.69)	3.39 (3.43)	3.22 (0.57)	3.46 (0.46)	3.42 (0.69)
Pro-social behaviors	3.24 (0.63)	3.34 (3.41)	3.14 (0.54)	3.28 (0.44)	3.29 (0.52)
Interpersonal skills	3.26 (0.63)	3.05 (3.11)	3.16 (0.64)	3.02 (0.66)	3.17 (0.60)
How the world works	3.35 (0.56)	3.42 (3.44)	3.31 (0.60)	3.15 (0.52)	3.27 (0.55)
Sense of possibilities	3.35 (0.56)	3.42 (3.44)	3.31 (0.60)	3.15 (0.52)	3.27 (0.55)
Sense of purpose	2.96 (0.52)	3.20 (3.15)	3.19 (0.31)	3.05 (0.40)	3.05 (0.41)
Strong sense of identity	3.29 (0.74)	3.42 (3.55)	3.50 (0.60)	3.36 (0.56)	3.50 (0.91)
Ties to the community	3.23 (0.61)	3.18 (3.25)	3.11 (0.57)	2.83 (0.56)	3.01 (0.67)
Follows intrinsic interest	3.13 (0.59)	3.23 (3.26)	3.22 (0.45)	3.08 (0.51)	3.24 (0.54)
Attributes success to own efforts	2.95 (0.99)	3.05 (3.00)	3.04 (0.90)	3.48 (0.51)	3.19 (0.40)
Empathic orientations	3.05 (0.66)	3.18 (3.27)	3.27 (0.46)	3.17 (0.56)	3.00 (0.47)
Gets along with TWF better than regular school students	2.99 (0.88)	2.74 (2.77)	2.86 (0.92)	2.76 (1.01)	2.96 (0.92)
Academic integrity	3.23 (0.64)	3.28 (3.37)	3.13 (0.66)	3.18 (0.63)	2.88 (0.59)

behavior, interpersonal skills, beliefs about how the world works, sense of possibilities, sense of purpose, sense of identity, ties to the community, propensity to seek intrinsic rewards, empathy, attributions for success, and integrity.

Table 2.2 2014 Pro-social behavior scores by age and gender

Age	Girls	Boys
9–10	3.47	2.71
11–12	3.41	3.14
13–14	3.18	3.02
15–16	3.30	3.19
17	3.23	3.78

Comparing 2016 to 2014 Scales

As of 2016, we have a set of data to compare with the 2014 survey results. Averages from each of the sub-scales were calculated and compared across constructs, age groups, and gender. Notable differences were marked from 2014 to 2016 both by gains in scores as well as absences of gains within certain constructs and by gender. Table 2.3 represents a consolidation of the scale changes by gender. The darker boxes indicate significant gain. The table affords a side-by-side look at the data with girls' data on the left and boys' data on the right. This table reveals a clustering of scale gains in the lower half of the chart and shows major effects among five scales: sense of purpose, propensity to seek intrinsic rewards, integrity, sense of identity, and empathy.

Table 2.3 also points to areas where results differ markedly for boys versus girls. Girls had strong gains in sense of purpose and integrity in comparison to boys. Boys had stronger gains in sense of identity and empathy. Another interesting perspective in Table 2.3 is the total number of gains by age group. By far, the 13–14-year olds showed the most gains, with the girls of this age exhibiting gains in 7 constructs and the boys in 12 constructs measured by the survey.

Equally interesting to consider is the rank order of gains across constructs. As shown in Table 2.4, boys and girls combined showed robust growth across age groups in the following constructs: sense of purpose, propensity to seek intrinsic rewards, integrity, sense of identity, and empathy. The fewest changes occurred in the areas of self-concept dance, how the world works, and self-concept student, which ranked at 1, 1, and 0, respectively. At this point in the study, the researchers remain uncertain about how these scales behave and will pursue investigative piloting and discussion with TWF personnel before the 2018 data panel.

Results: Boys Only

The next table displays scale changes between 2014 and 2016 for the boys who completed both surveys. As listed before on the left margin are the 16 scales for which there was sufficient data for the analyses. Across the top

Scale	Pre / Post	Girls					Boys				Gains(n)
		9–10	11–12	13–14	15–16	17	9–10	11–12	13–14	15–16	
Self-concept dance	2014 / 2016										1
Self-concept Student	2014 / 2016										0
Creative Confidence Dance	2014 / 2016										3
Self-efficacy	2014 / 2016										2
Collaboration	2014 / 2016										4
Pro-social Behavior	2014 / 2016										3
Interpersonal Skills	2014 / 2016										2
How the World Works	2014 / 2016										1
Sense of Possibilities	2014 / 2016										4
Sense of Purpose	2014 / 2016										8
Sense of Identity	2014 / 2016										5
Ties to Community	2014 / 2016										2
Seeks Intrinsic Rewards	2014 / 2016										6
Empathy	2014 / 2016										5
Attributions for Success	2014 / 2016										4
Integrity	2014 / 2016										6

Table 2.3   2016 Longitudinal survey data, two-year gains, all groups

Table 2.4 2016 Rank order of scale gains

Sense of purpose	8
Seeks intrinsic rewards	6
Integrity	6
Sense of identity	5
Empathy	5
Attributions for success	4
Sense of possibilities	4
Collaboration	4
Creative confidence dance	3
Pro-social behavior	3
Self-efficacy	2
Interpersonal skills	2
Ties to community	2
Self-concept dance	1
How the world works	1
Self-concept student	0
Total gains	56

are the ages of the cohorts at the follow-up survey. The intention of the chart is to show which scales manifested gains over the two-year period and for which cohorts. Gains are shown as boxes with two numbers—the top number is the average pre-score for the indicated cohort, and the bottom number is the average post-score for the same cohort.

Using the topmost box as an example, this refers to pre- and post-scale scores in the domain "self-concept dance." The average pre-score on this scale for the 13- and 14-year olds was 225, while the average post-score was 261. These scores are simplified. They reflect a 2.25 average on a 4-point scale for the pre-score and, in 2016, 2.61 on the 4-point scale for the post-survey. It is easier to read scores and differences without the decimals. The increase can be read as the difference between 225 and 261, or 36 points. A 36-point scale gain is somewhat typical in this chart, but there are some that exceed this gain by a large margin and some that are smaller. For example, the pre- and post-scale scores for "how the world works" for the 11- and 12-year olds are 322 and 378, respectively, reflecting a 56-point gain. The same cohort shows a small gain of seven points for "creative confidence in dance."

Table 2.5 provides a comprehensive look at where and to what extent results on the student scales grew among boys from 2014 to 2016. One way this is depicted is in the number of gains per scale that is shown in the right column. The scale gaining in the most cohorts is "empathy," which gained in all four cohorts. In contrast, the scale "self-concept student" showed no gains.

Scale	Pre/Post	Age Group				Gains(n)
		9–10	11–12	13–14	15–16	
Self-concept dance	2014			225		1
	2016			261		
Self-concept Student	2014					0
	2016					
Creative Confidence Dance	2014		274	240		2
	2016		281	279		
Self-efficacy	2014	333				1
	2016	347				
Collaboration	2014	332		327		2
	2016	362		346		
Pro-social Behavior	2014			302		1
	2016			329		
Interpersonal Skills	2014			322		1
	2016			352		
How the World Works	2014		322			1
	2016		378			
Sense of Possibilities	2014	337			328	2
	2016	346			340	
Sense of Purpose	2014	248		327	289	3
	2016	358		346	320	
Sense of Identity	2014	310	338	338		3
	2016	346	346	356		
Ties to Community	2014			302		1
	2016			317		
Seeks Intrinsic Rewards	2014	275	309	309		3
	2016	320	330	322		
Empathy	2014	260	307	314	306	4
	2016	285	359	325	373	
Attributions for Success	2014			329		1
	2016			361		
Integrity	2014	310		294		2
	2016	333		319		
Total Gains by Age Cohort		8	5	12	3	28

Table 2.5 2016 Longitudinal survey data, two-year gains by age group, boys only

Table 2.5 also shows some clustering of gains. In general, the top scales in the chart show fewer gains with only one or two scale gains in each domain. The bottom half of the chart shows many more gains, with three or four cohorts realizing increases in several scales. For the boys, sense of purpose, sense of identity, seeking intrinsic rewards, and empathy are well populated with gains. Empathy is the one scale that grew for all four cohorts of boys.

Important to note is that the cohort of 17-year-old boys was dropped from the presentations for 2016 due to low participation rates. An insufficient number of students in this category participated, preventing the ability to analyze the results. TWF's student year-over-year retention during 2014–2016 was between 86–90%. However, when the study parameters were developed, student attrition during the two-year intervals was not accounted for. The attrition occurred due to student participation (both direct and indirect drops from TWF) or parents declining survey participation for their children. Missing data is an occupational hazard for longitudinal studies, such as what occurred here with the cohort of 17-year olds. There is some chance that the 2016 17-year olds will be brought back into the study if alumni surveys are deployed in 2018, or later, and if these students are found in college. For now, we choose to emphasize the full span of cohorts for which missing data was not a problem.

Results: Girls Only
The final table displays scale advancements between 2014 and 2016 for the girls who completed both surveys. While these changes are notable, they have not been tested for significance. Listed on the left margin are the 16 scales for which there was sufficient data to analyze. Across the top are the ages of the cohorts. The intention of the chart is to show which scales manifested gains over the 2-year period and for which cohorts. The format and layout mirror the previous chart. Gains are shown as boxes with two numbers—the top number is the average pre-score for the indicated cohort and the bottom number is the average post-score for the same cohort. The larger the difference between the two scores, the more likely the difference will prove significant.

Table 2.6 provides a comprehensive look at where and to what extent the girls' scales grew from 2014 to 2016. One way this is depicted is in the number of gains per scale shown in the right column. The scale gaining in the most cohorts is sense of purpose, which gained in all five cohorts. In contrast, the scales self-concept student and self-concept dance showed no

Scale	Pre / Post	Age Group					Gains(n)
		9–10	11–12	13–14	15–16	17	
Self-concept dance	2014						0
	2016						
Self-concept Student	2014						0
	2016						
Creative Confidence Dance	2014		312				1
	2016		317				
Self-efficacy	2014				316		1
	2016				322		
Collaboration	2014		319	322			2
	2016		326	328			
Pro-social Behavior	2014	324		314			2
	2016	338		320			
Interpersonal Skills	2014				302		1
	2016				323		
How the World Works	2014						0
	2016						
Sense of Possibilities	2014	335			315		2
	2016	346			318		
Sense of Purpose	2014	296	320	319	305	305	5
	2016	343	326	329	316	311	
Sense of Identity	2014	328	342				2
	2016	344	344				
Ties to Community	2014				283		1
	2016				305		
Seeks Intrinsic Rewards	2014	313		322	308		3
	2016	316		329	312		
Empathy	2014					300	1
	2016					326	
Attributions for Success	2014			304	344	324	3
	2016			380	367	330	
Integrity	2014	323	328	313		288	4
	2016	336	333	322		319	
Total Gains by Age Cohort		6	5	6	7	4	28

Table 2.6   2016 Longitudinal survey data, two-year gains by age group, girls only

gains in any cohort for the girls. At this point in the study, the researchers remain uncertain about how these scales behave and will pursue investigative piloting before the 2018 data panel.

Total gains by cohort are at the bottom of the chart. Gains were spread fairly evenly across the cohorts for the girls. As with the boys, a total of 28 positive scale changes resulted for 2016. Additionally, the chart shows some clustering of gains in similar scales—clusters that mirror the scale changes for boys. In general, the top scales in the chart show fewer gains, with only one or two scale gains in each domain. The bottom half of the chart shows many more gains, with three or four cohorts managing increases in several scales. In this section, sense of purpose, seeking intrinsic rewards, attributions for success, and integrity are well populated with gains. Sense of purpose is the one scale that grew for all five cohorts.

IMPLICATIONS

After two years of work, the researchers found promising, yet inconclusive, results in the data. However, there are clear implications for how to move forward. At the organizational level, TWF will continue to use data to inform organizational strategies and programmatic decisions. The researchers will take the lessons from the first panels of implementation to refine the study (instrument, survey administration plan, etc.) in preparation for the next data panel in 2018.

Using Data to Inform Practice

As collaborative partners, The Wooden Floor and the Centers for Research on Creativity engage in a dialogic relationship. Since the study began, regular, periodic consultations with CRoC have occurred in an iterative, reflective manner. The data have informed decision-making, and TWF will use the results, especially as the third and subsequent panels of data emerge, to explore the following:

- Trends in scales based on scale scores for each of the five age clusters
- Actual growth patterns over each two-year interval
- Cumulative growth patterns over multiple intervals
- Exploration of associative and potentially "causal" relationships between and among developments

Because the survey includes a wide range of popular measures, the data will continue to inform academic and social developments for years to come, with additional waves of data entering the database. Scholars interested in any of its scales will have opportunities to explore developmental conditions for each and to explore status relationships and dynamics or relationships between pro-social development and bonding to community values. The researchers will refine the academic and artistic self-concept scales before such explorations fully proceed. The results may be disseminated to other not-for-profit youth organizations and discussed at TWF and CRoC in order to lend some context to what emerges in TWF data.

This project contributes data that could inform a number of studies, such as relations between academic and creative self-concept. The study's research findings can also help shape how other practitioners view youth assets that contribute to development and achievement. Furthermore, as the study progresses, factors that help close the achievement and other gaps will be illuminated.

For TWF, the 10-year study has both instrumental and conceptual uses. Outcomes measured in two-year intervals will suggest the impacts of program practices. The TWF program may evolve in response to the data as the organization employs a continuous cycle of improvement to advance effectiveness and sustain high-impact outcomes.

Furthermore, the study will advance TWF's goals to scale its model locally and nationally. In November 2015, TWF signed its first national, licensed partner, CityDance DREAM in Washington, DC. Under a copyright license agreement, TWF provides curriculum, training, and consulting on its program model, as well as effective youth development strategies, and CityDance DREAM agrees to implement TWF's theory of change and programmatic model in full. Additionally, when TWF opens its second location, 100 new students will be enrolled in the longitudinal study for a total of 475 participants in the 2017–2018 data collection panel. TWF will determine if those 100 students will participate as their own cohort for comparative purposes, as part of the 2018 interval of the Longitudinal Study.

Implementation Lessons

Many lessons have emerged since the evaluation tool design phase and through the implementation of the first two panels of the longitudinal study. It is the hope of the authors that the goals and outcomes of this longitudinal study, including the complexity of the preparation and implementation process, will serve to inform internal stakeholders at TWF and a broader audience of researchers, practitioners, and leaders in the field of the arts and creative youth development.

Embarking on a 10-year longitudinal study is a considerable undertaking, and the rationale for conducting longitudinal studies is multifold. In the complex scenario of a person's life, it is statistically challenging to isolate factors that contribute to change. Longitudinal studies present an opportunity to observe changes over time, identify patterns, and present sound explanations or conjectures for why changes occur. When patterns are identified, inferences for why these factors have an effect, as well as implications for how to replicate those effects, can result. In a short-term study, the likelihood of confidently identifying factors that contribute to change is considerably smaller.

Through the course of this study, the researchers anticipate that the data will illuminate (a) appropriate indicators of success in the realm of creative youth development, (b) positive changes over time among these indicators for various age groups and for the two gender cohorts that participate in intervention programming, and (c) elements of curriculum and instruction that correlate to positive changes in student development.

There are many benefits to conducting this type of research; at the same time, the amount of effort required is significant. TWF created an ambitious plan to carry out the work. These activities included increasing the annual operating budget and fundraising to support the evaluation study at 2-year intervals; investing in professional development to build staff capacity and understanding of evaluation methodology and data management; coordinating logistics with the research firm; developing internal policies and procedures and training documents; and communicating the work with the Board of Directors, staff, faculty, students, and families at TWF.

TWF has three dedicated staff members involved in the Longitudinal Study to ensure that in the event of a staff departure, the study would have appropriate staffing and sustainability. During 2016, in fact, one of the three staff members departed, but the study was not affected due to redundancy measures and a new third staff member was immediately identified to join the team.

As the board and executive leadership of TWF look to the next 30 years, the organization is driven to respond to the overwhelming need to serve more youth. In 2009, when TWF envisioned the longitudinal study, there were no specific plans for growth and expansion. Since the first baseline study in 2014, TWF has definitive plans for scaling its model both locally and nationally. In 2017, TWF will expand its footprint to serve 100 more students between the ages of 8–13 for a total of 475 students.

As mentioned previously, once CityDance DREAM implements the full programmatic model, their own cohort of students will be encouraged to participate in the longitudinal study. TWF had to ensure that the evaluation tool was easy to implement and that CRoC could accommodate the analysis and data reporting for TWF and CityDance DREAM, both as individual organizations and combined.

CONCLUSION

TWF uses dance as a vehicle for student success because dance engages all the systems of the body. We are not sure at this point about whether the results so far are unique to dance as a programmatic intervention for youth. This will be a subject of inquiry as subsequent panels of data are attained. Creativity and expression are catalysts for positive change through the process of inventive art-making. Exploratory dance engages multiple intelligences and modalities within the body that encourage youth to think differently about themselves, to push through obstacles, and to emerge as strong and confident leaders. Success and feelings of accomplishment permeate and lift all areas of their lives, from academic engagement and proficiency to the dreams they hold for the future. As TWF students advance through the rigorous dance education curriculum combined with co-creation of art, dance-making processes, and the experience of live performance, they stand to gain:

- Creativity and resilience
- Discipline and motivation
- Physical health and well being
- Self-awareness and presence
- Access to the soul through the creative experience
- An embodied sense of community and team learning
- Confidence and a sense of safety to explore and express
- Awakened curiosity and attentiveness
- Problem-solving skills and patience with process
- Trust of their subjective experience
- Joy

The Centers for Research on Creativity and The Wooden Floor authors would like to thank the following people for their support of the longitudinal study: TWF Board of Directors and staff, dance faculty and program team, as well as study coordinators Derek Bruner (TWF) and Tamee´ Seidling (CRoC).

TWF believes in the power of dance as a catalyst for personal change and empowerment in order to move young people forward, with the confidence and gifts to know that from here, students can step anywhere. We will learn more and more about where they step as the study proceeds.

REFERENCES

Ames, C. A. (1990). Motivation: What teachers need to know. *Teachers College Record, 91*(3), 409–421.

Bradley, K. (2002). Informing and reforming dance education research. *Critical Links*, pp. 16–18. Arts Education Partnership, Washington, DC.

Catterall, J. S. (2009). *Doing well and doing good by doing art: Effects on the achievements and values of young adults.* Los Angeles, CA: I-Group Books.

Chapman University School of Education. (2008). *Analysis of the multidimensional self esteem scale data for Saint Joseph's Ballet.* Orange, CA: Chapman University.

Coleman, J. S., Campbell, E. Q., Hobson, C. F., McPartland, J. M., Mood, A. M., Weinfeld, F. D., et al. (1966). *Equality of educational opportunity.* Washington, DC: U.S. Government Printing Office.

Darby, J. T., & Catterall, J. S. (1994). The fourth R: The arts and learning. *Teachers College Record, 96*(2), 299–328.

Fredericks, J., & McColskey, W. (2011). *Measuring student engagement in upper elementary through high school: A description of 21 instruments.* REL Southeast Report 098, Southeast Regional Educational Laboratory. Retrieved from http://files.eric.ed.gov/fulltext/ED514996.pdf

Gandara, P., & Contreras, F. (2009). *The Latino education crisis: The consequences of failed social policies.* Cambridge, MA: Harvard University Press.

Graham, S., & Taylor, A. (2002). Ethnicity, gender, and the development of achievement values. In A. Wigfield & J. Eccles (Eds.), *Development of achievement motivation* (pp. 121–146). San Diego, CA: Academic Press.

Hagell, N. A. (2012). *Changing adolescents: Social trends and mental health.* Bristol, UK: Policy Press.

Johnson, D. W., & Johnson, R. T. (1989). *Cooperation and competition: Theory and research.* Edina, MN: Interaction Book Company.

Lopez, M. H., & Velasco, G. (2011). *The toll of the great recession: Childhood poverty among Hispanics sets record, leads nation.* Washington, DC: PEW Hispanic Center.

Pajares, F. (1996). Self-efficacy beliefs in academic settings. *Review of Educational Research, 66*(4), 543–578.

Raffini, J. P. (1993). *Winners without losers: Structures and strategies for increasing student motivation to learn.* Boston: Allyn & Bacon.

Rogoff, B. (2003). *The cultural nature of human development.* Oxford: Oxford University Press.

Salkind, N. J. (2008). Empathy. In *Encyclopedia of educational psychology.* Thousand Oaks, CA: Sage Publications.

Scholz, U., Gutierrez-Doña, B., Sud, S., & Schwarzer, R. (2002). Is perceived self-efficacy a universal construct? Psychometric findings from 25 countries. *European Journal of Psychological Assessment, 18*(3), 242–251.

Simpson, S., & Minear, N. (1998). *Impacts of Saint Joseph Ballet: A development asset model.* Irvine, CA: University of California.

Siri, J. (1993). *Creative intervention for at-risk youth: An evaluation of Saint Joseph Ballet's impact on inner-city youth.* Santa Ana, CA: Saint Joseph Ballet.

Stipek, K., & Seal, D. (2004). *Mentes motivadas: Como educar a tus hijos para Qque disfruten aprendiendo.* Spain: Ediciones Paidos.

The Pell Institute for the Study of Opportunity in Higher Education and The University of Pennsylvania Alliance for Higher Education and Democracy. (2016). Indicators of higher education equity in the United States. Retrieved from http://www.pellinstitute.org/publicationsIndicators_of_Higher_Education_Equity_in_the_United_States_2016_Historical_Trend_Report.shtml

The Wooden Floor. (2014). *The Wooden Floor: From here, you can step anywhere.* Santa Ana, CA.

Weiner, B. (2006). *Social motivation, justice, and the moral emotions: An attributional approach.* Mahway, NJ: Lawrence Erlbaum Associates Inc.

CHAPTER 3

Everyday Arts for Special Education: Impact on Student Learning and Teacher Development

Rob Horowitz

New York City's District 75, the special education district, received an Investing in Innovation (i3) grant in 2010 from the US Department of Education for the Everyday Arts for Special Education (EASE) program. EASE was a five-year program providing professional development and instruction in the arts in ten District 75 elementary schools, spread across multiple NYC sites. Instruction included activities in music, visual art, dance, and drama. The program was implemented in collaboration with the Manhattan New Music Project (MNMP) and Urban Arts Partnership (UAP). The program served 300 teachers and 5334 students (K-5) over the five years of the grant.

The teaching artists of MNMP and UAP had nine years of practical experience collaborating with District 75 through a series of federal professional development grants, beginning in 2001. Their success in improving

This research was supported by US Department of Education i3 Grant U396C100275 awarded to District 75, New York City Department of Education.

R. Horowitz (✉)
Center for Arts Education Research, Teachers College, Columbia University, New York, NY, USA

© The Author(s) 2018
R.S. Rajan, I.C. O'Neal (eds.), *Arts Evaluation and Assessment*,
https://doi.org/10.1007/978-3-319-64116-4_3

the communication and socialization skills of children with disabilities prompted the district to apply for the i3 grant, in order to reach more students and teachers, and to study the potential effects.

The evaluation design included two impact studies, a mixed-method and student assessment study, an implementation study, and case studies. The impact of the program on reading and math achievement and social-emotional learning (SEL) was investigated through a quasi-experimental design (QED) using the New York State Alternative Assessment (NYSAA) for reading and math scores, and the Student Annual Needs Determination Inventory (SANDI) for SEL. The mixed-method study included weekly student assessment by participating teachers, structured observations, surveys, and interviews. An implementation study examined patterns of teacher participation through instruction logs, professional development, teaching artist visits and mentoring, and curriculum development. Case studies were conducted in selected sites, examining student behavior and progress, and teachers' ability to implement instructional methods learned through professional development. Analysis included a multilevel regression model for the QEDs, extensive coding of qualitative data, and descriptive, correlative, and regression analysis for the surveys and observation data.

The program was determined to have an effect on reading scores, social-emotional learning, communication and socialization skills, and teachers' ability to implement arts-based teaching methods for students with varied disabilities. Students also made gains in time spent on task, classroom engagement, mastery of IEP goals, and arts proficiency. Teachers gained new skills in using the arts to engage students with varied disabilities.

The evaluation design presented unique challenges due to the diversity of the students, who varied according to disability and the degree of disability. There were many different stakeholders for the evaluation, including the US and NYC departments of education, the school principals, the partnering arts organizations, and the teachers, teaching artists, and parents. This chapter presents the most salient findings from the evaluation, while exploring the special challenges we faced and the solutions we provided. We invite the reader to consider how this study highlights complex issues inherent to a large-scale evaluation in special education and the arts, and whether our solutions are applicable to others' efforts, both large and small, national and local, and within and outside the arts and special education.

Context and Unique Challenges

EASE was funded through an i3 Development Grant to District 75, New York City's special education district. When the grant began in 2010, District 75 employed 4000 teachers in 56 schools within each of New York City's five boroughs. Of the District's 23,000 students, 71% were eligible for Title I support, 86% were from minority populations, 15% were English Language Learners, and 60% were assessed on New York State alternate academic achievement standards. Students' disabilities encompassed a wide range, including autism spectrum disorders, cognitive disabilities, emotional disturbance, severe learning disabilities, and multiple handicaps (physical and cognitive). The students required highly specialized educational programs and support systems.

The participating EASE students were all in elementary grades (K-5) within ten District 75 schools. However, the meanings of "district," "school," and "grade" were different than a conventional setting. District 75 is not a geographical district, but is instead an organizational structure across the entire city for students who require the special services available through the district. The EASE "schools" were not buildings, but instead were organizational structures, comprised of multiple sites, within various school buildings which might also have other programs. In total, the EASE program operated in 37 sites throughout NYC. While all students were in elementary grades, these grades did not reflect a level of academic achievement, but instead were based upon each student's physical age.

EASE students had four categories of disabilities: autism spectrum, intellectual disabilities, emotional disturbance, and multiple disabilities. Students varied in the range of severity of disabilities within each category. EASE instruction took place within each EASE teacher's classroom. The classes were sometimes grouped according to disability, but often contained various disabilities. EASE class sizes varied, as well, with up to 12 students per class. Most EASE classes had six students.

Therefore, the setting for EASE was unusual. The diversity of sites, students, disabilities, and class groupings did not readily lend itself to a rigorous impact study that could meet standardized evaluation criteria, such as those recommended by the What Works Clearinghouse (2014). Each EASE student and classroom was in fact quite atypical. The students all had an Individualized Education Plan (IEP) and teachers were expected to customize the instruction to meet each student's special needs. The EASE program provided extensive professional development (PD) for the teachers that included a repertoire of arts-based strategies that they could employ to address each students' IEP needs, particularly in communication, socialization, and related academic areas.

As is often the case with a complex arts partnership, there were many interested parties, or stakeholders, who comprised the "audience" for the evaluation. These included US and NYC departments of education, the school principals, the partnering arts organizations, and the teachers, teaching artists, and parents. Like the EASE students, each audience had its own interests and needs. The US Department of Education placed a strong emphasis on rigorous evaluation designs, with a preference for a randomized controlled trial (RCT) or quasi-experimental design (QED). Conversely, the diversity of sites and students lent itself to a mixed-method design with extensive qualitative study. We therefore decided to take a multiple-method approach to examine program impact while also investigating the unique experiences of teachers, artists, and students. This chapter primarily reports on the quantitative findings, while subsequent reports will more fully explore the qualitative data.

THE PROGRAM AND IMPLEMENTATION

EASE teachers learned strategies across multiple arts disciplines (music, dance, visual arts, and theater) through a series of professional development workshops and extensive in-school support. There were four key program components:

1. Professional Development Workshops (Teachers and administrators met with teaching artists for full-day workshops, where they learned a repertoire of arts-based instructional strategies to address students' IEP goals.)
2. Collaborative Classroom Modeling (Teaching artists collaborated with teachers to implement strategies learned in the PD workshops.)
3. On-Site Professional Development (Teaching artists conducted 45-minute on-site PD sessions with teachers, focused on differentiation and documentation of best practices.)
4. Classroom Instruction (Teachers addressed an IEP goal through an EASE instructional activity.)

The PD was led by Manhattan New Music Project (MNMP) and Urban Arts Partnership (UAP) teaching artists.[1] Teachers learned differentiated arts-based strategies designed to meet the communication, socialization, academic, and arts goals of each student's IEP across multiple arts. The strategies were developed through many years of experience by a core group of teaching artists, who had worked in other District 75 and special education projects. The strategies were codified at the outset of the program by a curriculum developer/program designer. The PD sessions were experiential, with teachers practicing the activities, both as "students" and instructors. Artist visits to each classroom provided modeling and on-site coaching.

A new cohort of 60 teachers and their students from the participating sites were added to the EASE program each program year, while ongoing PD and support was provided for previous years' participants. The level of direct teaching artist support was reduced in each subsequent year of teachers' participation as they became more capable of implementing the program without assistance. Upon reaching their fourth year, the most effective teachers were identified and trained to become mentor teachers, in order to help disseminate the EASE program to others.

Table 3.1 shows the levels of support for each year's cohort of teachers. Table 3.2 shows activities for each level.

Table 3.1 EASE teacher cohorts: Levels of program support over five years

Implementation year	Support level				
Year 1	Beginner level support				
Year 2	Intermediate level support	Beginner level support			
Year 3	Advanced level support	Intermediate level support	Beginner level support		
Year 4	Selected teachers become mentors	Advanced level support	Intermediate level support	Beginner level support	
Year 5	Selected teachers become mentors	Selected teachers become mentors	Advanced level support	Intermediate level support	Beginner level support

Table 3.2 Activities for teachers at different program levels

Level	Activities per level			
Beginner level	Teachers learn and implement EASE with extensive support from teaching artists	4 full-day workshops per teacher	20 in-class teaching artist visits per class	20 forty-five minute sessions per teacher
Intermediate level	Teachers implement EASE with new students, taking more responsibility from teaching artists	2 full-day workshops per teacher	16 in-class teaching artist visits per class	16 forty-five minute sessions per teacher
Advanced level	Teachers implement EASE with new students, requiring minimal support from teaching artists	1 full-day workshop per teacher	8 in-class teaching artist visits per class	8 forty-five minute sessions per teacher

EVALUATION DESIGN

Given the complexity and diversity of the program, we employed several distinct evaluation components, including two impact studies, a mixed-method study with student assessment, a fidelity study, and case studies of specific classrooms. The evaluation team included nine graduate students and postdoctoral researchers with experience in the arts, education, and qualitative fieldwork. The evaluation was guided by five questions:

1. Does the program increase teachers' ability to effectively apply multidisciplinary arts-based strategies for students with special needs?
2. Does the program improve students' communication and socialization skills through multidisciplinary arts activities?
3. Does the program improve students' arts proficiency through multidisciplinary arts activities?
4. Does the program improve students' academic proficiency through multidisciplinary arts activities?
5. Are there different effects among different sample populations, including students on the autism spectrum, students with cognitive disabilities, students with emotional disturbance, and students with multiple disabilities?

Academic proficiency was investigated through the impact studies, using the New York State Alterative Assessment (NYSAA). Communication and socialization skills were examined through a standardized measure of SEL (SANDI), teacher assessments of student development, and classroom observations by the evaluation team.

Design of Impact Studies: Reading, Math, and SEL

The impact studies employed a cluster (site) quasi-experimental design to examine the impact of EASE on special education students' academic achievement and social-emotional behavior. The studies were conducted in multiple sites within the ten EASE schools. At the outset of the program, District 75 schools were invited to apply for participation via a survey, with the following questions.

- State your current elementary-age population across all sites. (Pre-K through 6th grade)
- State the number of elementary-aged classes you currently have across all sites. (Pre-K through 6th grade)
- How many classes are served by these arts specialists, at which sites, and how frequently?
- List the cultural organizations which provided arts programs/residencies (if any) at your school for the past three years.
- How did you hear about EASE and why do you think your school will be a good candidate for participation in EASE?
- What changes do you expect to see in your students, teachers, and administration as a result of the EASE program?
- EASE may require schools to adjust their schedules from time to time in order to facilitate teaching artist visits, teacher meetings, in-school professional development, and interviews by the evaluation team. What do you see as the challenges to this?
- How will you address these challenges?
- EASE will require that participating teachers be released up to four times per year for mandatory all-day workshops. Although funds are available for hiring substitutes, schools sometimes find it difficult to release multiple teachers on the same day. How challenging is it for you to find substitutes?

- How many teachers do you feel you could reasonably expect to release on any given day?
- As part of the project's research component, participating teachers will be required to submit weekly online reports tracking students' progress in EASE activities. What strategies will you employ to ensure your teachers are compliant with this requirement?
- Although EASE training is provided to teachers, the program will function more smoothly with other school staff on board. How will you turnkey the knowledge and skills gained by teachers to administrators, related service providers, and paraprofessionals?
- The EASE program will require a school point person for EASE coordination. What are the qualities that would make an individual effective in this position?
- Who would be the EASE point person at your school?
- In addition to any grant-imposed teacher selection criteria, indicate the criteria you will use to select teachers for participation in EASE.

Applications were reviewed by District 75 and Manhattan New Music Project (MNMP) staff. The ten schools were selected based upon their capacity, leadership, and ability to sustain commitment to the program. Schools and teachers were not offered any incentives to participate beyond access to the grant activities. The program was implemented in 37 sites within the 10 schools.

The treatment groups for the QED impact studies were drawn from these 37 sites, based upon students matching the selection criteria described in the **Selection of Student Sample** section, below. The comparison groups were from the same ten schools, but in sites where there was no EASE participation.

Research questions for the impact studies included:

- What is the impact of two years of exposure to EASE on fourth grade special education (SPED) students' reading achievement as measured by the New York State Alternative Assessment (NYSAA)?
- What is the impact of two years of exposure to EASE on fourth grade SPED students' mathematics achievement as measured by NYSAA?
- What is the impact of two years of exposure to EASE on second–fifth grade SPED students' social-emotional behavior as measured by the Student Annual Needs Determination Inventory (SANDI)?

New York State Alternative Assessment (NYSAA) Academic achievement was measured through NYSAA, which contains a series of teacher-selected performance tasks. Only students with severe cognitive disabilities are eligible for NYSAA, based upon these criteria: (1) the student has a severe cognitive disability and significant deficits in communication/language and significant deficits in adaptive behavior; (2) the student requires a highly specialized educational program that facilitates the acquisition, application, and transfer of skills across natural environments (home, school, community, and/or workplace); and (3) the student requires educational support systems, such as assistive technology, personal care services, health/medical services, or behavioral intervention (New York State Education Department [NYSED], 2010). The study sample of students took NYSAA in reading and math each year, in the fall and spring.

When administering NYSAA, teachers selected indicators for each content area that was appropriate for each student. The indicators ranged "across a spectrum of complexity from least to most complex." An example of a less complex fourth grade ELA indicator was to "attend to or read literary texts" while a more complex indicator was "select and read literature for fluency for comprehension." The indicators were selected based upon the students' grade and age, the appropriateness of the challenge, the students' academic ability, and the school year's curriculum content. Teachers selected an assessment task that matched the indicator, that could be performed in one day, and that was observable and measurable. Teachers gathered two pieces of verifying evidence for each indicator, and scored the resulting "dataportfolios" on two dimensions: Connection to Grade Level Content and Performance. Level of Accuracy and Level of Independence were considered when scoring Performance. They were calculated as a percentage from 0% to 100% and then assigned to a level of 1 to 4 based upon the percentage of accuracy and independence (1 = 0–29%, 2 = 30–59%, 3 = 60–79%, 4 = 80–100%) on their performance tasks. Accuracy was determined by comparing the student's number of correct responses with the total number of expected responses. Independence was determined by dividing the number of steps or items not requiring prompts or cues by the total number of steps in the task (NYSED, 2010).

Student Annual Needs Determination Inventory (SANDI) Social-emotional behavior was measured using the Student Annual Needs Determination Inventory (SANDI), an 88-item survey of Performance Items completed by teachers. SANDI was developed by the Riverside

County, California, Office of Education, Special Education Unit as an assessment tool to determine students' functional skills. In addition, SANDI aids instructional decisions based upon a students' performance level, progress on IEP goals, and identification of educational needs (Riverside County Office of Education, 2008).

Students were asked to perform tasks that reflected IEP goals. Sample SEL items included "Turns, looks, and/or listens to show awareness of people in the environment 5 times a day" and "Uses self-regulating strategies to cope with 5 situations that are stressful to the student." SANDI items were scored according to four categories (Not Engaged, Engaged, Supported, Independent) which reflected the percentage of correct responses, considering additional scoring criteria such as the number of prompts needed to complete the task. The scores were used by the teacher to identify areas of need and to refine IEP goals. Based upon the scores, the students were assigned to one of four categories for each IEP assessed: Proficient, Basic, Below Basic, Far Below Basic (Cahill, Silva, & Chappell, 2012).

Selection of Student Sample The sample used to examine academic achievement included two cohorts of fourth grade students (2011–2012 and 2012–2013). Academic outcomes (NYSAA scores) were analyzed at the end of fifth grade (2013 and 2014, respectively). To be included in the analysis, students were required to meet these criteria:

- Student identified as an alternative assessment student (i.e., eligible to take the NYSAA)
- Student had a NYSAA third grade score (in order to have a pre-intervention measure of academic achievement)

The sample used to examine social-emotional behavior included two cohorts of students in second–fourth grade (2012–2013, and 2013–2014) that had fall pretest (2012, 2013, respectively) scores and spring posttest scores (2014, 2015, respectively) on the SANDI. Outcomes (SANDI scores) were analyzed at the end of third, fourth, and fifth grades, respectively (in spring 2014 and 2015).

Therefore, the treatment sample for academic achievement was fourth grade students after two years of exposure, and the treatment sample for SEL was second, third, and fourth grade students after two years of

Table 3.3   EASE impact study samples

	Schools		Sites	Students	
	EASE	Comparison	Grade(s)	EASE	Comparison
Academic achievement sample	8	28	18	4th	83	74
Social-emotional behavior sample	10	23	22	2nd, 3rd, 4th	190	569

exposure. The comparison sample included all students with pretests and posttests for NYSAA and SANDI in the same years, who had no exposure to EASE, and were in sites that had no EASE programming but were within the same ten schools. The counterfactual conditions were "business as usual" in these comparison sites. Identification of the treatment and comparison samples was at the student level, according to the criteria described above, and both groups were distributed across various sites within the ten schools. As shown in Table 3.3 the academic achievement (reading and math) analysis included 28 EASE sites and 18 comparison non-EASE sites (within 8 of the 10 schools implementing EASE). The analysis of social-emotional behavior included 23 EASE sites and 22 comparison non-EASE sites (in 10 of 10 schools implementing EASE).

The analysis sample was defined as being comprised of students with non-missing pretests and non-missing outcomes. Therefore, the analysis used casewise deletion for students that were missing pretests or outcomes. Estimates of the intervention's effects were based on analysis of data without any imputed outcome values.

Mixed-Method Study and Student Assessment

A mixed-method study was conducted for the entire EASE teacher and student population over the five-year grant period. Data collection included weekly student assessments, teacher surveys, exploratory and structured observations, and teacher interviews. Quantitative indicators were identified through systematic analysis of qualitative data, including ethnographic observations and teacher interviews from previous evaluation projects in District 75.

Each week EASE teachers assessed each of their students through an online survey. In the survey, the teachers described an IEP goal that they addressed through EASE, identified the EASE instructional activities they used that week to address the IEP goals, and rated the students on these dimensions: communication skills, socialization skills, following directions, time on task, engagement, arts proficiency, and progress toward the selected IEP goal. Ratings were on a 3-point scale (little or no progress, some progress, and significant progress). The ratings were conducted throughout the school year.

Between 40 and 79 EASE classes were observed each year by the evaluation team, for a total of 293 classroom observations. The number of observations increased per year as the program expanded to more teachers. An observational assessment protocol was developed after the first year. Each field researcher rated 12 teaching indicators and 4 student learning indicators through an online survey, on a software platform that linked data from multiple sources. Each researcher was asked to provide qualitative descriptions of teacher and student behaviors to illustrate or explain their ratings for each indicator. The submissions were coded for school site, teacher, artist, researcher, grade, and teacher level through the software. The researchers all had completed graduate coursework in qualitative methods, had extensive field experience in arts partnership evaluation, and met throughout the study to compare observations and review the indicators. Inter-rater reliability estimates of $r = 0.87$ were obtained through comparing observer ratings. The teacher and researcher ratings were submitted through the ArtsResearch software platform, developed for the EASE evaluation (Horowitz & Horowitz, 2016).

Implementation Study

A fidelity measure was developed that tracked teachers' participation in each program component. The program developers defined a minimal level of participation they considered essential for the program to be effective. For instance, teachers were expected to attend each PD session. Therefore, they received a score of 1 for attending all sessions, and a score of 0 if they missed a session. If 75% of teachers received a score of "1" then that was considered evidence of program fidelity for the PD program component. Similar formulas were developed for assessing fidelity in the other program components, based upon the degree of participation per level (i.e., beginning teachers attend at least 15 on-site PD sessions for a score of 1). Fidelity scores were then calculated at the teacher, site, and school levels. Analysis of the fidelity scores indicated consistent adherence to the overall program (Table 3.4).

Table 3.4   Fidelity of implementation

Program component	Component level threshold for fidelity of implementation	Component fidelity score (%)
Professional development workshops	Unit level score = 1: Teacher attends all PD workshops. Sample level: at least 75% of teachers across all schools have a score of 1	93.2
Collaborative classroom modeling	Unit level score = 1: Beginning teachers participate in > 14 collaborations; intermediate teachers > 11 collaborations; advanced teachers: > 5 collaborations. Sample level: at least 75% of teachers across all schools have a score of 1	91.9
On-site professional development	Unit level score = 1: Beginning teachers participate in > 14 collaborations; intermediate teachers > 11 collaborations; advanced teachers: > 5 collaborations. Sample level: at least 75% of teachers across all schools have a score of 1	90.4
Classroom instruction	Unit level score = 1: Teacher has weekly reporting indicating that he/she has implemented activities to address each student's IEP goal for at least 19 weeks. Sample level: at least 75% of teachers across all schools have a score of 1	75.4

DATA COLLECTION CHALLENGES AND SOLUTIONS

The evaluation design and data collection process presented several interesting challenges. Although these challenges are inherent to applied educational research and assessment, they seemed magnified in the EASE project.

EASE was one of the largest federally funded arts education/special education projects to date. It employed an exemplary cadre of NYC teaching artists, and used a pedagogy that was hard won over years of experience. District 75 had considerable experience in implementing these projects, although this was their largest funded arts program. The US Department of Education had detailed, specific requirements for evaluators and provided technical support for designing and analyzing rigorous statistical impact studies.

However, the standardization that these studies required did not match the non-standard students and classrooms, which were all unique in their own way, with customized, differentiated instruction the guiding principle for providing appropriate services for students with special needs. The program implementers were fond of saying that they worked in a context where "one size fits none." The EASE teachers were consistently urged to select the teaching strategies that would work best for each child. Therefore, EASE did not teach a set arts curriculum, but was instead best understood as a PD and instructional program that used a palette of arts-based strategies to engage each individual child. The "treatment," therefore, consisted of approaches to engaging students and teaching varied content, both academic and in the arts. A common thread, however, was that all the activities were arts-based and interactive, and helped children communicate and learn to socially interact with their peers and teachers through verbal, non-verbal, and artistic means.

Clearly, as evaluators we would need to spend observation time in the classroom, documenting student behaviors, and drawing inferences on children's potential development through EASE. At the same time, we would use overall standardized measures for the QED impact studies. Our selection criteria for the QEDs meant that our treatment sample size was relatively small and excluded most of the EASE students. We therefore understood that it was important to gather data in other ways that would reflect the experience of all EASE students. One key approach was to engage teachers in a demanding and continuous student assessment study, with teachers rating student development throughout the year. Another was to observe many classes in as natural and noninvasive manner as possible.

Teacher Buy-In

We wanted open access to EASE classrooms, so we could observe the program as it appeared naturally and not in response to our presence. We also wanted teachers to provide accurate ratings on the weekly assessments, and to not feel compelled to provide positive data for the benefit of funders or administrators.

We therefore placed a great emphasis on building trust with the teachers and continually explaining the evaluation process. We told the teachers we needed accurate data, and we needed their help to get it. Our team of field researchers already had extensive experience working in District 75 schools and observing various arts and education programs. We attended the PD sessions and spoke with teachers, explaining our note-taking and the evaluation process. The teachers were assured by senior District 75 staff that the raw observation and survey would only be seen by the evaluation team and would not be shared with administrators. The data would only be reported once it was aggregated, and individual teachers and schools would not be named. In no way would our EASE evaluation be used for teacher evaluation, and school and teacher performance would not be compared in public documents. These assurances were important, because we wanted to avoid any sense of competition among teachers and schools.

During the PD sessions, the evaluation team also facilitated discussions on the kinds of behavioral indicators they might observe that they could use in their survey submissions. These indicators could not be standardized across all of the EASE classrooms, due to the range of disabilities, so we wanted teachers to rate students based upon their knowledge of the students and then explain their ratings.

Software Development

It became apparent in the early years of the study that we needed to sharply upgrade our survey platform capacity. We used two common commercial software packages during the first three years, but teachers found the survey process to be overly repetitive and time consuming.

Each teacher was required to submit a survey for each student each week. It was challenging to get that level of responses using the commercial software platforms. They were resistant to using the survey platforms, which did not have the features to expedite timely responses. We decided to develop our own software to make it as easy as possible for teachers to respond on whatever platform they had available, and that would also facilitate our analysis.

We discussed with the teachers the challenges they faced and asked for recommendations. They requested software that would allow them to:

- Review, print, and analyze previous submissions
- Cut down data entry through having pre-populated student registration, disability data, and EASE activities
- Save partially completed surveys so they could return and write more detailed open-ended responses

These requests matched our own experience, through which we identified three primary challenges to using online surveys: (1) it can be difficult to gather responses, particularly from teachers who have multiple demands on their time and attention; (2) the available platforms did not easily allow for nested, or hierarchical, designs that included evaluation of teacher professional development and student assessment across multiple sites; (3) several steps were needed to export data to statistical software, analyze, create tables or charts, and embed them into reports (Horowitz & Horowitz, 2016).

We therefore developed our own survey platform for the project with the needs of the teachers in mind. Through the software, teachers uploaded student rosters and then accessed pre-populated surveys for each of their students, with due dates for each survey indicated on each teacher's home page. They were able to respond on any mobile platform. Using the software, we received over 30,000 survey responses in the last two years of the project. The resulting ArtsResearch software has now been used on over 100 different projects, including independently by other educational providers.

PROGRAM EFFECT ON STUDENT DEVELOPMENT

The program was determined to have an effect on reading scores, social-emotional learning, communication and socialization skills, and teachers' ability to implement arts-based teaching methods for students with varied disabilities. Students also made gains in time spent on task, classroom engagement, mastery of IEP goals, and arts proficiency. Teachers gained new skills in using the arts to engage students with varied disabilities.

Impact Studies: Reading, Math, and SEL

Baseline Equivalence For each contrast, baseline equivalence was established in the analytic sample (those students with pretest and posttest scores), using third grade NYSAA scores for the academic achievement contrasts, and the SANDI administered to students in the fall prior to the first school year of EASE exposure.

Baseline equivalence was examined using a modified version of the impact model with the pretest as the dependent variable and the inclusion of two independent variables: (1) a treatment indicator and (2) a cohort (block) indicator. The treatment-comparison difference in Table 3.5 is the

Table 3.5 Baseline equivalence of treatment and control groups

Contrast and measure	Treatment group N	Comparison group N	Unadjusted treatment group SD	Unadjusted comparison group SD	Unadjusted comparison group mean	Treatment-comparison difference	Standardized T-C difference
Reading proficiency (NYSAA)	83	74	0.896	0.846	3.68	−0.026	−0.03
Math proficiency (NYSAA)	83	74	0.480	0.404	3.88	−0.048	−0.11
Social-emotional learning (SANDI)	190	569	77.89	73.63	141.68	12.34	0.16

Table 3.6   Impact estimates

Contrast	Treatment group SD	Comparison group SD	Impact estimate	Standardized effect size	Impact standard error	p value	Degrees of freedom
Reading	0.549	0.771	0.278	0.42	0.139	0.054	33.34
Math	0.610	0.652	0.033	0.05	0.088	0.971	37.86
SEL	73.65	66.09	12.21	0.18	4.11	0.005	36.48

parameter estimate on the treatment indicator taken from the model. As shown in Table 3.5, baseline equivalence was established for each contrast.

Impact Analysis Analysis of the impact studies indicated a program effect on reading achievement and social-emotional learning. There was a substantively meaningful effect of the intervention on students' reading skills (Effect Size = 0.42) as measured by NYSAA. There was a modest but significant effect on students' SEL (Effect Size = 0.18) as measured by SANDI. Analysis of NYSAA math proficiency indicated indeterminate effects with no treatment-comparison difference ($p = 0.97$) (Table 3.6).

Mixed-Method Findings: Communication and Socialization Skills

As part of the EASE program evaluation, every participating teacher rated each of their students weekly on a 3-point scale (1 = little or no progress; 2 = some progress; 3 = significant progress) on these indicators: (1) communication skills, (2) socialization skills, (3) following directions, (4) time on task, (5) self-esteem, (6) engagement, and (7) arts proficiency. Teachers also identified an IEP goal for each student that they addressed through EASE teaching strategies, and indicated the degree of improvement toward meeting those goals. The criteria for progress in each area were determined by the teachers, who had the best understanding of the students' disabilities and IEP. Teachers used their professional judgment and knowledge of each student's disability (and degree of disability) to determine if the student was making progress. Teachers received professional development in developing criteria and rating students. The teacher ratings were submitted weekly for 23 weeks during the school year. The assessments were conducted online using ArtsResearch software. Teachers

Table 3.7 Student assessment

Assessment domains	November mean	May mean
Communication skills	1.64	2.05
Socialization skills	1.66	2.08
Follows directions	1.69	2.11
Time on task	1.67	2.09
Engagement	1.78	2.17

were also asked to provide qualitative examples of behaviors that demonstrated progress in each indicator.

Analysis demonstrated significant gains in each rated domain. Table 3.7 shows significant increases ($p < 0.001$) from November to May in the fourth year of the program, when most surveys were gathered and the program was up to a full complement of 180 teachers ($n = 19,689$ assessment surveys were gathered that year). Similar gains were made each year of the program.[2]

In the assessment surveys, teachers described behaviors that supported their high ratings in communication, socialization, and engagement. These included: taking turns, leading activities, successfully interacting with peers and teachers, responding to modeling, sharing materials, appropriately interacting, making eye contact, taking turns, verbalizing or physically expressing ideas, demonstrating self-control, focusing, staying on task, and using imagination and creativity when responding to a set of criteria in a sustained task. Teachers observed that students were better able to participate longer on challenging tasks.

Classroom Observations These findings were supported by computer-assisted qualitative data analysis of evaluator site reports. Evaluators observed up to 79 EASE classes per year, writing descriptions of student behaviors that indicated improvement in communication, socialization, academic, and artistic skills. Students practiced observation, recall, focused listening, and following a sequence of steps. Artists encouraged students to use their imagination and creativity. Students were encouraged to express their ideas verbally, physically, and artistically as they acquired skills in arts activities. We observed students who began to successfully interact and collaborate with their peers, who were previously unable to do so.

Student Engagement Through interviews we learned more about teachers' perspectives on their students' development through EASE. They most often spoke about improved student engagement, and their ability to "reach" students, sometimes for the first time. They attributed the students' engagement to their desire to participate in activities that were "fun" and interactive, providing a gateway to content learning.

> *It's so easy to do because there's so much speaking and listening, the foundational skills for our students. I get goose bumps because it's just so special to see how they take that initiative when it comes to EASE. And you see the independence. When it's something they want, they can participate.*—Level II Teacher

> *In special education, we're always looking to find where a student can have an entry point. The focus of EASE is engagement first. It's a better building block to go from.*—Level III Teacher

Teachers indicated that the students were learning to concentrate and focus for longer periods of time on challenging tasks, due to the interactive, social nature of the instructional strategies.

> *I have one student in particular that's been in EASE as long as I've been in the program. She's a student who has difficulty paying attention and interacting in a positive manner whenever we do group activities. But for some reason she's very alert during EASE activities. Very focused, attentive, and she's learning a lot of different ways to interact with her peers. She's able to basically come alive during these activities. She's much more attentive [as] opposed to just sitting behind a desk and learning a concept.*—Level III Teacher

> *Two third graders were having a really difficult time sitting still and focusing, but during EASE time they would be so focused. They were really involved every time.*—Level III Teacher

Teachers mentioned that students often viewed the EASE activities as "safe," enabling them to participate with less fear of failure.

> *I had a couple of students who were kind of shy at the beginning and they didn't really want to participate. We didn't force them, as EASE tells [us] not to. But then by the end of the activity they would definitely participate. They saw it was a safe environment.*—Level III Teacher

Teachers attributed the students' engagement to the kinesthetic, active quality of the arts activities.

We'd been working on certain words since September [and my student] couldn't do it. Present it in an EASE kinesthetic—running around the room and matching the word—she can look at that first initial consonant [snaps fingers] and get it like that! When it's presented in a flashcard, no interest. I see the progress. I see the socialization. The eye contact.—Level II Teacher

I was able to get all of my students involved and engaged. There are few times throughout the day when I can honestly say that every single one of my kids seems totally immersed in an activity quite like they are with EASE.—Level I Teacher

Social Skills and Emotional Development The interactive quality of the EASE activities helped develop students' social skills. Many of the activities involved taking turns or leading other students in structured interactions, such as passing an imaginary ball or "conducting" each other's musical expression.

I think there are a lot of great things that [EASE] taught me as well as the children. It helps to work on the goal of socializing, communicating, eye contact, respecting whoever is sitting around you, giving them a turn. There's a lot of turn-taking skills.—Level I Teacher

According to teachers, students with consistent exposure to EASE demonstrated improvement in social-emotional learning and developed a greater sense of ownership of the learning process.

After working with the artists there was a spike in focus, in communication, in turn-taking. We would go through different IEP goals ... One child was just absorbing everything so quickly. In the beginning, she was just kind of ho-hum. She did what she was told and then we moved on. Then, I would say after two months, definitely it was a total change. She would help me with the music. It became this whole other level. She understood all of the activities because she had been doing it for so long. And then the next step was independence. And she really soared.—Level I Teacher

TEACHER IMPLEMENTATION AND PROFESSIONAL DEVELOPMENT

Teachers received sustained and intensive professional development through a series of workshops, on-site sessions, and in-class teaching artist visits for collaborative classroom modeling. They learned a repertoire of strategies designed to engage students through the arts. The teachers identified an IEP goal for each student and specified an EASE activity that they would use to meet the goal. They reported these goals and activities through their weekly assessment surveys, providing a detailed profile of classroom implementation that could be compared with data from other sources, such as observations and interviews.

Examples of EASE activities, learned through PD, include: (1) **Coffee Filter Murals**, where children applied concentrated watercolor paint to coffee filters and then worked in groups to create murals by pasting the filters on poster paper, with the goals of encouraging self-expression, collaboration and sharing, tactile exploration, and the development of motor skills; (2) **Chair Sequence Composing**, where children sat in a row of chairs with instruments or found objects and played when a "conductor" (teacher or classmate) pointed to them with "ribbon wand" or used STOP and GO signs; (3) **Dynamics**, where children made sounds vocally, with their bodies, or with instruments, and varied the dynamics according to prompts indicated on cards held by the leader, with the goal of practicing appropriate vocal moderation and giving and taking directions; (4) **Cameras**, where children took photos of people and objects in their classroom, and then practiced identifying people, objects, shapes, and colors, and arranging time sequences of activities, with the goal of exploring perceptions of self and others, and remembering and communicating about past events.

Field researchers rated the teachers on 12 observable indicators of competence at applying EASE strategies in the classroom. The ratings were submitted through the evaluation team's dedicated ArtsResearch software. Table 3.8 shows the percentage of EASE classes where we observed each teaching indicator. These percentages are drawn from 169 observations over the final four years of the project. Some percentages are likely lower than others because the indicators were not as easily observable in certain classes (i.e., leading other students with severe disabilities) or the classes did not provide opportunities to observe a given indicator (i.e., mentoring). The field researchers also submitted rich description of teacher and student behaviors, to illustrate and explain their ratings.

The assessment survey and observation data were very positive, indicating strong gains in teachers' knowledge and application of arts-based teaching strategies for students with special needs. Systematic analysis of combined data indicated a high degree of competence at applying arts-based strategies and improvement in their ability to serve as mentors to other teachers.

Table 3.8 Researcher ratings of teaching indicators

Teaching indicator	Percent of classes observed (%)
Teacher begins the activity in a way that is comprehensible to students	79.9
Teacher creates an opportunity for students to help prepare the activity	66.1
Teacher leads a warm-up activity that ties in with the main lesson and/or builds upon foundational skills addressed in previous lessons	59.5
Teacher creates opportunities for students to make independent choices	74.0
Teacher creates opportunities for students to make creative/aesthetic choices	62.7
Teacher creates opportunities for student interaction	66.9
Teacher creates opportunities for students to lead activities or help peers	54.4
Teacher allows ample time for each student to experience the activity as fully as possible	88.2
Teacher challenges students	82.8
Teacher effectively paces activities	75.9
Teacher sets up transitions between activities or when ending the activities	64.5
Teacher mentors or supports other professionals' understanding and participation	65.2

Professional Development Workshops The PD sessions provided ample opportunities to observe the artists model the lessons and then try them out themselves, with their peers acting as students.

Actually seeing and doing the activities as children before we implemented it in the class really helped. Because just reading it on paper doesn't do it justice.— Level III Teacher

Some teachers didn't feel comfortable infusing playfulness or using unfamiliar theater exercises. But most teachers overcame their initial reluctance and improved through trying out the lessons.

*I don't like to be in front of people acting, and that's a big part of EASE, kind of putting on a show. It's easier in class with the kids, but I don't come from a theater background or anything. It's difficult for some of us to go up there and to have to act out something.—*Level I Teacher

The support of teaching artists was invaluable. Having someone to bounce ideas off of and to look objectively at the delivery was very helpful to me and certainly helped to bolster my confidence.—Level II Teacher

Adopting the EASE Approach Teachers were encouraged to accept a certain level of experimentation. They were advised to allow "wait time" for individual students to respond or explore at their own pace, and in their own way. Teachers were also encouraged to allow students as much independence as possible regardless of a student's perceived level of ability.

I feel like I've taken on the model of "wait," and "one thing at a time," and "focus on the important things and leave the rest behind." I use that now even in my academics.—Level III Teacher

Changes in Approaches to Teaching Teachers spoke about how the program opened them up to new perspectives to teaching and learning in special education. They became more adept at allowing students ample time to respond and explore ("wait time"), focusing on what's most important in a lesson, and encouraging students' independence.

The motto "what's important?" and to let go of the rest—to wait ... For example, with the paint brushes. Two of my kids are very low [functioning]—I wasn't sure if they would be interested, or know what to do necessarily, and they totally took to it. I waited for them to discover the paint brush and they just went with the flow of what everybody else was doing. It was really nice to see them participating, where I wasn't sure if they could, or if they would be interested in doing it. But they were.—Level I Teacher

Most teachers were open to making their style of instruction more dynamic when using EASE strategies, even when they did not have an arts background. They viewed the program as beneficial to their professional development.

The teaching artists really helped me see a different point of view by using EASE. They helped me a lot in terms of how to look at a lesson plan and make it fun. And I think that's where I don't know what to do, because I don't know how to make lessons fun. They come in to tell me, "Well, we can change it up by looking at the classroom. We can move tables." Moving tables—I didn't think of it! Using cameras—taking pictures and showing the kids what they did the day before as a review. And the kids get really excited once they see pictures of themselves. They're like, "Oh! We made that!" I think painting is another big thing. They love art. I get very skeptical about using paint in my classroom but the kids get really excited when they mix colors together. It's very calming for them. They give me a lot of advice on how to make the lesson fun, and I think that's where I'm starting to see where I need to work on my professional growth.—Level II Teacher

New Perspectives on Students EASE created opportunities for teachers to see their students in a different light. Several teachers mentioned that they were surprised by the types of activities that resonated with their students.

I was just surprised at the activities I expected certain kids to like or dislike. It didn't always work the way I thought. EASE is a little unpredictable. And they talked about it at the last EASE PD ... You think that a certain kid won't like this activity because of the noise—because of this or that—and it actually turned out to be opposite. It opens your eyes to [the fact that] they can make their own choices.—Level I Teacher

Two students in particular really took on a leadership role. They got excited. They wanted to be the leaders. And a few of them went to places that I didn't think that they would go. Some of the things that I wouldn't think that they would do, they did.—Level I Teacher

CONCLUSIONS AND FUTURE DIRECTIONS

The EASE program was challenging to implement, due to the number of participating teachers and artists, the geographical spread of sites, and the range of disabilities in the student population. Nonetheless, the program was quite successful in its implementation. The district and its partners, MNMP and UAP, accomplished what they set out to do, with remarkable fidelity to their grant application and the plans of the program designers. All ten schools stayed with the program for the full five years, despite political and policy changes with potentially competing priorities. New York City schools often have multiple outside programs and in-house initiatives, and yet District 75 was able to stay the course and keep the program stable. The fidelity data provided evidence of this adherence to the overall program design.

There were challenges. Scheduling was difficult, with so many players and moving parts. Getting teachers to PD sessions could be challenging, as substitutes had to be hired and schedules could conflict with other agendas. Teachers had to be continually engaged, as the program could only work if the teachers felt it supported their instructional needs. We determined that a large majority of teachers greatly appreciated the program and implemented the EASE strategies. However, some teachers were less successful, or not as interested, and didn't invest as much in the program. A key lesson from EASE is that the extensive PD sessions, artist in-school meetings, and artist modeling were essential for nurturing the active participation of teachers. The weekly online student assessment and documentation of their EASE instruction also helped keep their focus on EASE instruction and effects on student development, amidst competing priorities for their time and attention.

Similarly, the efforts we placed as evaluators on respecting the professionalism of the teachers and their knowledge of each student's abilities were essential for data collection. We repeatedly engaged the teachers, explained the research and how it would be reported, and assured them that the data would only be used for the overall study, and not for teacher evaluation. This could be a hard sell for long-term City teachers, who had "seen it all" and weathered multiple changes in leadership and direction. But we kept at it and thought the effort paid off. We tried to be as respectful as possible during classroom observations, not disturbing the flow of the class and not expecting a show for our benefit.

Our greatest challenge—beyond scheduling—was probably developing software quickly that could meet our needs. We wanted the weekly data, but also had to respond to the teachers' issues with using other software. It was also challenging to set up a rigorous QED given the diversity of the student population. It would have been very difficult to implement without our own software, which facilitated tracking student participation in the program.

The best part of the evaluation was undoubtedly watching the program in action, and seeing children's development firsthand. We observed students with disabilities gaining communication and socialization skills, making eye contact, successfully interacting with other children, and responding to the teachers. They were often excited to participate and express themselves through the arts, and without the program they might not have had that same opportunity.

Results of the QED impact studies showed a program effect on reading and social-emotional learning. These findings were consistent with our analysis of the survey and observation data. Our overall conclusion is that these findings are due to the engaging quality of the activities, which facilitated children's interacting in new ways and communicating through verbal, non-verbal, and artistic means.

We did not learn as much as we hoped about varying effects on different disabilities. The reading QED sample was composed largely of students on the autism spectrum. There wasn't a significant difference in SEL scores between children with autism and those with emotional disturbance. Continued exploration of the qualitative data may reveal more understanding on effects of the program on children with different disabilities. We also would like to know about which specific teaching strategies are most effective for each disability group.

Hopefully this study can point the way toward continued research on the effects of arts learning on students with disabilities. There is more to learn about which art forms are most likely to be successful with differing disabilities, which kinds of classroom settings work best, and how classes can be structured to provide the most robust effects.

For those who take on this work, we suggest that evaluators be open to using multiple methods, be flexible, respect diversity and cultural differences, and always keep in mind that each individual student, teacher, and classroom has a story to tell.

Notes

1. District 75's arts partner was MNMP for the first two years of the grant. MNMP was absorbed by UAP, which then became District 75's partner for the final three years.
2. Because students were rated on a 3-point scale, mean scores could range from 1 to 3.

References

Cahill, K., Silva, R., & Chappell, D. A. (2012). *SANDI training manual.* Riverside, CA: Riverside County Office of Education.

Horowitz, R., & Horowitz, A. (2016, October). *Demonstration of a hierarchical survey platform for program evaluation and student assessment.* Demonstration presented at the American Evaluation Association Conference, Atlanta.

New York State Education Department, Office of State Assessment. (2010). New York State Alternative Assessment: Administration manual 2010–11, pp. 1–31. Albany, NY.

Riverside County Office of Education, Special Education Unit. (2008). *Student annual needs determination inventory* (3rd ed.). Riverside, CA: Riverside County Office of Education.

What Works Clearinghouse: Procedures and Standards Handbook: Version 3.0. (2014). Washington, DC: U.S. Department of Education, Institute of Education Sciences.

CHAPTER 4

Learning Through Music: A Five-Year Evaluation of the Cleveland Orchestra's Learning Through Music Program

Hal Abeles and Mary Hafeli

In many US schools, music education is music performance education, with the goal of student ensembles being performance perfection. US elementary schools often have a full-time school-based music specialist teacher who focuses on general and choral music education, while music instruction in secondary schools emphasizes elective choral and instrumental ensembles. This chapter highlights a somewhat alternative approach to music education centered on a partnership between a group of schools and a professional orchestra. While some school-orchestra partnerships provide arts enrichment opportunities, such as a string quartet performance in a school auditorium, the partnership described in this chapter is more comprehensive—with music instructional experiences provided by a professional orchestra and intended to promote learning in music as well as in subjects outside of the music.

The Cleveland Orchestra developed *Learning Through Music (LTM)* as a partnership program in four Cleveland-area elementary schools. The participating schools were selected by the Orchestra's education

H. Abeles (✉) • M. Hafeli
Teachers College, Columbia University, New York, NY, USA

© The Author(s) 2018
R.S. Rajan, I.C. O'Neal (eds.), *Arts Evaluation and Assessment*,
https://doi.org/10.1007/978-3-319-64116-4_4

65

programming staff from an applicant pool of 22 schools, and the criteria for selection included the perceived commitment to the program of the school principal and music teacher. Two schools were located in the Cleveland School District, one was in the Lakewood School District and the other one was in the East Cleveland School District. In the year the *LTM* program began, the two Cleveland School District schools had enrolled 317 and 568 students, respectively, and had poverty indices of 69.9% and 92.6%, the school in the Lakewood School District had a poverty index of 40% and 376 students, and the school from the East Cleveland School District enrolled 567 students and had a poverty index of 94.4%. At the end of the project's third year, after extensive discussions with the principal and faculty at one of the Cleveland School District schools about the school's level of participation in *LTM* program activities, the Orchestra decided to dissolve the *LTM* partnership at that school. Three schools remained in the program for the rest of the five-year period of the evaluation.

The *LTM* program was designed to engage participating classroom teachers, music teachers, students, and orchestra musicians. The program vision focused on classroom teachers working collaboratively to integrate music concepts and skills into their existing curricula, with music teachers deeply involved as consultants in this process, making them valued, key resources in their schools and leading all participants to actively advocate for music education in their schools. With this vision in mind, the program aimed to increase classroom teachers' interest, skill, and confidence in using music regularly in their teaching. Students were expected to gain knowledge of a symphony orchestra and its instruments and repertoire, to build their appreciation for music, and to consider music as a life-long pursuit or interest. In addition, it was anticipated that students' involvement with *LTM* would increase the number of students who pursue skills-based music experiences, such as playing musical instruments.

LTM was also intended to provide the opportunity for musicians to develop personal relationships with community members, helping to break down barriers and transforming public perceptions. Musicians were expected to develop skills that would assist them in effectively communicating with students and supporting teachers in their instructional goals. Overall, the program hoped to increase students', teachers', and parents' interest in and value for a range of musical experiences.

The practical focus of the *LTM* program was the development of music-integrated instructional resources that supported the state of Ohio's existing standards-based curriculum. Participating teachers, consultants, and the Cleveland Orchestra's education staff collaborated to develop a music-integrated curriculum resource binder that included specific lesson plans (K–5) and instructional materials, such as children's books and CDs, that were used to support each of the lessons. In addition to curriculum resources, the program provided professional development workshops for classroom teachers and music specialists several times a year to assist them in integrating the *LTM* lessons into their curricula. At the participating schools, all of the grade level teachers as well as the music specialists were expected to participate in *LTM*.

The *LTM* program started with kindergarten and first grade classes and added a grade level each year, building toward school-wide (K–5) participation at the end of the five-year pilot program. As a key component of the program, Cleveland Orchestra musicians provided in-school presentations for each of the participating classrooms approximately six times a year. These school visits culminated in a yearly neighborhood concert that featured an ensemble of Orchestra musicians. Students also attended educational performances at the Orchestra's Severance Hall.

Early in the first year of implementation, a team from the Center for Arts Education Research (CAER)[1] undertook an assessment of the program. Based on the intended outcomes of the program for teachers, students, and orchestra members, the assessment design used a variety of data-gathering strategies, such as classroom observations, reviews of student work, and interviews with students, teachers, teaching artists, and program staff. The assessment focused on: (a) the effect of *LTM* on students, (b) teachers' skill and interest in using the arts to provide interdisciplinary instructional experiences, (c) teachers' personal interest in and value for music, (d) collaboration among teachers, (e) the effect of participating in the program on school-based music specialists, and (f) the effect of participating in the program on orchestra musicians. The assessment also sought teachers' perspectives on different components of the program, such as curriculum materials, as well as their views on how participating in *LTM* affected their students and themselves. The specific data-gathering strategies for the assessment with the outcomes they were intended to examine appear in Table 4.1.

The remaining sections of the chapter are organized according to four topics: the effect of *Learning Through Music* on students, the effect of *Learning Through Music* on teachers, the effect of *Learning Through Music* on schools and communities, and the effect of *Learning Through*

Table 4.1   Program goals and outcomes and assessment tools

LTM goals/outcomes	Assessment tools
Students' knowledge of a symphony orchestra and its instruments and repertoire	Student interviews and written tests Teacher interviews Teacher survey
Students' achievement in non-arts learning	Ohio State Proficiency Exam (OSPE) scores Student achievement pretests/posttests designed by assessment team
Students' interest in pursuing life-long learning in and their appreciation for music	Student vocational choice survey Student discretionary time survey Parent survey student interviews
Students' interest in pursuing skills-based music experiences, such as playing musical instruments	Student vocational choice survey Student discretionary time survey Parent survey student interviews
Teachers' collaboration in integrating music into the curriculum	Observation of workshops Observations of classrooms Interviews with teachers and principals Teacher surveys
Teachers' interest, skill, and confidence related to using music regularly in their classroom teaching	Observations of classrooms Interviews with teachers and principals Teacher surveys music teaching self-concept inventory
Role of music teachers	Survey of classroom teachers Teacher interviews Principal interviews Observations of workshops
Musicians' skills development	Musician interviews Teacher interviews Observations of musician presentations
Musicians' motivation	Musician interviews

Music on Cleveland Orchestra members. Each of these sections is further divided into subsections, which report the results of the different assessment tools used throughout the study and that appear in Table 4.2.

THE EFFECT OF *LEARNING THROUGH MUSIC* ON STUDENTS

An important focus of our assessment was to examine the program's effect on students through several different quantitative measures as well as observations, interviews with students, teachers, and principals, and a parent survey. Early in the program, we conducted classroom observations

Table 4.2   Timeline of administration of assessment tools

Program year	Assessment tool administered
Year 1 Four schools Grades K and 1	End of the school year teacher survey (n = 23, 64%) Musician presentations in classrooms (n = 10) Teacher interviews (n = 32) Principal interviews (n = 4) Student focus groups (n = 21) Musician interviews (n = 9) Music teaching self-concept inventory (n = 22)
Year 2 Four schools Grades K–2	End of the school year teacher survey (n = 26, 58%) Classroom observations (n = 13) Teacher interviews (n = 39) Principal interviews (n = 4) Student oral tests (n = 57) Student vocational choice survey (n = 86) Musician interviews (n = 12)
Year 3 Four schools Grades K–3	End of the school year teacher survey (n = 45, 66%) Classroom observations (n = 8) Teacher interviews (n = 44) Principal interviews (n = 4) Student interviews (n = 43)
Year 4 Three schools Grades K–4	End of the school year teacher survey (n = 34, 66%) OSPE scores (n = 146) Case study—classroom observations (n = 11) Student written pretest/posttest (n = 38) Teacher interviews (n = 39) Teacher journals (n = 22) Principal interviews (n = 3) Student discretionary time survey (n = 485) Parent survey (n = 114) Musician interviews (n = 6)
Year 5 Three schools Grades K–5	End of the school year teacher survey (n = 45, 72%) Classroom observations (n = 11) Teacher interviews (n = 35) Parent interviews (n = 22) Principal interviews (n = 3) Three parallel case studies Student written tests (n = 122) Musician interviews (n = 14) Music teaching self-concept inventory (n = 46)

and interviewed teachers, students, and principals in an attempt to identify student outcomes that were targeted by *LTM*, as well as outcomes that may not have been anticipated by program developers. Through this process, we identified likely outcomes and developed more targeted evaluation strategies.

The Development of Music Skills and Understandings

Through our conversations with students and from reports by teachers and principals, we noted that students were able to demonstrate that they learned concepts and skills targeted by the *LTM* curriculum. When talking with students, we observed that they were able to recall a variety of themes clearly associated with *LTM* activities. For instance, second grade students could describe in detail characteristics of musical instruments, as shown here: "He played the B-flat and E-flat clarinets, and the bass clarinet. That one kind of looked like the saxophone because it came up on a curve back."

In Year 2, we also employed oral tests to determine students' ability to recall, apply, and use analytical concepts presented in the classroom by their teachers and by musicians from the orchestra. We administered oral tests individually, using two testing protocols—one for use with the K–2 students and the other with third grade students. The protocol (Fig. 4.1) developed for students in grades K–2 sought to determine: (1) the amount of detail the child was able to report regarding *LTM* experiences and (2) the child's ability to demonstrate different levels of understanding regarding the concepts presented in the *LTM* curriculum. We used two criteria to score the students' responses to the test—responses that provided more detail were given higher scores, and responses that reflected the understanding of more complex concepts were given higher scores.

The Grade 3 test focused on an instructional unit on Duke Ellington. The first section of the test asked students questions about Duke Ellington's life and career. The next section of the test focused on Ellington's song *Take the A-Train*. Here, the students were asked both to interpret the title of the piece and to sing the melody if they could remember it. An excerpt of *Take the A-Train* was then played, followed by an excerpt of a classical piece performed by the Cleveland Orchestra. The students were asked to talk about the differences they heard between the two excerpts, and to identify the piece they preferred and give reasons for their choice. The

(Interviews with individual children must be done in rooms with the door open)

Center for Arts Education Research
Learning Through Music
Interview Protocol
Third Grade Students

Before interviewing students, find out which of the Duke Ellington units were implemented in the class. Ask the related questions below. Interviewer will need to provide paper and colored pencils for questions related to "Who is The Duke?" unit.

We're here to talk with you about some of your experiences in the Learning Through Music program, the work you did with the Cleveland Orchestra musicians and your teacher this year. (In addition to basic recall, we are looking for examples of higher-order thinking in the children's responses. Can they apply principles they've learned in LTM? Can they analyze? Can they evaluate and give reasons for their responses?)

Duke Ellington inquiry unit:

a. Did you study Duke Ellington this spring? What can you tell me about him? Do you know anything about "The Duke's" childhood? Do you know where he grew up? Where he lived? Do you know anything about his family?

Take the A-Train
a. Do you remember any of the pieces that his band played? (If they cannot remember "Take the A-Train", remind them about it.) Why do you think the tune might have been called "Take the A-Train"?
b. Let's listen to a little bit of The Duke's "Take the A-Train" (play 20 seconds). Now here's something from a different piece, performed by the Cleveland Orchestra (play 20 seconds). Can you tell me how the pieces are different? (Depending on the richness of the child's response encourage details.) Are the instruments in The Duke's Jazz Orchestra different from those in the Cleveland Orchestra? Can you tell me the differences? Which of the two examples do you like better? Can you tell me why?

The Color of Music
a. What can you tell me about Duke Ellington and Indigo?
b. Did you listen to The Duke's tune "Mood Indigo"? Let's listen to a little part of it. (Play 20 seconds.) What can you tell me about it? What words would you use to describe the music? What about the music made you choose those words?
c. Do you know of other tunes that The Duke wrote that were related to colors?
d. What would be the difference in the music between a tune that was one color, let's say red, and a tune that was blue? Is there anything else that would make them different?

Who is The Duke?
a. Did your class investigate: Who is The Duke?
b. What about The Duke did your group investigate? What are the different ways that your group used to get the information? (e.g., encyclopedia, internet, interviews)
c. Can you draw me a "mind map" that shows what you learned about The Duke? (prompt: for information regarding family, childhood, music, instruments, travel) Can you tell me more about...? (prompt: for areas specific to drawing) Which part did your group work on? Tell me about how the different parts of your mind map are connected.

Fig. 4.1 Third grade oral test interview protocol for Duke Ellington unit

students' responses were scored on a five-point scale by awarding more points for more complete and/or correct answers.

Between 40 and 50 children from kindergarten, first grade, and second grade classrooms were tested. We recorded students' responses on audiotapes which were then transcribed for analysis purposes. The average score at each grade level provided an index of the amount of detail that students could recall and their ability to apply and analyze concepts presented in *LTM* lessons. The kindergarten students' average of 1.80 indicated that many were able to recall specific information that is part of the *LTM* curriculum—for example, one of the kindergarten students we interviewed told us that the "bow is made of horse tail." The 2.45 average for the first graders indicated that they could recall specifics and demonstrate an understanding of the concepts presented during the *LTM* activities. For example, one student told us about a recent visit: "Mr. Alexander talked about vibrations and he used the tuning fork. He would hit it on something and then put it in water so we could see the water look like it was boiling. You could see the sound waves." Many of the second grade students were not only able to understand the concepts but also to elaborate on those concepts, demonstrating a deeper, or richer, understanding. One second grader commented:

> The Great Migration was about people who weren't slaves, but who were moving all around. They had to buy tickets to go to different states and cities. They wanted a better life. We studied Jacob Lawrence, the painter. He used a lot of colors in his paintings. Sometimes he used dark colors to show that it's gloomy, and sometimes he used light colors to show it's a happy picture. I painted the picture where there were people out picking cotton. I used red, green, yellow, blue, etc. I didn't write anything to go with the painting. I liked that activity because I like painting, but I want to be an archaeologist when I grow up.

Second graders' average score was 3.53.

This pattern of students reporting greater detail as they advanced in grade level should not be surprising. Students in the first and second grades had been participating in the program for two years and it may be that their understandings of concepts presented and their familiarity with the instructional approaches employed by the *LTM* activities had accumulated. Alternatively, as children develop they become more adept at forming complex understandings and may be better able to express those understandings. Clearly, the second grade students were more "conversational" during the tests, and their willingness and ability to converse about *LTM* alone was likely to increase their scores on an evaluation procedure.

Thirty-two children from third grade classrooms were also individually tested. Our examination of the results indicated that students demonstrated competence (scores of 3 or higher) in most areas that the test examined. Their abilities varied somewhat from task to task; for example, they were more able to give specific details about the life of Duke Ellington while they were less able to give specific information about one of his tunes, *Take the A-Train*. We were impressed with the students' ability to speak about the music and life of Duke Ellington, and with the distinctions they made between Ellington's music and that of the Cleveland Orchestra. When we asked students to contrast the two pieces, they said things like:

> I think the Cleveland Orchestra one was higher pitched, it had higher notes. The first one sounded more jazzy. The other one more classical. Let's just say jazzy is more crazy. Classical is more first-class. I'm not saying jazz is bad, it's awesome, it's a little more crazy.

Students' Learning: Teacher Survey Results and Student Interviews

On annual teacher surveys throughout the five-year pilot, between 80% and 90% of the teachers agreed or strongly agreed that "students' music vocabulary improved" and that students were "more critical and knowledgeable about music than they used to be."

In student focus groups, first and second graders were able to use instrument names correctly and tell to us about the instruments, for example, "the violin bow is made of horse hair." They were able to correctly identify the instruments that represented characters in *Peter and the Wolf*, and characterize musical styles as classical, jazz, or rock. When we spoke with fourth and fifth graders in Year 5, they were fluent with concepts about instruments and the orchestra. Some of them had developed unusual specific information, exemplified in this statement:

> Mr. Fisher came in with an English horn, which has much deeper sound than the oboe that he usually brings. He showed us the reeds of the two different instruments. They're both double reeds, and they were very different. The English horn reed is larger.

Our conversations with these older students tended to be different from our conversations with children in grades K–3. Two issues dominated these older students' impressions of *LTM*. The first was their increased interest in classical music and their interest in playing a musical instrument. Consistently, we heard comments like:

> We're all more interested in music now with LTM. I like Mozart and listening to classical music. I like to learn how to play an instrument. I like hearing this music at night when I go to sleep. Before LTM I only liked country music. But I'm interested in classical music now.

The other issue that the older students commented on frequently was how the classroom presentations of the Orchestra's musicians related to other subjects they were studying. As one student put it: "We learned about weather from LTM and things in science like simple machines. We also learned about solids, liquids, and gases. We learned about measuring things like water. We learned a little bit in math, and some writing, too."

The Development of Students' Interest in Music

Teachers and principals told us that students were "captivated" by Orchestra musicians' presentations, and commented that the children enjoyed the lessons and the concerts they attended. Throughout the pilot period, *LTM* continued to broaden the students' musical experiences. One teacher described this impact of *LTM* on the students this way:

> The kids are very excited, and they love it. They love getting to know the musicians, getting to know about composers and their lives and music. And just being able to go to Severance [performance venue for the Cleveland Orchestra] and have that exposure. I really don't think that some kids would ever walk inside Severance without this program.

It seems that the students' distance from the professional orchestra members, sitting on stage in a formal uniform, had been shortened as students had come to know that these men and women lead "normal" lives—they have children, eat pizza, and like to ride bikes. And, because students were hearing much more orchestral music, teachers perceived that they were beginning to realize that any stereotypes they may have had regarding classical music may not necessarily apply to individual pieces they had come to appreciate through the *LTM* program.

In addition to conducting interviews, we administered teacher questionnaires each year. The data obtained in these surveys supported students' positive interest in and value for the program and music. Once again, from 80% to 90% of the teachers consistently agreed with statements such as "My students are more interested in music as a result of their involvement in *LTM*" and "My students look forward with anticipation to *LTM* events and activities."

Students' Vocational Interest in Music

In the second year of the program, the Vocational Choice Scale (VCS), developed by Cutietta (1995) for use in assessing children's interest in different vocations, was completed by 286 students at three *LTM* schools and 200 students at two non-*LTM* schools. In this survey students were asked to choose three vocations that they thought they might "like to be" when they were adults. There were 18 different vocations represented on the scale, including Teacher, Doctor, Parent, Basketball Player, and Musician. The results were examined to determine if there were differences between the frequencies of Musician selections for the *LTM* and non-*LTM* students. Our analysis revealed that more than 6% of all of the vocational choices made by the group that participated in *LTM* activities were Musician, while slightly more than 2% of the vocational choices by the non-*LTM* students were Musician. *Pearson's chi-squared* test of statistical significance indicated that there was a statistically significant difference (*chi-square* = 7.99, $p < 0.005$) between the pattern of responses across the two groups.

The pattern of responses for both the *LTM* and non-*LTM* groups suggests that children at this age tend to choose vocations that they are exposed to or familiar with. Their most frequent choices were Parents, Teachers, and Basketball Players. This interpretation also seems to help explain the significant differences found between the students at the *LTM* schools and the students at the two other schools. While both groups of students participated in school-based music instruction, and both groups attended The Cleveland Orchestra's Education Concerts, students at the *LTM* schools were visited by members of the Cleveland Orchestra several times throughout the year. These visits were in their classrooms, close enough so that in many cases the students could actually touch musicians' instruments. Many of the students in the *LTM* schools had participated in these activities for three years, so the musicians' visits had become a normal or expected part of their school experience.

As children grow and are exposed to a wider range of vocational choices, they may eventually narrow their choices based on both school and life experiences. It seems clear, though, that this interest in music as a vocation was present as a result of the *LTM* program. While we should not expect that a large number of *LTM* students would grow up to be members of the Cleveland Orchestra, or be music majors in college, it seems likely that more of these students would choose to become involved in a school-based instrumental music program based on their experience participating in the *LTM* program.

Students' Use of Discretionary Time

To better understand the *LTM* program's impact on students' interest in music, as part of the Year 4 assessment, we examined the extent to which *LTM* students made different choices for their use of discretionary time than students who were not in the program. We developed a survey, based on Heath and Roach's (1999) study of students' extracurricular activities, that asked students to indicate the grades in which they participated in various activities. The list of activities included both arts activities, such as "acted in a school play," and non-arts activities, such as "played on a school sports team," as well as those activities that take place during the school day or after school or on weekends. A total of 485 fifth grade students at five different Cleveland-area schools responded, 273 students from the three *LTM* schools, and 212 students from two non-*LTM* schools. The two non-*LTM* schools were demographically similar to the three *LTM* schools.

The results showed that approximately 22% of *LTM* students took lessons on orchestra instruments at their school, while a little more than 12.3% of non-*LTM* students took school-based lessons, a difference that was statistically significant (*chi-square* = 7.72, $p < 0.05$). While there was somewhat less of a difference between the two groups when comparing their enrollment in instrumental instruction outside of school (13.2% (*LTM*) versus 7.1% (non-LTM)), the difference was also statistically significant (*chi-square* = 4.74, $p < 0.05$).

More than 53% of the students at the *LTM* schools participated in some in-school arts activity, compared to 33.5% of students in the non-*LTM* schools. This difference of almost 20% was also statistically significant (*chi-square* = 21.00, $p < 0.05$). This result underscored how students who attend schools with increased arts programming may be more likely to enroll in arts elective programs when these programs are available in higher grades.

Almost 44% of the students at *LTM* schools had attended a symphony orchestra concert, compared to 25% of students at the non-*LTM* schools—also a statistically significant result (*chi-square* = 18.02, $p < 0.05$). Students at *LTM* schools were also more likely to go to community arts venues in general (44.3% for the *LTM* group and 32.6% for the non-*LTM* group), which was again statistically significant (*chi-square* = 8.52, $p < 0.05$).

The results reported above indicate that there was a difference in students' arts activities and attendance patterns at schools that participated in the program when compared with schools that did not participate in the program. The results suggest that programs like *LTM* may foster continuing interest in symphonic music both in and out of school.

Possible Alternative Explanations for the Results To examine if students at the comparison schools were simply *different* in their overall activity patterns, we analyzed participation in other non-arts activities included on the questionnaire. These included in-school sports activities and after-school sports activities and scouts and/or boys and girls clubs. In each of these three activity areas, there were no statistically significant differences in the pattern of participation between the *LTM* students and the students at the two schools that had not participated in the program.

In studies like this that focus on the use of students' discretionary time, it is necessary to consider alternative explanations for the observed results. One competing reason for the differences observed may be the general nature of the three participating schools. Since these schools were selected from a pool of 22 applications, were there other arts-related characteristics of the *LTM* schools that influenced them to participate in the program initially, made their applications particularly appealing to the Orchestra, and that may have influenced the students' activity choices? In other words, were the arts already valued at the three *LTM* schools more than the two non-*LTM* schools that were used in this study of discretionary time? We do know that the comparison schools in this study were similar to the *LTM* schools in the number of arts teachers employed and in the general arts activities that were offered. However, other differences, such as classroom teachers' attitudes about and interest in the arts, were not known. Nevertheless, most of the differences reported above were statistically significant, and the results were congruent with other information gathered from students, teachers, and parents at *LTM* schools. If we consider the multiple sources of information from student, teacher, and parent interviews as well as the results of the use of discretionary time survey, there appears to be triangulation supporting the finding that *LTM* makes a difference in students' interest in and value for music and other art areas.

Student Learning in Non-arts Disciplines

Learning Through Music, as the name of the program suggests, was designed to support student learning in other subject areas. Consequently, the assessment project focused on this issue throughout the five-year pilot program and initially, we used qualitative evaluation strategies here. We relied primarily on teachers to help identify nonmusic learning outcomes that they saw evidence of in the classroom. In addition, during the first several years of the program, through student interviews, we were able to identify understandings from outside of music that students could demonstrate. Through the qualitative data we collected in the first three years of the program, we designed specific assessment tools in years four and five to more systematically examine learning outside of music. Also, in the fifth year, we analyzed the results of the Ohio State Proficiency Examination (OSPE) scores for students participating in *LTM*. During the period the assessment took place, the OSPE was administered only to students in the fourth grade.

Teachers initially reported that students were developing skills and ways of thinking, or habits of mind (Tishman & Perkins, 1997), through the *LTM* curriculum that might ultimately influence learning in other subject areas. Teachers reported on areas such as listening skills, cooperative learning, and justifying solutions. For example, in an interview, one first grade teacher described the impact of *LTM* on her students' general learning dispositions:

> Well, I think it sharpens their listening skills. They're not used to the music, some of the music that they hear and when Mr. Taylor[2] was having them find patterns in a melody, you know it heightens their attention for listening and that will affect all areas.

Early in the study, many teachers perceived that the *LTM* learning outcomes for their students were primarily "music-based," such as appreciation for different types of music or knowledge of different instrument families. Yet, teachers were also able to see direct connections between *LTM* activities and learning in other areas.

> We talk about the detail in music and layering in music and how the more lay- ers the more detailed the music sounds and that goes into our art. You know how a six-year old with just a little bit of detail and a picture with a lot more detail, it gives a clearer vision of what the performer or artist wants to say and then it goes into our writing. "There's a ball. I like to play." Well now you need to add more detail, add more layers and that's something that we worked on is adding, like getting the detail. We illustrated that for you in music.

In other words, these teachers perceived that particular lessons from the *LTM* curriculum helped reinforce general concepts they were teaching within other subject areas. In the words of another teacher, these lessons provided "another exciting, concrete vehicle to use in the classroom to demonstrate the concepts" being presented. We noted that in the last two years of the pilot implementation, teachers were able to be much more specific about the skills and understandings their students acquired in other disciplines through *LTM* lessons.

In general, when we asked teachers about the impact of *LTM* activities on non-arts learning, they were able to provide illustrations of student behaviors that support this area of student outcomes. Yet, teachers were somewhat less confident about these outcomes than they were about stu- dents' interest in and value for music.

Measures of Student Achievement in Non-arts Disciplines

During the fourth year of the program, we designed a study to examine specific skills and understandings in disciplines other than music that students developed through *LTM* experiences. We conducted a case study of one classroom in each of the three pilot schools, with the three teachers selected from the third and fourth grades. We chose teachers based on their experience and commitment to the program. For example, we selected teachers who reported in interviews that they had used multiple lessons from the *LTM* curriculum, had demonstrated their lessons at the *LTM* teacher development workshops, and were recommended by their school principal.

Our first meetings early in the school year with the three selected teach- ers helped us to understand how they planned to use the program through- out the school year—for instance, the general curriculum areas they expected to reinforce with specific *LTM* units. Then, in collaboration with the individual teachers and the *LTM* staff, we identified one lesson from the *LTM* curriculum to focus the case study in each of the classes. The lessons that were selected were judged by each of the classroom teachers to effectively develop student understandings in a discipline other than music. For example, in one fourth grade class that was part of the case study, a unit titled "Solid, Liquid, It's a Gas!" was selected. In this unit, fourth grade students learned about the properties of matter and about the speed at which sound travels through different media.

In close collaboration with the classroom teachers, we developed short written pretests, focused on nonmusic outcomes, and administered them for each of the selected lessons. In addition, we observed *LTM*-related classroom activities and any related lessons taught by the music teacher. Through these observations, supplemented by interviews with teachers, we were able to better understand the instructional experiences for the children in the case study classrooms. Soon after the completion of the last *LTM*-related instructional experience, teachers administered a posttest, which we designed to parallel the pretest. Differences between pretest scores and posttest scores were then analyzed statistically.

Two of the fourth grade case study classes in different *LTM* schools completed the *LTM* lesson titled *Just the 2×3 of Us*, which focused on the development of student writing by studying song lyrics. We designed a 15-item pretest and posttest to measure the nonmusic proficiencies for the lesson, including problem solving, using details, and staying on topic. The test included multiple choice questions as well as short answer questions designed to provide samples of students' writing. Sixteen students in the first class and 22 students in the second class completed both the pretest and posttest. In the first classroom, the average score for the pretest was 5.75 and the average score for the posttest was 10.87 (a score of 15 would be a perfect score). The difference between the averages was statistically significant ($F(1, 15) = 400.24$, $p < 0.05$). In the second fourth grade class, the average pretest score was 7.35 and the average score for the posttest was 11.40. Once again, the difference between the two averages was statistically significant ($F(1, 21) = 122.43$, $p < 0.05$).

These results reinforce the notion that students developed skills and understandings in non-arts disciplines through *LTM* lessons. Proficiencies that the students were unable to perform just prior to the presentation of the unit were demonstrated after the unit was completed indicating that *LTM* experiences complement students' learning of materials related to the Ohio Competency Based Curriculum on which the units in the *LTM* curriculum were based.

The Effect of Learning Through Music *on Students' Ohio State Proficiency Exam Scores*

Throughout the *LTM* pilot program, we monitored scores for the participating schools. There are five subtests that comprised the OSPE—Reading, Writing, Math, Science, and Citizenship. The results for schools are reported by the percent of students' performance scored as meeting proficiency. In the fifth year of *LTM*, the OSPE scores for the three pilot schools combined were below the Ohio State average on the Reading (Ohio 56%, *LTM* 51%), Math (Ohio 59%, *LTM* 51%), Science (Ohio 56%, *LTM* 54%), and Citizenship (Ohio 60%, *LTM* 42%) subtests, although on the Writing subtest the *LTM* average was slightly higher (Ohio 79%, *LTM* 81%). The average scores across the three *LTM* schools showed little variability.

During the five-year *LTM* pilot, the three partner schools participated in several programs in addition to *LTM* that were designed to improve students' scores on the OSPE exam. These support programs included after-school and extended-day programs, where tutoring was provided by teachers at the school, as well as individual tutoring by volunteers from corporate groups in the community. Because there was considerable effort at each school directed toward improving OSPE scores, it was difficult to attribute any changes in the scores to any one program.

One approach we used to try to uncover an *LTM* effect on OSPE proficiency scores was to examine whether or not the length of time that students had been involved with *LTM* was related to their performance on the OSPE, which was administered only to fourth graders in Ohio. Through an examination of available student records, *LTM* students' profiles were contrasted with those of fourth grade students who had not been involved with the program for all five years of the pilot.

We examined student records for the fifth grade students who completed the OSPE in the spring of the fourth year of the program, when they were fourth graders. Each of the three participating schools provided between 40 and 50 records for a total of 146 student OSPE scores, which were included in the analysis. In these reports, scores were reported for each of the five OSPE subtests—Reading, Writing, Math, Science, and Citizenship. The year in which students entered a participating school was used as the indicator of how long they participated in *LTM*.

To illustrate the approach that we used to examine the OSPE data, the details for the OSPE Citizenship subtest scores are provided. The three *LTM* school students' scores on the OSPE Citizenship subtest averaged 212.23. To be considered proficient in Citizenship, students had to achieve a score of 218. Students who had been at the *LTM* schools for four years or more averaged 217.66 on the Citizenship subtests, while average scores for students who had been at the schools for three years or less (210.09) or two years or less (208.95) were lower. An analysis of variance indicated that there were not significant differences between the averages ($F = 1.812$, $p > 0.05$).

The results revealed a very consistent pattern. On each subtest, students who had been enrolled at the *LTM* pilot schools for longer periods outperformed students who had been enrolled for shorter periods. But it is important to note that for no subtest did the statistical analysis indicate that these differences were significant. The direction of the data is consistent and parallels the findings of other researchers (Tanner-McBrien, 2010) who have focused on how mobility affects students' proficiency test scores. For instance, an analysis of test scores of 16,278 Cleveland Public School students, 1914 of whom changed schools at least once during the school year, indicated that these mobile students scored on average 5.12 points below other more stable students (Smith, 2003). Thus, mobility alone may explain the differences observed in this study's data.

THE EFFECT OF *LEARNING THROUGH MUSIC* ON TEACHERS

Throughout the implementation of the program, we observed *LTM* classroom teachers presenting *LTM* lessons to their students. We interviewed participating teachers each year and teachers also completed questionnaires that focused on the influence that participating in the program had on them personally and on their teaching. In the last two years of the pilot program, primarily through case studies at each of the three pilot schools, we closely examined classroom teachers' use of the resources provided and the role of music specialists in the program.

Teachers' Skills and Interest in Integrating Music into Their Lessons

Each year in the annual teacher surveys, we asked teachers to answer questions regarding the effect of the *LTM* program on their teaching. We found that a large majority of the teachers agreed that they had developed new music skills and understandings as a result of participating in the program. They also agreed that they had begun to integrate music into their curriculum beyond just the *LTM* supplied lessons. Case studies of *LTM* classrooms, which are reported in detail later in this chapter, provided additional evidence that supported the teachers' self-reports that many had learned to effectively incorporate the materials from the *LTM* curriculum into their ongoing classroom teaching.

The annual teacher survey data was also supported by our interviews with teachers and principals. It appeared that well-designed teacher workshops, lessons that were viewed as effective and directly related to the schools' curriculum, collaboration with other classroom teachers and with music teachers, and the active support of principals all contributed to teachers pursuing the development of these new skills. Principals reported changes in participating teachers. One principal stated, "I go into classrooms, and a lot of the teachers are playing music. Now I notice that music is being played on a daily basis, and not only that, but I see a lot more music being incorporated into lessons."

Music Teaching Self-Concept Inventory

An important goal of the program was for classroom teachers to gain confidence in using music and music concepts regularly in their classroom teaching. Although elementary classroom teachers in Ohio are required to have courses that focus on developing their skills and understanding of music as part of their initial teacher certification, music is not often well integrated into classroom instruction. To examine if participating in *LTM* changed teachers' confidence in using music in their lessons, we surveyed participating teachers both in the first year of *LTM* and again in the last year of the program.

The Music Teaching Self-Concept Inventory (MTSCI) was developed by the CAER and had been previously used in other assessment projects (Fig. 4.2). The inventory has 16 statements paired with five-option Likert-type response scales. Ten statements comprise the subscale that measures

CAER MUSIC TEACHING SELF-CONCEPT INVENTORY

School_____ Number of Years at Current School_____

This questionnaire contains 16 statements about your use of music in your classroom and your music background. Using the following five-point scale, please circle the response that best describes the extent to which you agree with each statement.

SA- Strongly Agree, A- Agree, N- Not Sure, D- Disagree, SD- Strongly Disagree

Please be sure to respond to each item.

SD D N A SA   1. I often use music in my teaching.

SD D N A SA   2. I studied a musical instrument or sang when I was younger.

SD D N A SA   3. It is difficult to make time for music in my daily class schedule.

SD D N A SA   4. I feel confident integrating music into my teaching.

SD D N A SA   5. Using music in my classroom has helped me grow professionally.

SD D N A SA   6. I don't feel comfortable enough with my music skills to use music in my classroom.

SD D N A SA   7. I had great music training when I was young.

SD D N A SA   8. . I come from a very musical family.

SD D N A SA   9. I need to acquire more skills in music before I will be confident of integrating music into my curriculum.

SD D N A SA   10. I've had very little background in music.

SD D N A SA   11. I'm not sure how to integrate music into my curriculum.

SD D N A SA   12. I am confident in teaching music concepts to my students.

SD D N A SA   13. I get anxious when I have to use my music skills.

SD D N A SA   14. I feel comfortable enough with my knowledge of music to integrate it into my curriculum.

SD D N A SA   15. I have attended a number of effective music workshops and/or courses.

SD D N A SA   16. I play an instrument or sing music recreationally.

Fig. 4.2   CAER music teaching self-concept inventory

confidence in integrating music into the classroom, for example, "I feel comfortable enough with my knowledge of music to integrate it into my curriculum." The remaining six statements comprise the "prior music experience" subscale, such as "I studied a musical instrument or sang when I was younger."

Based on four previous applications of the MTSCI in previous assessment projects, we expected that the average for both subscales would be about the same—that is, the extent of a teacher's previous background in music should parallel his or her comfort regarding integrating music into his or her curriculum. The scores generated by 22 respondents in the first year of *LTM* showed that teachers' average response to the confidence items (2.74) on the scale was higher than their average response to the background items (2.46). This suggests that these teachers were somewhat more confident about using music than their backgrounds might predict. In the fifth year of the program, a survey of 46 teachers from the same participating schools revealed that teachers' average response to the confidence items (3.65) on the scale was 0.88 higher than their average response to the background items (2.77), suggesting that the teachers participating in the program in the fifth year were more confident about using music in their classrooms than the teachers were in *LTM*'s first year of implementation. Twelve of the teachers from three of the participating schools responded to both the Year 1 and Year 5 administrations of the MTSCI. An analysis of their results showed that the increase in the teachers' average confidence score between Year 1 (2.74) and Year 5 (3.69) was statistically significant ($t = 3.017$, $p < 0.012$).

Teachers' Use of Learning Through Music *Curriculum*

Teachers viewed the *LTM* curriculum materials as being well designed and supporting the Ohio State Learning Outcomes. These characteristics appeared to be critical to the frequency with which the teachers used the materials. In Year 5, we looked at the use of the *LTM* curriculum resources with two questions in mind: "What are the characteristics of a curriculum unit that make it more likely to be used?" And "What is the frequency of use of the *LTM* materials?" We relied primarily on teachers' responses to survey questions and interviews conducted with teachers and principals to answer these two questions.

Responses to the teacher survey in the program's fifth year indicated that teachers believed the *LTM* materials were of high quality. Most of the teachers (72%) who responded to the survey agreed or strongly agreed that the quality of the lessons in the *LTM* curriculum was better than curriculum materials that they had received from other resources provided by the school districts. During interviews, teachers often made statements like the following:

> I think the units are very good. They're much better than average. Everything is laid out in those booklets and the lesson plans. It's all there, including objectives, what proficiencies are covered, the procedures. And if you want to do extensions, they're also included.

Eighty-five percent of the teacher survey respondents in *LTM*'s fifth year also strongly agreed or agreed that the materials "fit" well with their curriculum, and indicated that they were much more likely to use a unit that fit well with their curriculum. In interviews, many teachers told us that the lessons were "very clearly connected to the proficiencies."

The frequency with which teachers who responded to the Year 5 survey used the *LTM* resources depended not only on the characteristics of the materials, but also on the school and the background of the teacher. In our Year 5 survey, we found that as the teachers became more familiar with the program they tended to use more of the *LTM* curriculum units, as exemplified in this comment:

> I think it takes a couple of years to get familiar with it. I think when you teach the same grade level teachers tend to duplicate their lessons each year somewhat. Since this is a kind of new program I think it may take a little time to build it into the curriculum.

In addition, in our interviews with teachers, they reported that they were likely to use more of the materials in a particular unit as the number of years they participated in the program increased and they became more familiar with the units and how to better incorporate them into their curriculum. Teachers who were new to one of the participating schools, and therefore new to the *LTM* program, told us that they tended to use fewer units in their first year than did their colleagues, who had used the materials previously.

Year 4 teacher survey results showed that teachers reported that they used about 75% of the curriculum units provided by the program. From our interviews with teachers, we noted that in schools where there was considerable collaboration among grade level teachers, the *LTM* materials were more likely to be systematically included in teachers' plans. This collaboration also provided support for teachers who were new to the school and contributed to the likelihood that they would use the materials. Another factor that increased the use of the materials is the active participation of the schools' music specialists. Survey responses from teachers in schools where the music specialists provided strong advocacy and support for the program showed that they tended to use more of the units (mean response = 7.23) than did teachers in schools where the music specialist was less involved in the program (mean response 4.88).

The description of the planning process at one school reveals the strength of this interdisciplinary collaboration:

> The music teacher and all the fourth grade teachers got together as a team and we took all the units and the binder and we kind of broke them up according to our curriculum and where things fit in. The neat thing about it is not only do we do it in the classroom, but Lisa, our music teacher, ties everything in so they are really kind of getting a double whammy of it.

Factors that decreased the use of the *LTM* units included the introduction of other new curricula at the grade level or in the school. For example, some experienced *LTM* teachers reported that when a new reading/language arts curriculum was required, the use of the *LTM* materials was reduced.

Classroom Teachers' Interest in Music

Teachers reported on the annual survey that their interest in music and their understanding of music increased as a result of their experiences with the program. We measured this by examining teachers' responses to two specific five-option Likert-type scale items, "I've developed new music skills and understandings as a result of participating in *LTM*" and "I've become more interested in music through my *LTM* experiences." The average of teachers' responses to the first item ranged from 3.62 in the first year to 4.16 in the fifth year and on the second item from 3.92 in the first year to 4.32 in the fifth year. Each year, teachers agreed that they both developed new music skills and understandings and became more interested in music through their work with *LTM*.

When we interviewed teachers, many told us that the program affected their own interest in classical music, as exemplified here:

> I never thought I'd like an orchestra concert. Now, I would love to go to Severance again after going there for the first time. So the program has helped me, personally, to grow musically and to grow more interested in classical music. Music would not be something that I probably would have taught a lot in my classroom, if I hadn't had this program.

Collaboration Among Teachers

Principals told us that the *LTM* activities increased collaboration among teachers. In the second year of the program, one principal said:

> The program gives teachers reasons to plan together. The workshops provide a time for them, even on the trip back and forth to the meetings. I've noticed at some of their grade level meetings that LTM comes up more and more.

Our conversations with teachers also provided evidence of increased collaboration. Even in schools where collaboration was already a part of how teachers planned, *LTM* reinforced collaboration. As one fourth grade teacher put it:

> All of the fourth grade teachers work together anyway, so that really worked. The art and music departments are also trying to coordinate with us, and it works very well. Departmentalizing the lessons really helps with timing and curriculum. We all mapped out our plans on the calendar we were given.

One unique aspect of the *LTM* collaborations at several of the schools was the inclusion of the specialist teachers, in some cases both music and art specialists, in the curriculum conversations with classroom teachers. In general, it is unusual for these teachers to participate fully in the curriculum planning process. *LTM* provided them with this opportunity.

Participation of School Music Specialists

We noted early in the pilot program that in some schools the music specialist took on a central role in implementing *LTM*. It was the expectation of the program that music specialists needed to be involved, and in each of the pilot schools, the music specialist participated. In some schools, this solidified the role of the music specialist as an important part of the curriculum process, in other schools it gave the music teacher a new role in the curriculum process that had not been held previously.

In schools where music specialists were central to the program, they became a main factor for the widespread use of the program materials at the school. In such schools, classroom teachers described their planning with the music specialists in year-end interviews. Principals also noted a change in the role of the music specialists, characterized by one principal this way:

> I think that the program has reinforced and generated a more positive and central role for the specialists, particularly the music teacher in this building. I don't think that is the consensus throughout the district. I think specialists are not respected throughout the district, not as "real" teachers, but I think this building, particularly with the implementation of the program, it's different.

Principals' Perspectives on the Effects of the Program

Our conversations with principals throughout the program reinforced the notion that *LTM* had an impact on principals as well as on the school community in a variety of ways. First, it was clear that the principals of the *LTM* schools were all anxious to have the program continue at their schools beyond the five-year pilot implementation. They viewed *Learning Through Music* as having become an integral part of the school and had difficulty imagining the school without the program. While the principals generally had supportive views of the arts in the school curriculum prior to their involvement with *LTM*, the program reinforced this perspective. As one principal stated,

> Everyone knows that we're affiliated with the Cleveland Orchestra, and we take great pride in that. It is one reason that I stay here. The effect on the school will continue as long as the program continues. I will do my part to help it stay by having fundraisers and by encouraging the staff to participate.

We also noted that there were a number of arts-related changes in the three *LTM* schools during the period of the program's implementation. These included an increase in the number of music specialists in the schools (in one case a half-time music teacher was made full-time), increases in other music offerings (new instrumental music programs) at some schools, and the initiation of after-school music programs for students at another school. Fourth and fifth grade students at one school also began instruction on string instruments from students at the Baldwin Wallace Conservatory, an initiative established through the *LTM* program. We also learned of groups of teachers and principals applying for additional grants to bring other arts programs and artists to their schools. This activity clearly increased during the pilot years of *LTM*.

Finally, it appears that the program may have affected some of the participating principals in some of the same ways it affected many of the participating teachers. As the principal of one of the pilot schools told us,

> The program has helped me to appreciate classical music a bit more. I always had music appreciation classes, but I was never one to turn on the radio and listen to WCLV. But that has certainly changed. It is nice for me to meet the members of the Orchestra, and go to the community forum for the Orchestra. It has been a great benefit in my life.

THE EFFECT OF *LEARNING THROUGH MUSIC* ON SCHOOL AND COMMUNITIES

During the period of the *LTM* program's implementation and our evaluation, *LTM* schools looked and sounded different from non-*LTM* schools. The halls had photos of members of the Cleveland Orchestra hanging on the walls. Many of the classrooms had student projects resulting from the program displayed and some had "pin-ups" of "their" visiting musician on the bulletin board. Teachers told us that more music was being played in their classrooms. The program reached beyond the classrooms it served and the school's music program, to involve art specialists, librarians, and physical education teachers at several schools. Principals at some of the schools attended *LTM* workshops with their teachers. Music teachers at several of the schools showed their commitment to the program and their expertise, by demonstrating *LTM* lessons for other teachers during the workshops. Several teachers at these schools were thoughtful and articulate commentators on the program. Grade level planning appeared to become characteristic of several of the schools and as a consequence, teachers demonstrated a high level of collaboration.

The Program's Effect on the School Community

The Neighborhood Concerts were a specific time when the school community had the opportunity to become involved in the *Learning Through Music* program. Neighborhood Concerts were held every May at each of the schools during the five-year pilot program and we observed many of these performances. The concerts, usually held in the school's gym on a hot early summer evening, were exciting. In some schools, it was hard to imagine how more people might be fit into the performance space. The orchestra musicians, about 15 members of the Orchestra who were all participating in *LTM*, had the responsibility of talking to the audience about the music they were performing. The audiences were comprised of excited children, both elementary and preschool age, parents, and grandparents. The principals, teachers, and others from the community were also there. The program included students participating in several ways, often singing, playing instruments, and/or dancing. At all of the schools, the concert was an important highlight of the school year. Frequently, we were in the schools a day or two after the Neighborhood Concerts. It was clear that the teachers, principals, and students we interviewed on those days were still "buzzing" about the concert. One principal's comment described the positive responses of many principals and teachers:

> We had between 550 and 600 and as I said before that was very unusual for us. There is a level of excitement and ownership of this program among the parent community that I see and this would be more of the core group of parents that I work with versus those on the fringes, but the attendance was certainly a demonstration of the power of seeing that value.

Parents' Perspectives on LTM

During the fourth year of the program, parents attending the Neighborhood Concerts at pilot schools completed a survey that was designed to assess what parents knew about *LTM*. Questions on the survey sought to gather information about parents' familiarity with *LTM*, and their interest in other programs of the Cleveland Orchestra. The results of the questionnaire were based on the responses of 114 parents from the three pilot schools.

These parents seemed to be very aware of the program and its components. When asked if they "learned about the LTM program activities/

events from my child," 94% of the responding parents said *yes*, which suggested that the program affected the children to the extent that they wanted to share their experiences with their parents. Most parents (86%) also responded that their children's school also communicated with them about the program through newsletters. Parents appeared to know about the different, major activities of the program. Ninety-two percent of the parents reported that their children attended Cleveland Orchestra concerts at Severance Hall.

Virtually the same number (91%) knew that Cleveland Orchestra musicians visited their child's classroom, and only slightly less (89%) were aware that the Neighborhood Concerts were a part of *LTM*. On average, respondents had attended about two (1.92) Neighborhood Concerts, approximately one less than the number of years that their child had been attending the school. Parents also seemed to be generally interested in connecting more with the Orchestra, and possibly attending other Orchestra programs. More than half (52%) indicated that they would like to receive information about the Cleveland Orchestra Family Concerts and 43% indicated that they would like to know more about the summer outdoor concert series of the Cleveland Orchestra known as the Blossom Festival.

In addition to responding to questions on the survey, many parents also wrote additional comments attributing their children's increased interest in orchestra music and interest in learning to play an instrument to *LTM*. As one mother wrote,

> I truly appreciate that my children have the opportunity to experience a world-class orchestra. For family days, we now frequently attend music performances. My children now enjoy listening to all types of music at home and because of this program, my daughter will be starting violin this summer. Thank you very much. We could have never provided such an opportunity for our children otherwise.

THE EFFECT OF *LEARNING THROUGH MUSIC* ON CLEVELAND ORCHESTRA MEMBERS

The musicians and their visits to classrooms generated much of the excitement that circulated in schools around *LTM*. Students and teachers alike talked with great enthusiasm about the opportunities they had to be in close proximity to these "world-class performers." Musicians provided a personal link between *LTM* lessons and the schools and between the Orchestra concerts and the students. Throughout the pilot program, we observed musicians' presentations in classrooms and interviewed them to obtain their reflections on how participating in the program affected them. We conducted in-depth interviews with more than 40 members of the Orchestra. We also asked teachers, principals, *LTM* consultants, and members of the Orchestra's education staff about their perceptions of the musicians' role in the program.

Skills and Understandings Developed by Orchestra Members

We noted that musicians spent a considerable amount of time developing their classroom presentations. They understood the need to have a "tight" program, which seemed to parallel the approach they had to performing as a musician. All the *LTM* musicians seemed committed to keeping their presentations interesting and the students engaged. They appreciated the challenge in developing an effective program. According to one participating Orchestra member,

> The most challenging aspect has been learning how to present the program in the smoothest possible way. One can feel it when things are going well with the kids—when they're attentive, and the delivery is smooth. It has been a challenge to go in and speak confidently, but also to be playing at my best and presenting the material properly. I'm motivated to stay with the program because I want to get better at it, and I am getting less and less nervous about it.

According to many of the participating musicians, continued experience with the *LTM* program helped refine their presentations. It appeared that almost all of the musicians matured as teaching artists. They were more comfortable with young students, and enjoyed their interactions with them. Teachers were very positive about the skills and understanding the musicians demonstrated in their classrooms.

While musicians viewed the development of the presentations as hard work, several musicians told us that the program fulfilled them in ways that were different from performing in the orchestra. According to one musician,

> You can really be creative. There are very few outlets as an orchestra musician to feel creative, and this is a very creative experience. We are told constantly what to do [in the orchestra], so to have a place where we can have an opportunity to do something of our own design is wonderful.

Orchestra Members' Motivations to Participate in LTM

As reported earlier, some musicians found the development of their presentations to be a rewarding outlet for their creativity and/or a challenge, something that they wanted to work at to continue to improve. When we asked musicians about their reasons for participating in the program, in interviews during the fourth and fifth years of the program, we found that their responses could be categorized in two broad areas—one that focused on the musicians' value for interacting with students and the other that involved "social consciousness."

Many orchestra members reported specific anecdotes, or gave more general descriptions, of the positive interactions they had with children in the schools they visited. Musicians told us that the personal relationships they had developed with the children were very important to them. One musician related this experience:

> There was one class that I saw four times last year, and by the time I finished my presentation, they had brought cookies and balloons, and had written each of their names on a banner. And the hugs—every single kid came up to me and gave a hug.

Another musician described an interaction that he had with one student that he particularly valued.

> The moment was when a gigantic young man from what appeared to be an inner city, impoverished background came up to me and under his breath said, 'Don't tell anyone this, but when I grow up, I want to be just like you.' I thought that was pretty remarkable, that what are normally considered boundaries by society—such as race, socioeconomic status, age, and educational background—can be breached by the open-mindedness and the cooperation of people.

This comment also reflects the second major area that motivated musicians to be involved in *Learning Through Music*—social consciousness or community service.

Musicians told us about the importance of providing possibilities, by being a role model, for young people as they consider who they are and who they would like to become. Several musicians believed that some of the students "may not have a lot of positive things going on in their lives" that the *LTM* program can have a positive impact and that the musicians' presence in the students' lives "could swing it to the positive." Several musicians used phrases like "giving something back to the community, to people we often don't reach" as reasons for their continued participation.

Musicians told us they valued the program as a way that they could become part of the community, an opportunity for them to feel more involved. Other participating musicians linked the community service aspect of the program to the Orchestra:

> This is a worthwhile program for the kids and for the orchestra. This program is just another good thing that the orchestra is doing in the community. We're touching kids and parents. The group performs for the whole community—in schools and in halls. The parents and kids are getting involved and I think that's good for the orchestra; reaching out to help kids learn. Some of these kids or their parents may one day buy a ticket to come to one of our concerts.

When we spoke to Orchestra musicians who were not involved in *LTM* we found that many of them had positive views of the program and the participating musicians:

> It's hard to say if the participation of the orchestra members has affected the orchestra itself, but I am amazed at the commitment of those that do it. Being involved in the program must enhance their playing as well as their ability to communicate, as well as what is required to garner support for the orchestra. We need to keep this orchestra viable and I'm convinced LTM is one way to do that.

The *LTM* program affected the participating musicians in several positive ways. It provided them with new skills and challenges and it helped them to feel more closely linked to the community, and to children in the community. The musicians felt rewarded for their participation in the program, and looked forward to continuing in *LTM*.

REFLECTIONS: AN EVOLVING DESIGN FOR ASSESSMENT

While the *Learning Through Music* evaluation project examined a range of issues related to the implementation and effect of the program, the design of the evaluation was not set in stone at the beginning of the *project.* Prior to the beginning of each school year, we sat down with the Director of Education for the Orchestra and discussed the previous year's evaluation report. We reflected on what we had learned and what we still needed to know about *LTM*. Occasionally, we would add new assessment projects or remove assessment projects that had been planned, in order to better address an emerging issue. In some cases the assessment changed direction at the suggestion of the evaluation team and in some cases a new assessment project was added because of a need of the Orchestra's education staff. Over the five-year period of the assessment a feeling of trust was developed between the assessment team and the Orchestra's education staff, so that we all felt comfortable with negotiating changes to the assessment project. In addition, this approach provided the education staff with information that allowed them to make adjustments in the program as needed, which fit well with the nature of *LTM* as a pilot implementation. As a consequence, after five years of documenting the implementation of the pilot program, a relatively comprehensive perspective of *LTM* emerged.

In addition to conducting a series of data collections, program evaluators got to know the program in other ways. Our role as evaluators shaped the data collection as we observed the program in action. We sat with teachers during staff development workshops, and participated in the workshop activities. We had informal conversations with orchestra musicians, education staff members, principals, and students—sometimes in cars while traveling from one school to another, and sometimes during lunch breaks. Within the limitations of resources, we were able to develop a sufficient understanding of the program to generate results that were useful to the Orchestra's education leadership and members of the Musical Arts Association, which serves as the board that oversees the Orchestra.

There were challenges in this work as well. The logistical challenges presented by Severance Hall being over 450 miles from New York, where CAER is located, were managed in several ways. We were able to recruit experienced music education researchers from the Cleveland area to help with interviews and observations. Several of these researchers were able to participate in the evaluation for multiple years, which allowed them to become increasingly familiar with the program and with the evaluation strategies that CAER employed. In addition, those of us based in New York would arrange several week-long visits each year timed to attend important events, like teacher workshops, and to conduct focus groups, interviews, and observations.

Another challenge with undertaking a longitudinal project in an urban area was confronting higher than average school mobility rates. In some of the pilot schools, as many as one-third of the students would change schools during a school year, making it difficult to track student outcomes or undertake a simple beginning of the year to end of the year, pretest/posttest study. The advantage of longitudinal studies having a homogeneous subject pool is often lost with such high mobility rates.

It is important to highlight again that the title of this program is *Learning Through Music* and it was emphasized to schools wishing to join the program that *LTM* was designed to enhance student learning in areas outside of music. The Orchestra education staff members therefore were very concerned that an evaluation project should examine the relationship between participating in *LTM* and OSPE scores. With the help of the classroom teachers from the participating schools, the *LTM* materials were designed to parallel the learning objectives tested on the OSPE and teachers reported that students demonstrated learning from *LTM* experiences that would likely enhance students' OSPE performance. However, the strongest evidence we collected showed a positive relationship between *LTM* materials and the substantial changes in students' and teachers' understanding of, interest in, and value for music and a positive effect on school communities. These outcomes show that carefully designed programs can have multiple positive effects on music learning that may have a long-term effect on the role that music plays in the lives of the *programs'* participants.

As of the fall of 2016, the *Learning Through Music* program continues to be offered by the Cleveland Orchestra Education and Community Programs Office. *Learning Through Music* evolved throughout the pilot program and continued to change once the assessment was concluded. In many ways it reflects what was learned through the information that was collected during the assessment. One important outcome of a long-term assessment project like the one described in this chapter is that the administrators responsible for directing the program may develop a multidimensional critical perspective to guide the program and other educational initiatives the arts organization may undertake.

NOTES

1. The Center for Arts Education Research is an interdisciplinary group founded to stimulate and support basic and applied research in the arts, art education, and the arts in education located at Teachers College, Columbia University. Assessment teams are comprised of both faculty members and doctoral students. The Center has engaged in numerous arts-in-education assessment projects since its inception in 1993.
2. pseudonym.

REFERENCES

Cutietta, R. A. (1995). *Evaluation report.* St. Paul, MN: Saint Paul Chamber Orchestra.
Heath, S. B., & Roach, A. (1999). Imaginative actuality: Learning in the arts during the non-school hours. In E. Fiske (Ed.), *Champions of change: The effect of the arts on Learning* (pp. 19–34). Washington, DC: Arts Education Partnership.
Smith, A. M. (2003). *The relationship between student mobility and school district performance accountability ratings in Ohio* (Order No. 3099423). Available from ProQuest Dissertations & Theses Global (305343383). Retrieved from http://eduproxy.tc-library.org/?url=/docview/305343383?accountid=14258
Tanner-McBrien, L. (2010). *How does school mobility impact indicators of academic achievement for highly mobile students?* (Order No. 3404937). Available from ProQuest Dissertations & Theses Global (518838224). Retrieved from http://eduproxy.tc-library.org/?url=/docview/518838224?accountid=14258
Tishman, S., & Perkins, D. N. (1997). The language of thinking. *Phi Delta Kappan, 78*, 368–374.

CHAPTER 5

Aging and the Healing Power of Choral Music: A Community-Responsive Evaluation of Vintage Voices

Daren Nyquist and Kylie Nicholas

About Vintage Voices

VocalEssence has served as one of the nation's strongest advocates for choral music since its founding in 1969. The organization seeks to "transform lives through the experience and power of singing and the choral tradition"—and it has realized that vision by creating award-winning choirs and introducing new audiences to choral music through unique community engagement programs. VocalEssence runs a number of professional vocal ensembles that have earned prestigious awards and regularly tour internationally. Despite its global presence, the group has maintained a strong focus on using the arts to improve the lives of Minnesotans.

As part of its overarching mission, VocalEssence has made a strong commitment to helping older Minnesotans rekindle their love for choral music. The VocalEssence team understood years ago that Minnesota's once strong choral music tradition is slowly diminishing as the state's population ages. They realized that seniors who once loved being part of church choirs or community singing groups have fewer opportunities to

D. Nyquist (✉) • K. Nicholas
The Improve Group, Saint Paul, MN, USA

© The Author(s) 2018
R.S. Rajan, I.C. O'Neal (eds.), *Arts Evaluation and Assessment*,
https://doi.org/10.1007/978-3-319-64116-4_5

99

sing as they experience new health challenges, lose the ability to drive, or move into nursing homes and assisted living facilities. Above all, they recognized the need for a choral music program designed specifically for seniors facing a wide range of age-related conditions, from diminished vision and mobility challenges to dementia.

To help fill that void, in 2012 VocalEssence launched the Choral Pathways program with new funding from the Minnesota State Arts Board. Led by then Director of Community Engagement, Kimberly D. Meisten, and Education Manager, Robert Graham, Choral Pathways engaged participating seniors in a music appreciation class, a group sing-along, and a field trip to a performance by a VocalEssence professional choir. Operating Choral Pathways was a tremendous learning opportunity for the VocalEssence team. Kimberly and Robert began to understand the complexities and challenges of working with an aging population. At the same time, they were able to witness first-hand the extraordinary joy choral music brought to program participants. Although Choral Pathways was not funded for a second year, it solidified the commitment of the VocalEssence team to developing a dynamic choral music program designed specifically for seniors.

To deepen their understanding of the connection between arts and aging, Kimberly and Robert also took part in a professional development program created by ArtSage, which trains organizations on how to use arts-based programming to support senior communities. Through ArtSage, they learned about the groundbreaking work of geriatric psychiatrist Dr. Gene Cohen, who brought to light the powerful connection between creativity and healthy aging. Cohen's Creativity and Aging study (Cohen, 2006) was the first controlled study showing that community-based art programs run by professional artists can boost disease prevention efforts and promote better health. Through four day-long ArtSage seminars, the VocalEssence team learned best practices for developing arts-based programs that meet the unique needs of aging adults. These ArtSage trainings helped VocalEssence create the framework for its new choral music program, Vintage Voices.

Unlike Choral Pathways, which offered more limited opportunities to sing, Vintage Voices was designed to provide participants with a deeper and longer-term choral music experience—as well as the ability to learn new skills and build new relationships with fellow singers. VocalEssence began by partnering with local assisted living facilities and senior centers that had interest in creating a choir for their clients and residents. Robert worked closely with the activity directors at each facility to recruit at least 20 members for each choir. Choir members agreed to attend weekly rehearsals for three months, leading up to a final performance for family, friends, and caregivers.

The focus of Vintage Voices is entirely about improving quality of life for participants. According to Kimberly, the choirs "aren't about being perfect, or about hitting every note. It's about the process and experiencing the joy of singing. The driving force behind this program is helping older people enjoy the benefits that can come from raising their voices together."

Vintage Voices is designed to break down the barriers that prevent seniors from participating in a professionally run choral music program. It brings highly trained artists directly to assisted living facilities and senior centers, meeting people where they live and recreate. As the choir director, Robert is able to adapt programming and materials to work for those with a wide range of physical and mental health challenges. Vintage Voices' weekly rehearsal structure builds trust and creates opportunities for increased social engagement among choir members and program staff. Indeed, through this ongoing, interactive approach, VocalEssence is working to connect seniors with the healing power of music—to improve health outcomes, reduce depression, increase social engagement, and improve self-esteem.

CAPTURING "VINTAGE VOICES": INTEGRATING EVALUATION INTO THE PROGRAM

VocalEssence knew that evaluation would be essential to demonstrating how Vintage Voices improved the lives of senior participants. Kimberly and Robert turned to The Improve Group to design an evaluation framework and activities that could be integrated directly into Vintage Voices programming, beginning with its very first choir. By launching evaluation activities immediately at the start of the program, The Improve Group team could identify early program successes and challenges—and help VocalEssence refine and strengthen the program as it developed.

For VocalEssence, there were two fundamental goals for the evaluation: to identify opportunities for program improvement and to clearly demonstrate the program's value to external funders and other stakeholders. The primary audience was internal, and included organizational leaders and staff. They wanted evaluation activities to lead to improved programming design and implementation—so that Vintage Voices could have a more meaningful impact on the lives of participants. As Kimberly shared,

"Program improvement was really the most critical purpose behind this evaluation. We wanted to make Vintage Voices the best experience it possibly could be, and make sure we were achieving the goals we set out to achieve."

Meeting the needs of external audiences was also an important factor. VocalEssence needed to satisfy evaluation requirements as part of the Minnesota State Arts Board grant that funded Vintage Voices. In addition, it wanted to articulate program successes for board members, partner organizations, and other possible funders. However, VocalEssence also wanted to contribute to the increasing amount of evidence linking arts- and music-based programs with improved health outcomes for seniors. By demonstrating the power of choral music to improve quality of life for aging adults, VocalEssence could spur support for Vintage Voices as well as for similar programs across the country. As such, when the first three Vintage Voices choirs launched in the spring of 2015, evaluation activities were already built directly into the program.

EVALUATION APPROACH AND METHODOLOGY

The Improve Group's overarching goal was to capture authentic, qualitative reflections to reveal how the choir experience affected participants' quality of life. We developed evaluation methods and tools that could effectively engage choir participants living with a range of physical and mental health conditions, including mobility and sensory challenges, as well as memory loss and depression. To ensure the best possible results, we used our **Community-Responsive Approach**[SM] to evaluation as an overarching framework and philosophy.

Community-responsive evaluations ensure that all methods and instruments align with the realities facing the populations or communities at the heart of any research questions. Community-responsive evaluators design data collection methods that are accessible and engaging to respondents— and identify ways for community members to be a part of the evaluation design and data collection process. By being responsive to each community's distinct characteristics, evaluators are more likely to hear authentic experiences, concerns, and results. In this case, using a community-responsive approach helped to capture the voices and perspectives of choir participants, regardless of their physical or mental health status.

We also needed to provide the VocalEssence team with continuous feedback, in order to help them refine Vintage Voices' program design and implementation. For that reason, we used a developmental evaluation model to create our evaluation instruments. **Developmental Evaluation** (DE) is a method created by evaluation expert Michael Quinn Patton to support social innovators working in complex, fast-moving environments who want ongoing feedback to guide program development (Patton, 2010). While not appropriate for every evaluation, DE is an effective approach for measuring newly created programs, organizational changes, policy reforms, and systems interventions. DE can be used to quickly test new iterations of a program or policy and to surface challenges and opportunities in real-time so that they can immediately be addressed. In this case, using DE allowed us to evaluate the unique impact of each new Vintage Voices choir—and to provide program staff with a continuous stream of information to improve implementation.

Evaluation Inception and Design

To launch the evaluation, The Improve Group team facilitated a series of meetings with the VocalEssence team to identify their primary research questions. These questions were framed to draw out in-depth insights on quality of programming and its impact on participants and partnering organizations. They included:

- What benefits do participants get out of the choir experience?
  - How do these benefits compare to the goals of participants and the project?
- How did Vintage Voices address barriers to participation the senior community faces?
  - How was the choir experience customized to meet the needs of different communities or medical conditions?
- What do participants say were the benefits of the program? What do they say could be done to improve the program?
- How does Vintage Voices use music, participating in music, or singing together to create community?
- What do participating organizations want/get out of the activity?
- What are the advantages to participants for using trained artists to implement the choral experience?

We then completed a comprehensive stakeholder analysis—a critical initial step in any community-responsive evaluation. Through this process we identified all key stakeholders who could inform answers to our research questions (see the "Sources of data" column in Table 5.1).

Table 5.1 Vintage Voices evaluation work plan

Evaluation questions	Data collection methods	Sources of data	Evaluation roles	What we hope to find out
What do participants get out of the choir experience? How do these benefits compare to the goals of participants and the project?	• Singer profile • Wrap-up sessions	• Participants	• The Improve Group creates tool • VocalEssence implements and records data into MS Excel or similar • The Improve Group analyzes data	Participation has a positive social and mental health benefit
Was the choir experience customized to meet the needs of different communities or medical conditions?	• Activity director interviews	• Activity directors • Program dropouts		Program improvements to strengthen participation in the future
How did Vintage Voices address barriers to participation the senior community faces?	• Singer profile • Wrap-up sessions • Activity director interviews	• Participants • Activity directors • Program dropouts		Identification of barriers that must be addressed
What do participants say were the benefits of the program? What do they say could be done to improve the program?	• Wrap-up sessions • Activity director interviews	• Participants • Activity directors • Program dropouts		Broader understanding of the program's strengths and weaknesses
How does Vintage Voices use music, participating in music, or singing together to create community?	• Wrap-up sessions • Activity director interviews	• Participants • Activity directors		Information that can be used to increase senior engagement
What do participating organizations want/get out of the activity?	• Activity director interviews	• Activity directors		Organizational self-interests that can be understood for future marketing
What are the advantages to participants for using trained artists to implement the choral experience?	• Maple Nuts interview • Activity director interviews	• Maple Nuts choir director • Activity directors		How customizing the music improves engagement and participation

Working together with the VocalEssence team, we discussed targeted strategies to collect data from each separate stakeholder group. Based on their specific needs and preferences, we anticipated the best ways to engage the full spectrum of stakeholders, from partner organizations (including the staff of senior centers and assisted living facilities that served as sites for Vintage Voices) to internal staff at VocalEssence. We focused specific attention on developing methods to engage choir participants—as well as their families, loved ones, and caregivers—about the Vintage Voices experience.

Our stakeholder analysis helped us to identify the kinds of data collection instruments we would need to design to ensure a successful evaluation. While interviews could be used to collect information from program and facility staff, we needed a straightforward, accessible way to connect with participants with a range of physical and mental health conditions. Based on our findings, we created two initial tools for data collection. First, we created a survey to track the perceptions of choir participants at the beginning of their 12-week session and then at the conclusion of the session. This five-question survey used a Likert Scale to assess the participant's mental health status, social connections, and quality of life during the first few weeks of choir practice—and then to identify changes in their mental health, social engagement, and quality of life after the final performance was completed. Questions were intentionally broad: for example, on a scale from strongly agree to strongly disagree, participants had to assess whether they had "a positive attitude toward life" or whether their "overall quality of life" was good.

We also developed an interview protocol to gather insights from the activity directors at each Vintage Voices site. It included 11 open-ended, primary questions—plus additional follow-up questions—designed to draw out insights about the quality of Vintage Voices programming and its effect on participants as compared to other arts-based programs available through each partner organization. For example, activity directors were asked:

- Why did you bring Vintage Voices to your organization?
- What are some of the factors that keep people at your site from participating in programs or activities? (For example, medical conditions, culturally specific needs, lack of opportunities.)
  - How was the choir adapted to make it easier for singers to participate?
  - Were there any barriers to participating that were not addressed? If yes, what were they?

- Have the choir participants given you any feedback about the choir? What have the participants said they've gotten from singing in the choir? What have they said could be better?
- How did the choir meet or not meet your expectations?

Through these conversations, activity directors had a chance to reflect on the changes they saw in choir participants—and how the overall experience created a sense of community and wellbeing.

In addition to these primary data collection tools, we created methods for Vintage Voices to track weekly attendance and to record the reasons why some choir participants dropped out of the program.

To complete the evaluation work plan (seen in Table 5.1), we identified roles and responsibilities to guide the data collection process. While The Improve Group team created all data collection tools and conducted interviews with activity directors, we agreed that the VocalEssence team would work with participants to conduct the pre- and post-choir survey. This would allow participants to feel more comfortable with the evaluation process and to build trust with program staff. The VocalEssence team would then record survey data to inform our analysis.

Data Collection

The VocalEssence team began using the choir participant survey as initially planned with members from the first three Vintage Voices choirs. Almost immediately, we realized the survey had some significant shortcomings as a data collection tool. Choir participants with certain health conditions were unable to complete the survey: For example, respondents with memory loss had difficulty understanding the survey questions and were unable to assess their experiences over time. Other choir members with physical disabilities were unable to write on the survey to record their answers. And others simply did not see the value or purpose in the survey, despite our program staff's best efforts to engage them.

As a result, the first surveys provided very little information about choir members' quality of life or their hopes and expectations for the Vintage Voices experience. In discussions with the VocalEssence team, we decided to complete the post-participation survey at the first three choir sites, in case they picked up any measurable change in the quality of life of choir participants. But we also set out to refine our data collection strategies to better align with the needs of choir members.

Table 5.2 Protocol for Vintage Voices post-performance participant focus groups

1. What was your favorite thing about the choir?
2. What could we do to make the choir a better experience (prompts are listed below)?
   (a) *Warm-ups or activities*
   (b) *Physical space or location*
   (c) *Number or variety of members*
   (d) *The performance*
3. Does coming to choir practice change your mood? How?
4. If we do Vintage Voices again in the future, what are some songs or styles of music you would like to learn or perform?
5. What are three words you would use to describe Vintage Voices?

To replace the survey, we developed the protocol for engaging choir participants in an open focus group discussion immediately following their final Vintage Voices performance (Table 5.2).

We designed these discussions to be facilitated by choir director Robert, someone with whom choir members already had an established relationship. These conversations were meant to fit more naturally into Vintage Voices community-focused programming: they took place in the same rooms where choirs practiced, and encouraged free discussion among choir members and staff. Ultimately, we were able to create a safe, comfortable environment in which choir members could reflect back on the Vintage Voices experience and how it changed their quality of life.

The VocalEssence team led these sessions to capture insights from choir participants—while The Improve Group team provided strategic facilitation support, listened in on conversations, and recorded extensive notes. Working together, we were able to collect high-quality, qualitative data from choir participants living with a wide range of physical and mental health challenges. The reflections we gathered from both choir participants and activity directors provided the rich information we needed to conduct a comprehensive initial analysis. As Kimberly explained,

In our experience with evaluation, we've used a range of different tools, from focus groups and observations to surveys. But working with The Improve Group, we realized that different participants responded to different tools—and we needed to shape our evaluation activities around seniors. What was really wonderful about the evolution of our evaluation for Vintage Voices was the creation of the wrap-up focus group conversations that Rob is able to lead. Those conversations don't feel like evaluation—they simply feel like an opportunity for participants to reflect on this 12-week experience. It's an important step, and creates closure for the singers. And it really helps us hear, in their own voices, how they benefited from singing with us.

Data Analysis

Our evaluation team reviewed and analyzed all the data from focus group discussions and interviews as it was collected through the spring, summer, and fall Vintage Voices sessions. In conducting ongoing analysis, we were able to provide VocalEssence with a steady stream of information to strengthen the development of each new choir. We collected useful quotes from both choir participants and activity directors and continuously updated a shared document highlighting new feedback. The data from our early surveys did not prove useful—and we made a final decision to discard the survey and focus our efforts on capturing qualitative insights from primary stakeholders.

Our wrap-up focus group conversations provided exactly the kind of in-depth and meaningful reflections we were seeking. They allowed us to hear choir members speak openly about how singing improved their health and their overall quality of life. As each focus group and interview was completed, we scheduled regular calls and meetings with VocalEssence staff to share our thinking and reflect on the information gathered. Each subsequent conversation deepened our understanding of what made a choir successful and what program components needed to be refined.

At the end of Vintage Voices' first year, based on the data gathered from eight interviews and seven wrap-up sessions, we completed a final analysis and drafted our findings. We facilitated an emerging findings meeting with the VocalEssence team to review and reflect on the data together, to sharpen our interpretation, and to collectively validate our evaluation conclusions. While our analysis relied on a relatively small amount of qualitative data drawn from our focus groups and interviews, we were able to identify significant trends and concrete findings.

EVALUATION FINDINGS

Program Successes

Our evaluation of Vintage Voices' first year unearthed several powerful conclusions about singing and its ability to improve health, expand social connections, and enhance quality of life. We relied on qualitative reflections from choir participants and activity directors to draw these conclusions (Table 5.3):

Table 5.3 Qualitative evaluation findings

Reflections from choir members	Reflections from site activity directors
"I couldn't sing before so I was very reluctant to join but I was happy to be a part of it because I did learn some things. Sometimes I lip-synced but I love music and I feel really encouraged and want to continue to take lessons because I want to sing."	"Set it up so everybody can come regardless of vocal ability. Rob was very sensitive to people with diminished voices, or people who were not sure of the part they sang. He was very nimble in placing them next to someone with a stronger voice."
"You had the patience to work with everyone with varying ages. A lot of younger people don't have the patience like you and I commend you for it."	"Even the people who were not in the choir came to the concert and sat in the front row and cheered them on. There was a lot of bonding."
"Sometimes I think I can't do it. But we get someone like you and we can do anything."	"I think it's just a beautiful opportunity. ... It's a learning opportunity, but it's also very therapeutic. Learning new skills, and specifically arts, expands the brain and fends off dementia."

Choir Members Experienced Improvements in Physical and Mental Health Choir members and activity directors both indicated that the Vintage Voices experience helped to improve mental and physical health. Singing—as well as learning to read sheet music and performing in front of a live audience—stimulated the memories of many choir members. Participants who suffered from significant memory loss or had suffered a stroke experienced some of the most noticeable changes. Many choir members found themselves singing after rehearsal, and several activity directors said that choir members with dementia could still hum the tunes of their choir's songs. In addition, people who had trouble speaking following a stroke began to sing more clearly. Other members gained physical stamina and energy, including the increased lung capacity necessary to sing longer phrases without running out of breath.

Customized Programming Helped to Meet Choir Member Needs Vintage Voices adapted programming to align with participants' needs. To support choir members with vision problems, they provided music in larger print. For those in wheelchairs, staff provided music stands to place sheet music at eye level. And because many choir members live with dementia and Alzheimer's disease, Vintage Voices staff use seating charts, nametags, and other resources to better serve those with cognitive challenges and memory loss. Participants said the choir director and accompanist were extremely patient and adjusted the pace if they noticed anyone was struggling. Participants were able to engage fully and enjoy the experience because programming was customized to meet the needs of aging adults.

Choir Members Had More Opportunities to Deepen Social Connections By participating in Vintage Voices, members had more opportunities to connect with each other, with family members, and with people from the community. Choir members created friendships during regular rehearsals and concerts that lasted well beyond the 12-week session. In addition, activity directors observed choir members strengthen their relationships with people outside the Vintage Voices program. They invited family, friends, and community members to attend their final performance at the end of their 12-week session. Those who came to watch and support a singer said they were able to see that person in a new light— not defined by their particular health problems, rather, stronger, capable, and more independent.

Choir Groups Formed Strong Community Bonds that Extended beyond the Program Over the course of each 12-week session, groups of singers developed a strong, collective bond. Members voted on a name for their particular choir, and Vintage Voices provided customized polo shirts and branded music packets to strengthen each group's identity. These connections changed community dynamics outside rehearsals as well. Activity directors reported that, as a result of their participation in the choir, memory care patients were more frequently included in outside activities like card games.

Partner Organizations Recognized the Program's Extraordinary Value Vintage Voices' partner organizations saw tremendous value in being a part of the program. Activity directors recognized how singing in the choir lifted participants' spirits and improved their overall health. In addition, Vintage Voices eased the burden on activity directors by managing recruitment and logistics. All of the activity directors said that working with Vintage Voices was an extraordinary experience they would love to do again.

Trained Artists Made the Program Effective and Dynamic Vintage Voices staff are professional artists who have been trained to work with older populations. As a result, they were able to help choir members learn new skills and experience the joy of singing in a safe, supportive environment. Activity directors and choir members valued the preparation that went into each rehearsal. By providing labeled binders and sheet music in large print, Vintage Voices staff were able to ensure that all members could participate fully.

Opportunities for Improvement

Members of each unique stakeholder group expressed a shared appreciation for the Vintage Voices program. The data showed that the program's activities and structure provided significant benefits to choir members as well as their loved ones and caregivers. But it also revealed some clear opportunities for program improvement:

New Recruitment Strategies to Engage Singers of All Abilities Are Needed In order to reach participation goals, Vintage Voices is now working closely with activity directors to reach prospective choir members of all abilities. Men in particular were hesitant to join and were underrepresented among participants—something that happens frequently in senior arts programs and choirs of all ages. Recruiting a core group of men to join the choir would likely encourage others to follow. In addition, some prospective members were reluctant to join because of their diminished voices. Recruiting volunteer singers to participate in the choirs would add vocal support—and provide senior singers with added confidence. In addition, it would more actively engage VocalEssence singers in the organization's community-based programs.

To Engage Choir Members More Fully, Music Selection Should Be a Collaborative Experience We found that choir members were extremely interested in the music selection process—and that engaging them in that work helped to deepen their commitment to the Vintage Voices program. In addition, because choir members come from different geographic and cultural communities and have varying skill levels, music selections should be tailored to each particular choir. Today, Vintage Voices is involving all choir members in selecting the pieces to be sung at the final performance. The team also asks about music selection in the wrap-up focus groups and uses responses to inform subsequent choir sessions.

Stronger Partnerships with On-Site Staff Can Help Reduce Barriers to Participation We found that program directors who were committed to the Vintage Voices program were more actively involved in recruiting participants and reminding them to attend rehearsals. In addition, partnerships with transportation providers helped to ensure that choir members could attend rehearsals held at senior centers. VocalEssence staff is now focusing on strengthening relationships with all partners involved.

NEXT STEPS FOR VOCALESSENCE: SHARING FINDINGS AND EXPANDING EVALUATION CAPACITY

The Improve Group developed a clear, concise report outlining the evaluation's findings. Although the report is only two pages long, it provides a full overview of the evaluation process, methods, and the conclusions we were able to draw. In addition, it highlights raw data in the form of direct quotes from choir participants and activity directors. VocalEssence has shared the report widely, not only with funders and partners but also with participants, family members, and caregivers. According to Robert, the evaluation and the report itself are helping to underscore the program's value to a range of stakeholders:

> We've used this tool for showing why and how the program made such an impact on the lives of singers who participated. To show activity directors in particular that their residents want this—that there's now proof that the experience was really beneficial and made a positive impact on their lives and on their overall mental, emotional, and even physical health. We're using that as leverage to gain their support, and encourage them to devote their own dollars to this kind of high-quality programming.

With Vintage Voices well into its second year, VocalEssence has deepened its commitment to evaluating the program. The Improve Group is now conducting another developmental evaluation to track second-year outcomes, build on early successes, and strengthen program implementation going forward.

Working closely with VocalEssence, we are refining evaluation techniques to draw out more in-depth and compelling findings. For example, given the success of our wrap-up focus group conversations, we are now facilitating similar discussions with new choir members before rehearsals begin. These early conversations are helping us understand new members' quality of life as well as their hopes and expectations for the Vintage Voices experience. Capturing these early reflections—and then following up after the final choral performance—is allowing us to identify how singing with Vintage Voices changes participants' attitudes and health outcomes over time. It is important to note that we did not use clinical assessments: We analyzed health outcomes based on conversations with participants themselves and from observations collected by activity directors about participants' behavioral changes.

At the same time, as a result of this work, key members of the VocalEssence team recognized the critical importance of evaluation in both improving programs and effectively articulating their impact in the community, to funders, and to other target audiences. After losing the significant grant that initially funded the Choral Pathways program, VocalEssence leaders found they were able to make a much stronger case to funders using the findings from this evaluation of Vintage Voices. As a result, they decided to take on an even greater role in the evaluation process—and to build the organization's internal capacity to support evaluation work going forward. During the first year of evaluating Vintage Voices, the VocalEssence team recognized they needed more staff and volunteers to support evaluation activities. At their request, The Improve Group designed a comprehensive evaluation training for all VocalEssence staff. Over the course of two days, we helped the VocalEssence team learn critical evaluation skills, including how to build logic models, conduct interviews and focus groups, and complete qualitative analysis. According to Robert, the training has deepened the entire team's commitment to high-quality evaluation.

> It was incredibly productive and valuable to have the entire staff come together and learn about things like building a logic model—how a tool like that can ultimately help us demonstrate the value of our programs. VocalEssence is a small organization—with only nine full-time staff members—and we do a lot with relatively limited resources. And now everyone across the organization can see how evaluation gives you key information to make informed decisions about the direction we need to go in.

With this expanded capacity and knowledge, VocalEssence is already imagining new ways to use evaluation to measure future outcomes. For example, they hope to use evaluation to understand how Vintage Voices' final performances help to build community in assisted living facilities, and to understand how the benefits of singing improve relationships between choir members and their families and loved ones. Although they recognized the benefits of evaluation before, they now feel empowered to use evaluation more independently—to pursue new funding, to recruit more conductors, and to improve the lives of more seniors through choral music.

CONCLUSIONS: USING EVALUATION TO STRENGTHEN ARTS-BASED PROGRAMMING

Evaluating the Vintage Voices program presented The Improve Group team with an extraordinary opportunity to reveal how the creative process can improve health and change lives. In addition, it helped us to identify some key lessons and best practices for using evaluation to strengthen arts-based programming.

Understand How Programs Intend to Use Evaluation Findings Working closely with program staff—and understanding how they need to use data—is essential to a strong evaluation. During the first Vintage Voices sessions, we were in frequent contact with program staff to learn how evaluation activities were working and to hear feedback from host sites and choir members. Those regular meetings and check-ins allowed us to refine our evaluation approach throughout the year to meet VocalEssence's needs. We identified ineffective tools—like the pre- and post-choir survey—that were not providing the organization with useful information to strengthen Vintage Voices. We learned that gathering in-depth, qualitative reflections was critical, and we shifted our data collection strategy to draw out those insights from all key stakeholder groups.

When Working with Older Adults, Remain Nimble and Ready to Adapt Methods and Tools Being prepared to refine the evaluation approach so that it meets the needs of affected stakeholders is always crucial. Through this evaluation, we developed a deeper knowledge about the unique needs of older adults and how best to collect authentic insights and perspectives from aging populations. Our initial quasi-experimental design for this work was far too onerous for stakeholders. When we discovered that our pre- and post-choir surveys were ineffective, we immediately connected with the VocalEssence team to identify the problem and brainstorm solutions. We adapted the design by simplifying our approach and focusing on a series of simple—yet very meaningful—wrap-up focus group conversations. As a result, we were able to gather genuine feedback from stakeholders to answer questions about the power of music in the lives of older adults.

Build Internal Evaluation Capacity Wherever Possible Building the evaluation capacity of arts-based organizations can help them do more with less. The VocalEssence team already had a deep commitment to evaluation, and they were willing to take on new and challenging evaluation tasks in order to get more from their relatively modest budget. Their enthusiasm and ability to go beyond their initial comfort zone allowed us to build much more than we ever expected into the evaluation process. For example, VocalEssence initially had some trepidation about facilitating the wrap-up focus group conversations with choir members. We provided needed support and training to build the team's confidence. Ultimately, they led the facilitation process and unearthed some of the most important conclusions about Vintage Voices. And today, the VocalEssence team regularly introduces new ideas for integrating data collection into the choir experience in order to deepen evaluation findings.

Build Strong, Collaborative Relationships with Program Staff Developmental evaluation is meant to provide continuous feedback as new programs evolve—and the process requires frequent and open discussions about both program strengths and program weaknesses. By building a strong relationship with the VocalEssence team early in the evaluation, we were able to sustain a meaningful, continuous conversation as new challenges and opportunities emerged. Instead of isolating ourselves in our role as evaluator, we worked closely with the VocalEssence team as partners and encouraged them to take a leading role in the evaluation process. Ultimately, this collective, collaborative effort made the evaluation more productive—and the findings more powerful.

REFERENCES

Cohen, G. D. (2006). The Creativity and Aging Study: The Impact of Professionally Conducted Cultural Programs on Older Adults. Retrieved from https://www.arts.gov/sites/default/files/CnA-Rep4-30-06.pdf

Patton, M. Q. (2010). *Developmental Evaluation Defined and Positioned*. New York: Guilford Publications.

CHAPTER 6

Cultivating Sustainable School Culture: Tilling the Soil and Nourishing the Seeds Through the Arts

Ross Anderson and Christine Pitts

Arts integration is a creative opportunity to respond to the cultural elements of a school and explore the limitless design possibilities for teaching and learning, but it is not just one step (Corbett, Wilson, & Morse, 2005). Which steps are critical to transfer the benefits of arts integration from the classroom experience to a sustainable shift in school culture? What evaluation methods can help identify those steps early in the development of a model to support sustainability and impact? The evaluation presented in

This research was supported by a grant from the U.S. Department of Education (PR/Award No. U351D140063) and a grant from the Oregon Community Foundation.

R. Anderson (✉)
Educational Policy Improvement Center, Eugene, OR, USA

C. Pitts
Educational Policy Improvement Center, Eugene, OR, USA

University of Oregon, Eugene, OR, USA

R.S. Rajan, I.C. O'Neal (eds.), *Arts Evaluation and Assessment*,
https://doi.org/10.1007/978-3-319-64116-4_6

117

this chapter responds to these two driving questions through a mixture of methods and data sources.

The arts-based school reform model evaluated in this chapter situated school culture as a construct with overarching influence on all aspects of the school experience. School culture influences how an organization, as a whole, evolves and the way that teachers interact with students, collaborate with colleagues, approach instruction and curriculum, take risks with new ideas, engage in training, and share leadership responsibilities. By injecting struggling schools with a creative and artistic catalyst, the model sought to change instructional behaviors and curricular decisions as well as the culture supporting those features. As Guskey (1986) described, for new practices to sustain, attitudes and beliefs need to shift first. In schools suffering from a history of competing, short-term initiatives with little sustained improvement, those shifts may depend largely on a supportive school culture. Given this rationale, our evaluation of one arts-based school reform approach targeted the factors undergirding school culture—factors that both influence the promise of sustained change and become shaped by the arts integration experience.

THE ARTCORE MODEL

In the pursuit of an adaptable schoolwide arts integration model, the ArtCore project partnered with five middle level schools predominantly serving students who have been historically marginalized in K-12 education. This chapter documents the implementation during the first two years of a four-year model development, research, and evaluation grant-funded Arts in Education Model Development and Dissemination project. The project sought to reach more than 2000 students in five middle level schools with arts integrated opportunities in visual arts, music, and theater and core academic content areas. The project's goals were to boost academic achievement, motivation, engagement, and creative potential of students. To achieve those goals, the project aimed to increase the capacity of 50 middle school teachers to design, create, and deliver new pedagogy and arts integrated curricula. To ensure feasibility and sustainability of that objective the project focused on affecting positive schoolwide culture through a far-reaching unifying framework of student outcomes. The project aimed to establish the procedures, theory, and frameworks that can accelerate fragmented arts integration toward a coherent, sustainable, and adaptable schoolwide transformation model uniquely contextualized to schools.

Conceptually, the arts integration approach built on theories of creative learning (Beghetto, 2016), motivation (Bandura, 1986, 1997; Skinner, Furrer, Marchand, & Kinderman, 2008), and school engagement (Martin, 2012) to shift pedagogical priorities and enhance school culture. Incorporation of the Studio Habits of Mind (SHOM) prioritized the development of metacognitive strategies that underlie creative thinking and artistic learning (see Hetland, Winner, Veenema, & Sheridan, 2013). Teacher and teaching artist teams attempted to emphasize learning objectives in the arts and academics equally, choosing the standards and disciplines that best fit their context and student needs. By implementing with a team of teachers in one grade at a time, the project provided an intensive level of embedded professional development followed by support and feedback. These best practices (Salas, Tannenbaum, Kraiger, & Smith-Jentsch, 2012) targeted ownership, self-efficacy, and locally grown practices alongside simultaneous development of a cohesive and supportive school culture (Fullan & Quinn, 2015).

Depicted in Fig. 6.1, the theory of change driving the ArtCore model suggests when teachers are given modeling, guided practice, tools, and structured collaboration with a teaching artist and supportive colleagues, they will increase skills and self-efficacy related to arts integration and creative teaching strategies. The intervention's effect on teacher attitude, effort, and satisfaction may depend on their school's culture for organizational learning and school leadership's commitment. Teacher skill development and collaboration will affect student motivation, engagement, and creativity when teachers approach professional growth proactively. Enhanced student motivation, engagement, and creativity in school will affect their academic achievement. As teachers recognize this effect, their self-efficacy grows to a level where practices become sustained and modeled for others. The evaluation presented in this chapter will explore early evidence regarding the school and teacher elements of this theory of change—the prerequisite factors to sustained student outcomes.

EVALUATION APPROACH

The evaluation described in this chapter illuminates the early developmental phase to understand the adoption and adaptation of a schoolwide strategy and to provide opportunities to improve the approach. Evaluating the

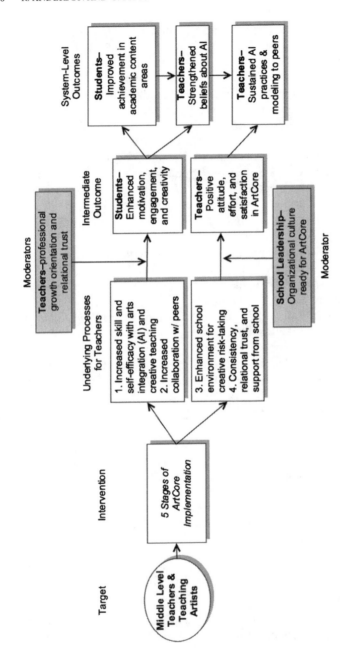

Fig. 6.1   ArtCore model theory of change

impact requires knowing *what* the intervention entailed and *how* schools interpreted and implemented the intervention differently. We employ an implementation framework where each step builds capacity and ownership of schools to become implementation and evaluation partners (Fullan & Quinn, 2015) and to clarify clear measurement parameters for the final summative evaluations (Blase, Fixsen, Sims, & Ward, 2015). In this developmental evaluation study (Patton, 2011), we sought to highlight the contextual irregularities of each unique implementation site rather than ignore these variations. Potential irregularities might include competition for time and resources of other initiatives or change in school leadership during implementation—potentially critical factors.

Given the complex and innovative nature of developing and evaluating a schoolwide model, the developmental evaluation approach allows for evaluators to synthesize ideas across the project. To learn from multiple angles that can inform continued innovation and improvement, we conducted (a) observations, (b) surveys, (c) interviews, (d) focus groups, (e) reflections, (f) self-assessments, (g) product reviews, and (h) video documentation throughout the year and across contexts. During this early stage of development, the research and evaluation team responded to needs and opportunities with the development of measures and tracking mechanisms aimed at detecting patterns across data and articulating the adaptation variability.

In order to evaluate the efficacy of an arts integrated school change model in future studies, our work in this current study first sought to understand how the development of school culture, supportive of arts integration, interacts with teacher mindset, affect, and behavior. This focus allows for school and community partners to know what aspects of early implementation, such as the development of shared values, may be highest leverage for sustained practice. The following questions guided the developmental evaluation.

1. Is there evidence that the ArtCore arts integration model may have affected teacher-level outcomes driven by a shift in school culture during the developmental phase?
2. How did the ArtCore implementation cycle work differently compared to the proposed model and across implementing schools? Does this cycle appear to support positive school change? If so, what were the catalysts? If not, what were the barriers?

3. How did the design of arts integration flexibly fit the unique context, assets, and needs of each school?

Hypotheses

We generated working hypotheses based on the theory of change undergirding the model—student-level effects depend on teacher-level effects, which in turn depend on the development of a supportive school culture driving adaptation in the arts integration model. We expected that some evidence would suggest effectiveness for shifting teachers' perspective, skill, and practices, but that the degree of this shift would vary across schools. We hypothesized that the work done to develop and align organizational culture may play an outsized role influencing the attitude and behaviors of teachers. Further, we believed that the implementation cycle and the design of arts integration would vary widely between schools. Establishing these hypotheses a priori required clarifying the theory of change driving the development of the model—a process that would allow alternative explanations to emerge. Testing these hypotheses explicitly supported refinement of the theory of change to improve future efficacy of the model.

Schoolwide Creative Engagement

The current education landscape is littered with school improvement approaches that often lack coherence with the preexisting context and fail to account for necessary adaptation (Fullan & Quinn, 2015). In contrast, a comprehensive arts-based intervention may create clarity and common purpose through the consistent integration of art disciplines across systems in the school that determine instruction, school climate, and interdisciplinary collaboration. Numerous evaluations of arts integration demonstrate promising links to student achievement in reading, math, and science for underserved populations (see Robinson, 2013, for recent meta-analysis). Few of these evaluation studies approached the variation in implementation as a potential means to learn what steps are most critical to sustain the effort (e.g., the proportion of teachers trained or number of disciplines integrated). Captured in a retrospective book (Noblit, Corbett, Wilson, & McKinney, 2009), the most comprehensive approach to date resulted from the Whole School Initiative in Mississippi. To gauge the effect of implementation on student outcomes in that initiative, evaluators collected data from multiple perspectives. For instance, a teacher survey, complemented by school observations, compiled the extent of arts integration in the school, the variety of instructional approaches, professional development opportunities, and alignment to schoolwide planning.

Not surprisingly, evaluators of the Whole School Initiative found that high levels of implementation associated with higher rates of meeting achievement growth by school. Corbett, Wilson, and Morse suggested that staff endorsement of the initiative, opportunities for skill development, presence of skilled coaches, and continuity of efforts represented "front-end" developments in implementation (2005, p. 19). Their work provided strong recommendations for future models and left more questions regarding the structures and supports and overall school culture in place prior to implementation in the most successful schools. Additionally, understanding the role that practitioner mindset, attitude, and belief might play on implementation and the tension between adoption and adaptation may be key. Given the paucity of further investigations, especially in middle schools, our evaluation study aimed to begin to fill this gap.

To reach sustainability, arts integration must move from the status as a singular program toward a composite of adapted and sustained norms and practices embedded in and supported throughout the school. The premise underlying this assertion emerges from organizational theory where the development of shared values and a unifying theoretical framework about teaching, learning, and student success takes on powerful symbolic meaning to influence individual beliefs and behaviors and organizational culture (Bolman & Deal, 2013; Fullan & Quinn, 2015; Nathan, 2011; Senge, 2006). As such, this element received attention in this evaluation across three interdependent levels: (a) the organizational culture shaped by a school's history and context, (b) collaboration within a professional community of practice, and (c) individual teacher attitude, pedagogy and design of the classroom environment. Just as the theory of change driving the ArtCore model specified the role that each of these three levels play, the evaluation used data from each level to look for evidence of change and potential interactions between levels.

METHOD

Our study is a mixed-method design that consists of multiple phases to answer a set of research questions (Creswell & Plano Clark, 2011). In this interactive design, a team of embedded researchers pursued evaluation questions that were connected and aligned to the program development of the study using qualitative and quantitative strands. To clarify the rationale for this approach, the use of quantitative data would demonstrate the degree to which the model shows promise, and in specific phases of the study, the qualitative data would illuminate potential mechanisms of change, illustrating perspectives independently of the quantitative data. During the phase of the evaluation represented in this chapter, both qualitative and quantitative data sources informed the findings and interpretation.

Schools

School and teacher-level data were collected from one rural and four urban middle schools in the Pacific Northwest. The five middle schools, within four school districts, participating in the intervention served high percentages of students identified as minority and low-income, compared to the average demographic makeup of the other schools in the state and participating districts. In four out of five schools, this early phase of the ArtCore project was implemented with a subgroup of sixth graders and their classroom teachers; in the remaining charter school (serving grades 7–12), the seventh and eighth graders and their teachers were included in the sample. All of the participating teachers from each school ($n = 17$) consented involvement in the research.

Measures

Our rubric, the ArtCore Measure of Adoption, Intensity, and Adaptation (AMAIA) provided the means for school and project administration to document the activities and efforts related to each implementation stage. The evaluation team designed this measure by adapting the National Implementation Research Networks' (2013) Stages of Implementation Framework and Implementation Drivers: Assessment of Best Practices measure (Fixsen et al., 2015). This adaptation aligned to the ArtCore stages of implementation, (a) organizational culture, (b) social capital and innovation, (c) adoption—adaptation, (d) schoolwide enactment, and (e) reflection and refinement.

Informed by the model's original design as well as features of implementation science, the details of the measure emerged inductively during the developmental phase, driven by how sources of evidence could triangulate behaviors, attitudes, and artifacts for the indicators of each component. Early in implementation, each school's context varied widely and informed how components were operationalized in each case study (see Table 6.1).

To complete the AMAIA, evaluation team members used qualitative and quantitative evidence collected to identify the quantitative score for component indicators on a scale from zero to two, where zero indicates "Not yet in place", one indicates "Partially in place", and two indicates "In place". Then, team members described and referenced evidence that supported the score given. The AMAIA provides a predetermined, quantitative scale that accounts for differences in adoption and adaptation, incorporating evidence, such as activities, artifacts, teacher and administrative efforts, organizational practices, beliefs, attitudes, and shared vision. Figure 6.2 illustrates the procedures for how to implement the AMAIA in practice.

In addition to administrative records of activities and document analysis of teaching and learning artifacts, quantitative data from the ArtCore teacher survey protocol provided more evidence of indicators' level of implementation within AMAIA stages. This teacher survey is an integration of multiple scales that measure teachers' reported beliefs about, (a) teaching for creativity, (b) the value and efficacy of arts integration, and (c) orientation to teaching and school culture. The validated Teaching for Creativity Scale solicited teachers' beliefs about their own self-efficacy, student potential, and societal value, as well as perceived environmental encouragement for creativity at their school (Rubenstein, McCoach, & Siegle, 2013).

Identified in Table 6.2, we adapted some of the scales employed to be retrospective based on recent experiences in the project; others were general to their teaching experience. Additionally, we developed the *Teaching for Creative Engagement Scale* where teachers documented the frequency that they employed metacognitive and modeling approaches for students' creative learning—two strategies unique to the ArtCore model. The *Value and Efficacy of Arts Integration Scale* and the scales measuring orientation to teaching and school culture were adapted from the My School, My Voice Survey validated by the Chicago Consortium on School Reform (2014). On these scales teachers provided responses about relational trust and school climate, collaboration, consistency of reforms, enjoyment of teaching, and orientation to professional growth opportunities, retrospectively.

Table 6.1   Component definitions of the ArtCore measure of adoption, intensity, and adaptation

Components	Definition
1. Organizational culture	Teachers, administrators, and the broader school community develop, evaluate, and refine a shared vision. A common set of values and norms is agreed on that all personnel use to drive their personal and professional decision-making in the school. A unifying framework of student-learning and inclusion strategies are intentionally designed, planned, and applied. Formal and informal decisions are consistently evaluated for sense-making and strategic decision-making processes.
2. Social capital and innovation	School leaders and educators develop adaptive and strategic capacity in content-specific areas, learning skills, and leadership. Voluntary participation taps the unique skills of different educators. An action-oriented learning cycle frames teacher collaboration. Supportive leadership encourages risk-taking and innovation.
3. Adoption-adaptation	Assessment of student and educator assets and needs drives the adaptation of instructional and curricular models. Alignment of inputs and processes to common goals and outcomes is intentional. Authentic, challenging, and supportive student engagement ensures that student voice and choice remain at the center of design work. Formative feedback about the learning experience and skill development provides opportunities to continue to adjust and adapt.
4. Schoolwide enactment	Professional learning communities arise across content and grade level teams. Professional development is differentiated based on teacher interests but builds on a schoolwide unifying framework. Policies and practices are implemented based on an evaluation of resources, support, and opportunities for innovation. Continued Implementation is designed and implemented with consideration for existing politics, roles, and relationships.
5. Reflection and refinement	School leaders and teachers consistently evaluate their practices based on their shared vision and celebrate efforts and progress. Documentation of collaboration, strategies, and ideas informs future implementation cycles. Reflection builds greater coherence and community across a school of trusting and receptive learners.

Note: This implementation cycle builds from the School Success Model developed at the Educational Policy Improvement Center (2017)

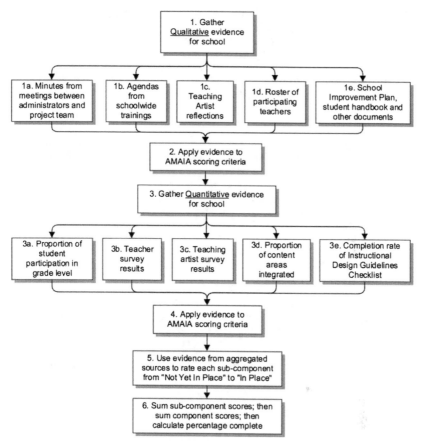

Fig. 6.2 Procedures for AMAIA implementation in practice

Student-level variables of interest correspond to teacher-level effects, but our focus for this chapter will be on the school- and teacher-level changes that we posit influence student-level effects. Though our larger program of inquiry includes student-level factors, those results are only preliminary and will be reported in future publications. As embedded members of the innovation team, researchers and evaluators learned lessons from multiple angles and data sources. Using our multiphase mixed methods research design we anchored quantitative findings to case study narratives, illustrating a developmental approach to evaluation. A rigorous

Table 6.2 Descriptive results of teacher-level factors included across implementation framework components

Factor	Mean (SD) across schools	School mean range
Retrospective measures ("Since participating in ArtCore, I feel...")		
Satisfaction and preparedness	4.97 (0.42)	(3.54–6.00)*
Arts integration positive effect on student engagement	4.88 (0.92)	(4.21–5.81)*
Improved relational trust of faculty	5.19 (0.38)	(4.54–5.67)**
Improved openness to collaboration of faculty	4.49 (0.56)	(3.94–5.50)*
Improved consistency of initiatives in school	4.14 (0.55)	(3.90–4.27)
Cross-sectional general measures (not specific to ArtCore)		
Teaching for creativity: self-efficacy	5.64 (0.80)	(5.39–5.71)
Teaching for creativity: environmental encouragement	4.33 (1.56)	(3.95–4.67)
Teaching for creativity: societal value	6.06 (0.28)	(5.72–6.41)
Teaching for creativity: student potential	5.12 (2.40)	(4.75–5.31)
Professional enjoyment	6.22 (0.42)	(5.81–6.63)
Perspective on professional growth	5.94 (0.43)	(5.25–6.38)*
Cross-sectional TFCE measures (frequency scale: "How often do you employ...")		
Practices for metacognition	3.50 (0.37)	(3.42–3.72)
Practices for modeling	3.66 (0.27)	(3.56–4.00)

Note: Responses are on a 7-point Likert scale for all factors except Teaching for Creative Engagement (TFCE), where 1 equals "totally disagree" and 7 equals "totally agree". For TFCE, responses are on a 5-point frequency scale where 1 equals "never" and 5 equals "very often". School mean range refers to the lowest and highest school averages. Symbols denote a statistically significant difference between the low and high means

$*p < 0.05;$ $**p < 0.10$

but responsive approach at this phase of evaluation provided lessons for model improvement.

FINDINGS

Findings focus on our three main research and evaluation questions. We address variations in the implementation cycle and the process of collaborative design to explore how the schools' organizational culture supported the growth of creative engagement at each level. We report on which elements of school organizational culture appeared to be most powerful in catalyzing or crippling this progress and how the process appeared to relate to shifts in perspectives and experiences of teachers. We provide comparative analysis of each case study school and summative analysis across schools.

Teacher-Level Impressions

On the teacher survey, teachers answered three forms of questions outlined in Table 6.2. The teacher survey included retrospective measures regarding teachers' reported satisfaction with the project, feelings of support and trust across their school since the project began, and opinions about the school's efforts across various schoolwide improvement initiatives. Cross-sectional measures documented teaching for creative engagement that asked about their perceptions of arts integration, as well as beliefs about their own self-efficacy for creative teaching, school-based environmental encouragement for creativity, the role of creativity in society, and student creative potential. A frequency scale measured how often teachers practiced instructional techniques that explicitly engaged students' creative metacognition or modeled strategies for creative learning. The aggregate mean for all participating teachers is reported for each scale in Table 6.2; we reported the range from lowest to highest mean disaggregated by school, illustrating patterns of statistically significant variation between schools.

Retrospective Measures

Generally, the means for each retrospective scale, ranging from 1–7 (totally disagree to totally agree), were above a neutral level; however, the findings provided some evidence of both systemic changes and hindrances. Although teachers' satisfaction with ArtCore and feelings of preparedness were at $M = 4.97$ (somewhat agree) across participating schools, the school-level variation ranged from a low rating of $M = 3.54$ (indifference) to a high rating of $M = 6.00$ (agree). The highest scale among the retrospective measures was for improved relational trust with colleagues and principals ($M = 5.19$ or somewhat agree). In addition, since the range across school means was small, we can consider that the collaborative arts-integration experience contributed to improved rapport, generally. On average, teachers reported indifference about the improvement of the consistency of schoolwide initiatives ($M = 4.14$); this score was the lowest average among all of the retrospective scales indicating that any potential effect of greater coherence was not yet realized.

Cross-Sectional General Measures

Across the respondent's reported perceptions, they consistently reported that their professional teaching experiences were enjoyable (M = 6.22 or agree) with a positive orientation to professional growth (M = 5.94 or agree). Additionally, teachers reported, on average, that they believe in the societal value of creativity (M = 6.06) and feel self-efficacious supporting creative learning experiences (M = 5.64). However, teachers reported uncertainty about the school-based environmental encouragement to take instructional risks (M = 4.33) and personal beliefs about students' potential for creative learning (M = 5.12). Based on the large standard deviations (SD = 1.56 and SD = 2.40, respectively) and nonsignificant statistical difference between school averages, their individual perceptions varied widely across teachers but not across schools. On average teachers' showed uncertainty in regard to their perceptions of students' creative potential, a result that could indicate narrow conceptions of creativity or a lack of opportunities to witness the complete spectrum of creative thinking, behaviors and performance.

Cross-Sectional Frequency Scale The last two scales represent the frequency that teachers engaged students through metacognitive learning and modeling of explicit strategies for creative engagement. Teachers responded to questions about how often they engaged in each instructional practice on a scale from one, "never", to five, "very often". On average, teachers across the schools reported modeling creative learning behaviors "sometimes" to "regularly" (M = 3.66), just slightly more than they reported engaging students in metacognitive learning (M = 3.50). For each scale, there was little variance across individual teachers and school-level reports. The results provide evidence that teachers may need continued professional learning opportunities and guided collaboration to reinforce awareness about high-leverage strategies that engage students metacognitively and creatively.

ArtCore Implementation Cycle

AMAIA results from this developmental phase indicated that each school's adoption, intensity, and adaptation differed depending on the implementation component. In this developmental evaluation, we operationalized each component into a measured indicator based on the original design of the model as well as inductively during the

Table 6.3 Results from the ArtCore measure of adoption, intensity, and adaptation during the ArtCore developmental evaluation study in five middle schools

Components	School A (%)	School B (%)	School C (%)	School D (%)	School E (%)
1. Organizational culture	33	25	42	58	75
2. Social capital & innovation	40	40	70	70	90
3. Adoption-adaptation	72	56	78	67	61
4. Schoolwide enactment	25	13	50	38	75
5. Reflection & refinement	40	30	80	60	80
Total	48	36	64	62	74

Note: The percentages represent the number of elements in each component that a school completed. The scale range for each component differed. Component 1 ranged from 0–12; Component 2 ranged from 0–10; Component 3 ranged from 0–18; Component 4 ranged from 0–8; and Component 5 ranged from 0–10. Total scores range for AMAIA is 0–58

process of evaluating adaptation by each school (U.S. Department of Education, 2017).

As such, the overall quantitative results, presented in Table 6.3, from our early phase of implementation encapsulate indicators of each component in the AMAIA. These results illustrate how each component plays out in practice with anecdotal evidence from each case study school. Overall, in schools that showed consistent levels of adoption, adaptation, and intensity across components during the first year and a half of implementation, practices began to sustain and produce positive attitudes.

Organizational Culture

During the exploration stage, school community members and program developers first explored the possibilities for program design examining their own beliefs and attitudes about why arts integration can work for their students. As with other components and in line with implementation science best practices, each indicator included in the AMAIA was (a) related to an observable process or event, (b) a measured attitude or behavior, or (c) connected to a tangible artifact of teaching and learning. As can be seen, participating schools ranged from 25% to 75% complete for this component reflecting a range of prioritization of time and energy. The outcomes were widely different, in part, because some schools weren't able to align or negotiate the commitments to other initiatives with this stage of implementation. This step to define the rationale for each school operationalized differently across schools but focused commonly on alignment of shared beliefs, attitudes, and values with an undergirding unifying framework. According to indicators on the scale, in three out of the five schools, school administration dedicated time to focus on clarifying the purpose of arts integration early in implementation; records show that two of those three schools included the entire faculty and the other included a majority of staff. In the remaining two schools, a full-day workshop was held late into the developmental phase of implementation at one school and at the other school these schoolwide opportunities were scheduled and canceled twice due to competing priorities. Table 6.4 provides information about who participated in key activities for each component.

Social Capital for Innovation

The recruitment, selection, and early design phase of the arts integration work was a time for schools to recruit and sustain participation across a grade level team of teachers. At varying degrees from school-to-school, participation was voluntary. As seen in Table 6.3, it appears that when teachers weren't aware of the purpose of the project and how it fit into the school's culture, social capital remained a largely untapped resource. At the heart of social capital and innovation, a long-term, community-based

Table 6.4 Participation at each school across different activities included in each component

Components	School A	School B	School C	School D	School E
1. Development of unifying framework	7 Teachers 1 Principal	–	All teachers 2 Principals	–	All teachers 1 Principal
2. Design team or school leadership team	–	7 Teachers 2 Principals	7 Teachers 2 Principals	–	8 teachers 1 Principal
3. Participation in cross-site trainings	6 Teachers	4 Teachers 2 Principals	8 Teachers	4 Teachers	7 Teachers
4. Participation in school-based trainings	–	–	All teachers	All staff	All teachers
5. Collaboration with teaching artist	4 Teachers (4 subjects)	4 Teachers (2 subjects)	5 Teachers (5 subjects)	4 Teachers (4 subjects)	4 teachers (4 subjects)
6. End-of-year reflection	1 Principal	2 Principals 1 Teacher	All teachers 2 Principals	All staff	All staff

teaching artist, or *ArtCore Weaver*, served as chief instigator, integrator, and creative catalyst, threading the strategies through the grade level team and potentially the school. Though level of experience and artistic discipline varied across assigned *Weavers*, each had demonstrated prior skill as a teaching artist in different disciplines and contexts. According to their reflection logs, each *Weaver* accommodated teachers' schedules and communication procedures, built the capacity of teachers to integrate the arts independently, and asked for feedback from their teacher partners, regularly. After recruitment, the *Weaver* engaged in facilitated face-to-face training and collaborative design. At one school, not only did the first cohort of teachers (6th grade) include the entire grade but members of this cohort also took leadership roles in planning a schoolwide strategy for continued growth and transformation. At the other end of the spectrum, another school struggled to engage members from the first cohort of teachers, consistently. Based on interview and survey data, these teachers reported being overwhelmed with the trauma of initiative overload and felt little organizational coherence across their responsibilities—they also served the highest concentration of historically marginalized and underserved students.

Adoption-Adaptation Once a team was formed, the AMAIA results show consistently adequate levels (>50%) across schools for this component, ranging from 56%–78% of the component indicators rating as fully developed. The ArtCore instructional design guidelines (Fig. 6.3) emerged from this developmental phase based on the common strategies employed; we analyzed a sample of teaching and learning modules from each site for evidence using this checklist. Based on that analysis, each site demonstrated evidence of developing rigorous arts integrated teaching and learning opportunities, which translated to higher scores for this component on the AMAIA. According to Weaver logs, during the collaborative design and instruction phase most Weaver-Teacher teams appeared to make meaningful efforts to develop the efficacy of the classroom teachers (e.g., shared teaching responsibilities and manageable art projects). To account for behaviors in our assessment of this component, we incorporated the scores from an observation protocol designed to measure the metacognitive and creative strategies integrated into teaching and learning. Comparing the quantity and quality of teacher practices that support creativity and student engagement, an independent-sample t-test demonstrated a large effect in arts integrated lessons across schools compared to traditional lessons; $t(56) = 7.37$, $p < 0.000$ (Pitts, Anderson, & Haney, in press).

artcore

Instructional Design Guidelines

Collaboration

I. Norms and Agreements

- _____
- _____
- _____

- _____
- _____
- _____

2. Co-Teaching

☐ One teaches, one supports   ☐ Station teaching
☐ Parallel teaching   ☐ Team teaching
☐ Alternative teaching

3. Content Emphasis

☐ **Art Discipline(s) / Standard(s):**

_____

☐ **Academic Content Area(s) / Standard(s):**

_____

☐ **Creative integration:**
Are students creating and demonstrating their understanding of and through one or more art forms? Describe: _____
☐ Is classroom teaching leading design and guiding collaboration?

checked: _____

Module Design & Instruction

I. Creative Arts Integration Strand: These strands can overlap in practice considerably. Based on the needs and assets of your school and your students, select your focus that can drive the design work. (If you are feeling ambitious, select and define all three)

☐ **Standards-based**—Arts and academic learning objectives
Define:_____

_____

☐ **Metacognitive**—Studio Habits of Mind (SHOM) thinking objectives
Define:_____

_____

☐ **Social-Emotional Skills**—Motivation and engagement objectives
Define:_____

_____

Fig. 6.3   ArtCore instructional design guidelines

Across the participating schools, arts integrated assessment approaches ranged from (a) an exhibition of learning with authentic community audience members to give students feedback, (b) self-assessment of the SHOM, (c) creative or reflective performance in front of peers and adults, (d) an arts history competition of ancient Greece, (e) concept mapping about creative learning, (f) memory recall, and (g) pre- and post-reflection on levels of anxiety in the face of math learning and assessment. According to interviews and observations, this authentic demonstration appeared to make several critical factors visible to participating teachers: (a) the rigor of quality arts integrated learning, (b) high levels of student thinking and engagement demanded through this approach, and (c) the latent creative potential of students.

Schoolwide Enactment
This component had the widest range within this sample of schools (13%–75% completion). At this point in the developmental adaptation of the model across schools, those farthest along in this component had developed a unifying framework and incorporated that framework into pedagogical innovations, vernacular for student feedback, staff meetings, strategic vision for the school, and other teacher and student supports.

Reflection and Refinement
Using a journey map, video, or photographs that captured the evolution of the work in each school, two of the five schools isolated time to complete a reflection as a staff. In other schools, reflection occurred between school leaders and project partners, using this reflection to set a course for the following year. In its furthest development, this stage systematically reviewed the accomplishments, challenges, and growth in skills, behaviors, and attitudes during the first cycle of implementation.

Three Strands of Arts Integration

As Fig. 6.4 illustrates, a tripartite model of arts integration emerged from the theoretical framework for instruction and the resulting teaching and learning modules created in ArtCore during the developmental phase. Intentionally, we asked Weavers to follow their instinct and respond to the assets and needs of the landscape—the students, the classroom setting, and the teachers. In response to these conditions, a common approach developed that integrated multidisciplinary arts learning and metacognitive

Fig. 6.4 Tripartite
model of arts integration

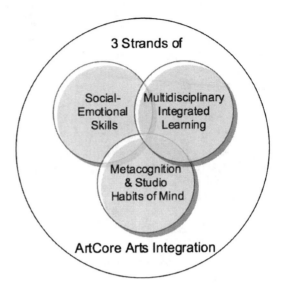

habits of mind within interrelated academic and social-emotional themes. The model established the concept of creative engagement—where learning is charged emotionally, aesthetically, and metacognitively—as a heuristic to guide the design of coteaching experiences (Anderson, 2017). The collaborative design sparked new student-learning opportunities. Based on the documentation of these modules, these experiences simultaneously connected art and academic skills, creative dispositions, and adaptive motivational orientation.

Each school built a unique take on one of the three strands incorporating culturally specific factors of the school: (a) social-emotional learning, (b) multidisciplinary integrated learning, or (c) metacognitive habits of mind. Their arts integrated approaches operationalized the ArtCore module design guidelines to varying extents with integrated standards, shared instructional efforts, authentic learning experiences, and authentic classroom-based assessments. One module that focused on socio-emotional skills aimed to reduce students' anxiety around math learning and assessment by guiding students through a process of manifesting their "anxiety monsters" with sculptural depictions, naming and describing them, and confronting them with expressive strategies. In another example, the integration of academic and arts standards drove module design and instruction. In this standards-based module, students learned science concepts behind the water cycle, plate tectonics, and ecology as well as illustration techniques in order to create national park coloring books for neighboring elementary school students.

The metacognitive SHOM were the focus of a student-centered "starburst book" in one school where students described, illustrated, and explained attributes about their unique identities through different media. The Weaver and teachers supported students' self-assessment of their books and mastery of the SHOM and ultimately gathered community members for a public screening and discussion of their work. In another school, students studied the anatomy of different insects, drawing scientific pictures in preparation for sculpting enlarged versions of their insect out of clay. When one of the sculptures exploded during firing, damaging the rest of the pieces, students and teachers practiced the habits of *persistence* and *exploration* improvising with wire and other materials to remake their sculptures into far more interesting hybrid creatures than the original works. Similarly, at the fifth school students integrated ecology, design, and engineering to design solutions to ecological disasters, practicing the SHOM at each stage of the process. Although these examples depict only one set of lessons from each school, they describe the consistent trend across each school's designed modules. Though a cohesive focus at each school began to emerge as distinct strands of arts integration, they overlapped considerably in practice. These strands appeared to complement the styles proposed by Bresler (1995) and extend those styles to focus the purpose of arts integration around different aspects of the learners' experience, skill development, assets, and needs.

DISCUSSION

This developmental evaluation aimed to investigate the factors both driving and thwarting adoption, adaptation, and implementation of arts integrated practices in five middle schools. Our initial analysis aimed at determining how the ArtCore project implementation cycle varied across schools. Given the overarching influence that classroom teachers have on student opportunities for creative engagement in learning, this evaluation aimed to learn about the relationship between aspects of implementation and teacher-level outcomes. We tested the ArtCore model theory of change through a variety of methods and data sources appropriate to developmental evaluation. We crafted research questions that targeted different features of the theory of change and built hypotheses from the literature that supported the theory of change. We recommend that evaluators consider these steps during the developmental phase in collaboration with implementation partners. By testing the hypotheses concerning organizational, implementation, and teacher-level aspects of the theory of change at this developmental stage, continued refinement may add to precision of future analyses of student-level outcomes.

As organizational theory led us to predict, it appears critical that a school community refer to a locally grounded unifying framework early in the process of implementation. This foundational piece seems to provide a common target and a shared purpose across learning environments and the constellation of initiatives in a school. The arts create an accessible, expressive, and inquiry-based approach for school teams to discover their own framework. Early experiences in the ArtCore model appear to have had a positive effect on the professional community and school culture experienced by teachers. In spite of teachers' lingering doubts about their schools' support for risk-taking, they indicated the highest level of agreement in the area of their own professional enjoyment and openness to growth—two critical assets on which arts integration programs should build. In contrast, our finding that some teachers felt uncertain about the creative potential of students requires greater attention. Arts integration programs might consider creating more opportunities to make the many dimensions of creativity visible in all learners. Measuring these perceptions in an evaluation may provide key moderators to test student-level effects.

School Culture and Social Capital

According to our results, in the three schools furthest along in the organizational culture component, the first had a unifying framework that underwent a consensus-building process of renewal and clarity. The second school made steps toward adoption of the SHOM, and the third school began an intensive process to get input from stakeholders on a new framework, aligned to the SHOM. In order to develop a locally grounded unifying framework (i.e., profile of a learner or habits of a successful graduate), examples were provided to all schools. This step appeared to be critical because it clarified a common target for student learning and expectations and norms for the adult community of practice. Most importantly, it created the opening for how the ArtCore model could enhance school goals. Based on the results of each AMAIA component, lack of progress in this component appeared to have thwarted progress in other components, especially schoolwide enactment.

Across schools, the intervention focused on cultivating the social and intellectual capital across teachers, teaching artists, and administrators within the school. Not surprisingly, we found that the three schools that developed the organizational culture component in depth alongside social capital showed the most evidence of sustainability—greater participation, enhanced collaboration and risk-taking, professional growth, and intention to continue efforts. In the organizational landscape where social capital was low, system-wide sustainability appeared tenuous. Communication between cohorts of teachers at cross-site professional development opportunities may have laid a foundation of common understanding and alignment. The three schools scoring highest in the schoolwide enactment component allocated school professional development time to the project during the school year to engage the entire faculty—including classified staff on occasion—in refining the unifying framework and integrating the ArtCore model to their shared vision for their school. Possibly due to consistently strong adoption-adaptation of instructional practices in each school, all schools appeared to attain higher levels of *reflection and refinement* compared to the early component of organizational culture. For instance, though School B scored the lowest on most components during this early phase, they completed the most effective reflection and refinement of their approach in preparation for the next year of work. They committed five half-days of schoolwide professional development to exploring drama-based arts integration as a staff.

Based on results from this early phase, a coherent, supportive organizational culture and commitment of leadership may moderate the effect of the ArtCore intervention on teacher outlook, future effort, and overall satisfaction and openness most profoundly. The greatest threats to accessing social capital appeared to be the perception of competing initiatives, a pervasive *either-or* attitude about arts and traditional academics, and the lack of a unifying framework to converge seemingly disparate content areas and programs under a coherent focus. Underlying some of these barriers may be a shallow understanding of the nature of arts learning. In their phenomenological study of the teacher experience in an intensive arts-based reform project, Lackey and Huxhold (2016) suggested similar explanations. As past efforts demonstrate, a unifying framework that echoes shared values, recognizes student creative potential, clearly defines the role of the arts, and undergirds an assets-based approach that can bridge teaching and learning across a large school (Nathan, 2011). Sites that committed to this effort consistently demonstrated such potential. In practice, evaluators should consider the influence of organizational culture on the creative risks that teachers are willing to take to shift practice.

Fidelity Versus Flexibility

One of the major challenges facing this evaluation effort was measuring the implementation fidelity of a model early in its development in five schools in four different districts. Although a few past studies identified supportive conditions that appear to associate with successful arts integration (e.g., Catterall & Waldorf, 1999; Peppler, Catterall, & Bender, 2015), results often focused on student-level outcomes rather than teacher- or school-level implementation. Given this limited past research, this current evaluation sought to understand more about implementation drivers and the tension between fidelity and flexibility.

This natural tension leads evaluators and researchers to question how to measure implementation fidelity while prioritizing adaptation based on context. To this end, we framed our developmental evaluation around key ideas from the field of implementation science (Blase et al., 2015), organizational change, and adaptation of innovations (e.g., Fullan & Quinn, 2015; Hall & Hord, 2014) to build capacity and strengthen school organizations through implementation. Implementation science, which examines the explicit functions that scale up evidence-based interventions for sustainability, provides us with important schema for understanding the organizational drivers that matter during implementation. Inherently, evaluators must be concerned with the fine balance between fidelity to prescribed practices and adaptation to existing contexts—potential moderators of program effects.

The approach to schoolwide integrated arts learning in the ArtCore model required continual documentation of implementation functions throughout the cycle. Contrary to common belief, evidence-based programs with tightly prescribed steps are not a sure-fire way to achieve implementation success across contexts; indeed, school-based adaptations may increase the likelihood participants will engage in the program and improve the outcomes of interest (Martinez & Eddy, 2005). Early in evaluation design, evaluators should consider aspects of their models of interest that may require extensive adaptation and plan to account for that adaptation in their measurement of implementation. The National Implementation Research Network (Fixsen et al., 2015) employs a 6-stage developmental implementation framework for researchers and policymakers to investigate, apply, and evaluate new programs across a variety of contexts with culturally specific evidence. We adapted that framework to our own emerging implementation cycle. As our investigation aimed to do, other evaluators of arts initiatives should describe contextual irregularities within schools rather than explain them away.

Adapting Arts Integration

Arts integration, generally, can be thought of "as an approach to teaching in which students construct and demonstrate understanding through an art form ... a creative process, which connects an art form and another subject area and meets evolving objectives in both" (Silverstein & Layne, 2010, p. 1). One of the challenges to evaluating the effects of arts integration is the different form it can take. Bresler's (1995) framework classified arts integration by style and suggested that efficacy of arts integration would depend on style and application. Though this evaluation did not compare the efficacy of different styles, one of the evaluation questions in this study did focus on how different settings adapted the arts integration approach. Based on their relevance across disciplines and their integration of metacognitive and social-emotional dimensions of learning, the set of eight SHOM appear to provide a framework that both arts education program developers and evaluators could make central to their approach.

Our findings show that each school adapted arts integration by concentrating on different elements of creative engagement as a focus. They centered their design work on one strand and incorporated the others in response to the unique conditions of their school. In the two schools that adopted the SHOM most intensively as teachable and transferrable skills, the vernacular spread across content areas and even became part of the homeroom experience for students. In these schools, the SHOM emerged inductively from the collaborative teaching and learning experience as an optimal unifying framework. In fact, students came up with the definitions adopted by the school. As potentially critical factors that may moderate student achievement in the arts and academics, metacognitive and social-emotional skills should be considered in the designs of arts program evaluators. Importantly, evaluators can manage adaptation of programming if there is a set of core strategies and techniques that encompass the various approaches that evolve.

Growing a Culture for Creative Learning

Metaphorically, the arts-based school change process that we described in this chapter mirrors the efforts to transform a besieged landscape into a thriving, self-sustaining garden. When you plant a garden to grow diverse fruits, vegetables, shrubs, and flowers, you undertake a design process that is inherently collaborative between the gardener, the plants, and nature's elements. Before you begin, you must first turn the soil, let it breathe, and discover what you are working with. This soil—the organizational culture of a school—will determine the health and longevity of the landscape you plant. As a landscape designer, you are both constrained and empowered by the attributes of the soil, the natural features of the site, and the seeds you will nurture—your students. The seeds you grow determine your decisions. As plants, some of the seeds may need an abundance of water, others may need shade, some will fix nitrogen to the soil, and others will demand it. In arts integration, we found that these decisions will drive the emphasis of your approach—social-emotional, metacognitive, or multidisciplinary integration.

In the garden, you envision a hybrid design with the hope to grow plants that support each other in a self-nurturing and evolving ecosystem. Your long-term aim is to develop the garden slowly and strategically so that, in time, it does most of the work for you. You develop the skill to practice integrative designs that will set up a diverse garden that mutually thrives as a symbiotic whole. Once planted, you plan for the ongoing care and support that will be needed at different stages of growth—leafing, rapid growth, rooting, blooming, fruiting, and drying. In arts integration, the water will be the nurturing of artistic skills and aesthetic awareness and the fertilizer will be boosts of metacognitive habits of mind and social-emotional skills for learning.

As the garden grows, the different zones must be planned in a cohesive way so that the soil remains healthy across the landscape. As a gardener you must observe thoroughly with all senses, taking note of what worked well and what you would change in the future. The more you harvest, the more you learn. In arts integration, performance assessments produce formative feedback, depicting what boosts in skills and awareness each learner needs. You watch in awe as small seeds turn into giant blossoms and as the elements transform your design into a new interactive composition. You retest your soil and identify the next zone of your landscape to design and cultivate. The interactive cycle continues and a thriving landscape takes shape, where diverse plants feed back to boost the health of the soil.

Conclusion

Should evaluators measure implementation fidelity by a checklist of activities or by the behaviors, attitudes, and artifacts that result from those activities and are critical for uptake and sustainability? Do teacher beliefs perhaps play an outsized role in how the arts are perceived and applied as a teaching and learning tool? These are tough questions for arts program innovators and evaluators to wrestle with in developing, assessing, and improving models to become powerful forces of change in schools and communities. Developing a school into a thriving landscape of creative learning takes careful planning and nurturing. Rushing through a step early on, ignoring the state of the soil or the pressures of the surrounding elements, or failing to water the adult learners with arts learning opportunities can stunt growth and result in defeated efforts to build capacity. In fact, many efforts, as we learned, may not take root and instead be washed away by the torrent of initiatives—a common fate in school improvement efforts. On the other hand, when the right balance of attitude, adaptation, and alignment is present, student motivation thrives, thinking becomes visible, and the classroom buzzes with the flow of creative learning from teachers and students alike. School leaders shift priorities and teachers open up to unexplored possibilities in their craft, adapting new perspectives and practices.

Evaluators of arts programming in schools should consider what dimensions of school culture the programming may depend on for implementation to be successful and sustained and what influence the program may have on this school culture, in turn. Although implementation science suggests that programs focus on finding communities well-poised to make fundamental changes in their practices, some schools in most need of uplifting interventions, like arts integration, may not meet the minimum standards in that initial screening. In those schools, the infusion of the arts into the early stage of organizational culture development may need to be intense for the adults in order to pump the soil full of nutrients before planting the seeds for students. Indeed, in schools enduring mounting pressures from test-based accountability and shrinking funding, a revolving door of leadership, and a constant demand for reform, the soil may need considerable turning and breathing, using the arts as a means to reflect, come together, create, and explore a shared future. Through this developmental study, we learned early on that the focus must begin first with a shared understanding of *why* the arts matter as a universal entry into learning rather than *how* it must be done. Then, as our results suggest, arts-based school change can move from programmatic to systemic, growing into a symbiotic landscape of creative possibility.

REFERENCES

Anderson, R. C. (2017). *Creative engagement: An embodied approach to making meaning in learning.* Poster presented at the annual convention of the American Psychological Association, Division 10: Society for the Psychology of Aesthetics, Creativity, and the Arts, Washington, DC.

Bandura, A. (1986). *Social foundations of thought and action: A social cognitive theory.* New Jersey: Prentice Hall.

Bandura, A. (1997). *Self-efficacy: The exercise of control.* New York: Freeman & Co.

Beghetto, R. A. (2016). Creative learning: A fresh look. *Journal of Cognitive Education and Psychology, 15*(1), 6–23.

Blase, K. A., Fixsen, D. L., Sims, B. J., & Ward, C. S. (2015). *Implementation science: Changing hearts, minds, behavior, and systems to improve educational outcomes.* Oakland, CA: The Wing Institute.

Bolman, L., & Deal, T. (2013). *Reframing organizations: Artistry, choice, and leadership* (5th ed.). San Francisco, CA: Jossey-Bass.

Bresler, L. (1995). The subservient, co-equal, affective, and social integration styles and their implications for the arts. *Arts Education Policy Review, 96*(5), 31–37.

Catterall, J., & Waldorf, L. (1999). Chicago arts partnerships in education: Summary evaluation. In E. Fiske (Ed.), *Champions of change: The impact of the arts on learning* (pp. 47–62). Washington, DC: The Arts Education Partnership; The President's Committee on the Arts and Humanities.

Corbett, D., Wilson, B., & Morse, D. (2005). *The arts are an "R" too.* Jackson, MS: Mississippi Arts Commission.

Creswell, J. W., & Plano Clark, V. L. (2011). *Designing and conducting mixed methods research.* Thousand Oaks, CA: Sage Publications, Inc.

Educational Policy Improvement Center. (2017). The School Success Model. Retrieved from http://www.epiconline.org/projects/school-success-model/

Fixsen, D. L., Blasé, K., Naoom, S., Metz, A., Louison, L., & Ward, C. (2015). *Implementation drivers: Assessing best practices.* Chapel Hill, NC: National

Implementation Research Network, University of North Carolina at Chapel Hill.

Fullan, M., & Quinn, J. (2015). *Coherence: The right drivers in action for schools, districts, and systems.* Newbury Park, CA: Corwin Press.

Guskey, T. R. (1986). Staff development and the process of teacher change. *Educational Researcher, 15*(5), 5–12.

Hall, G., & Hord, S. (2014). *Implementing change: Patterns, principles, and potholes.* New York, NY: Pearson.

Hetland, L., Winner, E., Veenema, S., & Sheridan, K. (2013). *Studio thinking 2: The real benefits of visual arts education.* New York, NY: Teachers College Press.

Lackey, L., & Huxhold, D. (2016). Arts integration as school reform: Exploring how teachers experience policy. *Arts Education Policy Review, 117*(4), 211–222.

Martin, A. (2012). Part II commentary: Motivation and engagement: Conceptual, operational, and empirical clarity. In S. Christenson, A. Reschly, & C. Wylie (Eds.), *Handbook of research on student engagement.* New York, NY: Springer Science+Business Media, LLC.

Martinez, C. R., Jr., & Eddy, J. M. (2005). Effects of culturally adapted parent management training on Latino youth behavioral health outcomes. *Journal of Consulting and Clinical Psychology, 73*(5), 841.

Nathan, L. (2011). *The hardest questions aren't on the test.* Beacon, MA: Beacon Press.

Noblit, G. W., Corbett, H. D., Wilson, B. L., & McKinney, M. B. (2009). *Creating and sustaining arts-based school reform: The A+ schools program.* New York, NY: Routledge.

Patton, M. Q. (2011). *Developmental evaluation: Applying complexity concepts to enhance innovation and use.* New York, NY: Guilford Press.

Peppler, K., Catterall, J., & Bender, S. (2015). *Learning and achieving through the arts: Executive summary and evaluation report.* Bloomington, IN: Indiana University.

Pitts, C., Anderson, R., & Haney, M. (in press). Measures of Instruction for Creative Engagement: Capturing what eludes traditional teacher observation measures. *Learning Environments Research.*

Robinson, A. H. (2013). Arts integration and the success of disadvantaged students: A research evaluation. *Arts Education Policy Review, 114*(4), 191–204.

Rubenstein, L. D., McCoach, D. B., & Siegle, D. (2013). Teaching for creativity scales: An instrument to examine teachers' perceptions of factors that allow for the teaching of creativity. *Creativity Research Journal, 25*(3), 324–334.

Salas, E., Tannenbaum, S. I., Kraiger, K., & Smith-Jentsch, K. A. (2012). The science of training and development in organizations: What matters in practice. *Psychological Science in the Public Interest, 13*(2), 74–101.

Senge, P. M. (2006). *The fifth discipline: The art and practice of the learning organization.* New York: Doubleday/Currency.

Silverstein, L., & Layne, S. (2010). *Defining arts integration.* Washington, DC: The John F. Kennedy Center for the Performing Arts.

Skinner, E. A., Furrer, C., Marchand, G., & Kinderman, T. (2008). Engagement and disaffection in the classroom: Part of a larger motivational dynamic? *Journal of Educational Psychology, 100,* 765–781.

University of Chicago Consortium on School Research. (2014). My Voice, My School Teacher Survey [Measurement instrument]. Retrieved from https://consortium.uchicago.edu/sites/default/files/uploads/survey/2014%20Teacher%20Survey%20codebook.pdf

U.S. Department of Education. (2017). ArtCore: An immersive, studio-to-school arts integration and schoolwide transformation model. Retrieved from https://ed.gov/programs/artsedmodel/2014/springfieldschooldistrict.pdf

The Arts and Socioemotional Development: Evaluating a New Mandate for Arts Education

Steven J. Holochwost, Dennie Palmer Wolf, Kelly R. Fisher, Kerry O'Grady, and Kristen M. Gagnier

What is the mandate for arts education? Why does it matter if students receive an education in the arts? The most familiar argument, now enshrined in public policy, is that the arts are part of a "well-rounded education" (Every Student Succeeds Act, p. 807). This legislation asserts that just as we would consider a student's education incomplete without English language arts or science, we should regard an education without the arts as incomplete, given that without arts education students are denied access to a broader literacy that includes the ideas captured in art works and the traditions of other cultures.

A second, more instrumental argument is that arts education confers benefits to students' academic achievement. However, while this has been and remains an attractive advocacy position, the experimental literature

S.J. Holochwost (✉) • D.P. Wolf
WolfBrown, Cambridge, MA, USA

K.R. Fisher • K. O'Grady • K.M. Gagnier
Johns Hopkins University, Baltimore, MD, USA

© The Author(s) 2018
R.S. Rajan, I.C. O'Neal (eds.), *Arts Evaluation and Assessment*,
https://doi.org/10.1007/978-3-319-64116-4_7

demonstrating a *causal* link between arts education and academic achievement is limited (Winner & Cooper, 2000; Winner, Goldstein, & Vincent-Lancrin, 2013) and suggests that these effects may require years of sustained instruction to realize (cf., Costa-Giomi, 1999; Holochwost et al., 2017). Moreover, this portrayal of arts education as a handmaiden to academic achievement is vulnerable to criticisms of inefficient investment and a disregard for the expressive, figurative, and creative impulses central to the arts (Eisner, 1998).

One alternative argument for the value of arts education is that it may contribute to the development of socioemotional skills, which accumulating evidence indicates are central to school and life success (Zins et al., 2004). For example, arts education may foster students' persistence, defined as the capacity to continue engaging in an activity despite setbacks or challenges (Peterson & Seligman, 2004). In the serious study of any art, challenges abound; however, so too do opportunities to meet and overcome those challenges (Winner & Hetland, 2008), and therefore the argument can be made that arts education could foster persistence, though its capacity to do so may be contingent on the intensity and duration of instruction.

In this chapter we present the results of an evaluation that explored this expanded mandate. The evaluation investigated whether arts education programs—offered to diverse students across an array of disciplines and formats—were associated with improvements in selected socioemotional domains. As we discuss below, our findings speak not only to the promise of arts education to benefit participants' socioemotional development but also the importance of considering how student and program factors may render the fulfillment of this promise more or less likely.

CONTEXT FOR THE EVALUATION

Unlike many of the other evaluations presented in this book, the evaluation we conducted was not designed to examine the effects of a single program. Rather, it was designed to evaluate the impact of a heterogeneous portfolio of arts education programs representing the four major artistic disciplines (visual arts, music, theater, and dance) that varied in the intensity of their "treatment," with some programs offering short-term, in-school residencies and others providing after-school instruction for most of the school year. The students served by these programs were comparably diverse, ranging in age from 8 to 18 (enrolled in grades 3 through

12). The majority of the students were of color, and all students attended public schools in a city in which under-investment in education has restricted access to activities that may foster socioemotional development (e.g., athletics, after-school programs, and arts programs).

The programs shared a common set of stakeholders, which included:

- Students the programs served, as well as their families.
- Teaching and administrative staff in the schools students attended.
- Leadership of the school district.
- Program staff (e.g., teaching artists) and leadership.
- The staff and leadership of the foundation that funded the programs and this study.[1]

The Goals of the Evaluation

One goal for the evaluation was to contribute to our knowledge regarding the potential benefits of arts education for low-income students of color, given that much of the literature in arts education cannot be generalized to racially diverse groups of students from low-income families. This limitation has two origins: first, arts education is disproportionately available to more affluent, majority-Caucasian students, and arts education must obviously be offered to students in order for its effects to be evaluated. Second, even when arts education programs are offered to more diverse groups of students, there are substantial challenges to conducting rigorous evaluations in schools serving students from families of low income.

Another goal was to assess the programs in the portfolio with respect to a common set of outcomes. We arrived at the set of domains to be included in the study through two processes: a "top-down" approach in which we reviewed the developmental and educational literature to identify how arts education might provide a context for socioemotional learning (SEL) and a convergent "bottom-up" approach in which we conferred with program leadership about the specific domains of socioemotional development that they believed their programs were most likely to influence. During these discussions we focused on a subset of socioemotional outcome domains that might be unique to the experience of arts education—as opposed to those that could result from extracurricular activities more broadly, such as athletics—but that were *not* likely to be specific to a single arts discipline. Given the need to employ a survey measure approach to collect data from the large number of students with whom we anticipated working, we also led program leaders to focus on domains of socio-emotional development that are best measured through self-report, such as self-concept and self-efficacy, rather than domains that may require observation, such as social skills.

In both our initial conversions with program leadership and our review of the literature, we first focused on distal versions of each of these socio-emotional domains, defined as versions of these domains that were either general (i.e., not specific to the arts, such as perseverance) or specific to the school or academic context. This was done, in part, to allow us to address the question of far transfer: whether a program intended to teach students about music, for example, can yield benefits to another context such as school (Barnett & Ceci, 2002). This resulted in the following set of distal domains:

Perseverance Perseverance refers to one's ability to exert sustained effort in the face of obstacles or in the course of difficult or lengthy tasks (Peterson & Seligman, 2004). Although perseverance is thought to be a relatively stable personality trait, Winner and Hetland (2008) have argued that an education in the arts may provide opportunities to engage in challenging but nevertheless rewarding tasks and that repeated experiences of this type may foster perseverance in the context of the arts over time.

However, to date only a small number of studies have yielded empirical evidence to support the argument that arts instruction may lead to increased perseverance in more general contexts. Participation in both visual arts and music activities over the course of three years was associated with more rapid growth in teacher reports of persistence among Scandinavian elementary-school children (Metsäpelto & Pulkkinen, 2012), while South African adolescents from low-income families reported higher levels of perseverance following a program of musical instruction (Devroop, 2012). Scott (1992) found that young children (ages 3 to 5 years) who had taken either private or group Suzuki-based violin instruction for at least five months scored higher on measures of perseverance than their control-group peers. Thus, while there is some support in the literature linking arts education to perseverance, that literature is drawn from a small number of studies, most of which feature music education.

School Engagement School engagement is a multifaceted construct that includes students' participation in extracurricular activities, feelings about school, and investment in and valuation of learning (Fredricks, Blumenfeld, & Paris, 2004). Multiple researchers have proposed that school engagement influences success in school by reducing absenteeism and fostering students' commitment to their studies (Connell, 1990; Finn & Voelkl, 1993), and indeed higher levels of school engagement have been found to predict lower rates of school dropout, better grades, and higher standardized test scores (Fredricks et al., 2004; Marks, 2000). Both correlational (Heath, 1998) and experimental (Walker, Tabone, & Weltsek, 2011)[2] studies have indicated that participating in arts instruction predicts fewer absences from school among middle- and high-school students, even among high-school students deemed at risk for dropping out of school (Horn, 1992), and studies using assessments of students' self-reported school engagement have yielded similar results (Elpus, 2013). Two large, quasi-experimental studies have also supported the potential for arts education to foster school engagement, revealing that both drama education (DICE Consortium, 2010) and whole-school models of arts integration (Smithrim & Upitis, 2005) were associated with higher levels of school engagement (though for Smithrim & Upitis, this finding held only for girls). Thus, there is both correlational and quasi-experimental support for a link between arts education across disciplines and higher levels of school engagement.

Growth Mindset Growth mindset refers to the extent to which an individual sees their intelligence as mutable, as opposed to fixed (Dweck, 2000). According to a motivational model of achievement, those who see their intelligence as open to change will be more inclined to seek out challenges and thereby maximize their potential. Conversely, those who believe their intelligence is fixed will be more likely to avoid situations in which their limitations may be exposed, such as challenges beyond their current skill level, limiting one's opportunity to improve and resulting in the fixed mindset becoming a self-fulfilling prophecy. However, research has demonstrated that students' implicit theories of intelligence are open to change, and that embracing a growth mindset predicts better academic performance (Aronson, Fried, & Good, 2002). An education in the arts may alter students' implicit theories of intelligence, as they experience firsthand a change in their own artistic skill or understanding as they proceed through arts programs. However, the capacity of arts instruction to have this impact would be contingent upon the provision of encouragement and feedback that fostered a growth mindset, and at present no study has assessed this possibility.

Goal Orientation Goal orientation is a very broad concept that describes why and how people are compelled to achieve an objective (Anderman & Maehr, 1994; Kaplan & Maehr, 2007). Generally, three types of goal orientations are recognized: performance-approach, performance-avoidance, and mastery goals. Of these, an orientation toward mastery goals—a desire to develop competence, rather than to appear intelligent (i.e., performance approach) or avoid appearing foolish (i.e., performance-avoidance)—has been most consistently associated with behaviors that support learning and academic achievement (Ames, 1992). Only one study has examined the change in mastery goal orientation as a function of arts education: French-Canadian middle-school students who participated in a French-immersion, drama-based course of instruction exhibited higher levels of growth in one self-report measure of motivation orientation than students receiving a more conventional (but still French-immersion) course of instruction on the same topic (Bournot-Trites, Belliveau, Spiliotopoulos, & Séror, 2007). Thus, the literature linking arts education to mastery goal orientation is quite limited.

Self-Concept Another aspect of achievement motivation is self-concept, which is similar to self-esteem, but is generally considered specific to a particular domain, such as academics or peer relations. Correlational studies have revealed an association between courses of multi-arts (Burton, Horowitz, & Abeles, 2000; Catterall, 1998), dance (Carter, 2005), and music (Degé, Wehrum, Stark, & Schwarzer, 2009; Shin, 2011) instruction and higher levels of academic self-concept. McPherson and colleagues extended these findings to a large sample (over 2500) of middle- and high-school students studying music (McPherson, Osborne, Barrett, Davidson, & Faulkner, 2015).

Despite this promising correlational evidence, to date few studies have employed quasi-experimental or experimental methods to investigate whether participation in the arts may *cause* higher levels of academic self-concept. Lee (2007), for example, demonstrated that dance instruction yielded higher levels of academic self-concept in a sample of school-aged students in South Korea, while Rickard and colleagues reported similar results for general self-concept among a group of young children (age 8) participating in a school-based music education program (Rickard et al., 2013).

In summary, there is both correlational and quasi-experimental evidence for a link between arts education and academic self-concept, though it is difficult to generalize the results of the quasi-experimental studies to instruction across disciplines given that this evidence is drawn from smaller studies examining the relation between instruction in one arts discipline and either academic (Lee, 2007) or general (Rickard et al., 2013) self-concept.

Self-Efficacy Like self-concept, self-efficacy—one's belief in his or her ability to succeed—is generally considered to be domain specific, and like self-concept, higher levels of self-efficacy in a particular domain predict better performance in that domain, above and beyond actual capacity (Bandura, 1986). In quasi-experimental studies, Lee (2006) and Rapp-Paglicci (Rapp-Paglicci, Stewart, & Rowe, 2011) observed increases in academic self-efficacy among students receiving instruction in dance or multiple arts, respectively. Catterall and colleagues reported similar results for *general* self-efficacy among third-grade Latino and African American students who participated in a program of high-quality visual arts instruction (Catterall & Peppler, 2007) and among middle-school students from similar demographic backgrounds who participated in an after-school drama program (Catterall, 2007). Hence, there is quasi-experimental evidence for a link between arts education and self-efficacy, though the findings that are most generalizable to our study, based on sample composition, report a link between arts education and general, rather than domain-specific, self-efficacy.

The Benefits of Arts Education to Proximal Domains

We were also interested in whether arts education programs might influence self-awareness domains—goal orientation, self-concept, and self-efficacy—in the context in which they are offered. Ironically, less is known about whether arts education programs might influence artistic self-awareness or the development of *artistic* goal orientation, self-concept, or self-efficacy. For example, might a program of music education influence how students see themselves in the context of music or how efficacious they feel regarding their ability to learn about music? Previous research has found that children at risk for educational failure (Shields, 2001) and male students who were incarcerated (Kennedy, 1998) who received musical instruction reported significant increases in musical self-concept and that teacher reports of higher musical aptitude predicted more rapid growth in students' musical self-efficacy over time (Zelenak, 2015). But beyond these studies only one of which we are aware reported an association between instruction in an artistic discipline other than music and artistic self-concept (visual arts; King, 1983).

Given this, we included measures of students' *artistic* goal orientation, self-concept, and self-efficacy among our measures, aligned in each case to the artistic discipline(s) in which instruction was offered. These measures were based on the measures of *academic* goal orientation, self-concept, and self-efficacy cited below. However, we administered these measures only to older students (i.e., those in high school), as we judged that these students would be most capable of distinguishing between academic and artistic contexts.

Guiding Questions

With our domains of socioemotional development selected, we identified four guiding questions for our evaluation:

1. Would participation in a program of arts education be associated with higher levels of socioemotional development in the distal domains of perseverance, school engagement, growth mindset, and academic goal orientation, self-concept, or self-efficacy?
2. Would participation be associated with higher levels of development in the more proximal domains of artistic goal orientation, self-concept, and self-efficacy?
3. Would these associations be contingent upon student factors, such as age or prior exposure to the arts?
4. Would these associations be contingent upon factors that varied by program, such as dosage?

METHODOLOGICAL CHALLENGES

Our expectation that it was possible to assess a diverse set of arts education programs with respect to a common set of outcomes was based, in part, on the concept of equifinality, which we borrowed from the field of developmental science. Equifinality describes the potential for complex systems—here, the students being served by the programs—to reach the same end or set of outcomes through different means (Bertalanffy, 1969). For example, offering a program of arts education to students as part of their school day may enhance students' engagement in school, regardless of whether the program is offered in music, visual arts, theater or dance. The discipline may not matter (or may not matter enough) to influence whether increases in school engagement are observed, in which case the effects of the arts program on engagement may be said to be equifinal with regard to artistic discipline. Note, however, that other factors—such as whether teaching artists interact productively with students—may produce divergent outcomes.

The concept of equifinality is particularly useful in an evaluation such as this one, in which programs differed by artistic discipline, setting (in or out of school), and dosage, as well as the age and demographic composition of students served. Reducing the diversity of programs (e.g., by omitting those offered in a certain discipline) or students would undermine the purpose of the evaluation, which was to examine the foundation's portfolio of grantees. By invoking the concept of equifinality, we were able to fulfill this purpose and to further our understanding of how *the extent* to which a program achieved a given outcome was contingent upon program or student factors.

However, fulfilling the purpose of the evaluation presented us with two challenges, one of design and another of measurement. The design challenge was how to tailor our evaluation to fit the varied implementation approaches and schedules of the programs that comprised the foundation's portfolio while maximizing the internal validity of our design. The measurement challenge was how to reliably assess socioemotional development across a sample of students ranging in age from 8 to 18 years. In the following sections, we present our efforts to address both of these challenges.

Overcoming the Design Challenge

In the context of our evaluation, internal validity refers to the extent that the arts education programs in which students participated could be said to have *caused* any changes in students' socioemotional development that we observed. All else being equal, randomized-control evaluation designs are preferred over alternative designs because they maximize internal validity. But in the context of our evaluation, all else was not equal: programs varied greatly in their implementation schedules and the proportion of students in a given school they served, and therefore employing a single, randomized-control design for the entire evaluation was not possible. To overcome this design challenge we employed two variants of a pre-program/post-program measurement approach: (1) a quasi-experimental design with a matched comparison group; and (2) a delayed-implementation design featuring random assignment.

Quasi-Experimental Design with a Matched Comparison Group We used a quasi-experimental design when a program was being offered to a subset of students at a school that had chosen to participate in the program. For example, one program offered in-school elective courses in dance to students in grades 3 through 8. The disadvantage of this design, relative to a randomized-control alternative, is that the same factors that led students to choose to participate in the dance elective might also explain any observed differences in socioemotional outcomes. This disadvantage is often referred to as self-selection bias.

The use of a matched-comparison group helps to reduce this bias (though it cannot eliminate it). If treatment and comparison groups vary widely in composition—in gender or age, for example—then observed differences in socioemotional outcomes may be attributable to these differences. Matching the treatment and comparison groups on such characteristics reduces the likelihood of variation in sample composition, and thereby reduces the degree to which this variation may plausibly explain observed differences in outcomes. In this example, the comparison group was comprised of students who selected a different elective, but who were matched to the students who selected the dance elective in terms of gender, classroom, and grade in school.

The collection of data at two points in time—before and after the program—can also help reduce the likelihood of alternative explanations for results such as selection bias, which constitute threats to internal validity. Consider an alternative data collection schedule, in which data were collected only after the program. It is quite plausible that selection bias might explain any observed differences in socioemotional development at a single point in time. But with data collection before and after the program, group differences in initial scores are accounted for, and thus selection bias applies only to differences *in the degree of change* from pre- to post-program measurements.

Delayed-Implementation Design with Random Assignment This approach was feasible only in those cases where students did not self-select into a particular program. This was most common when a particular program was going to be offered to all the students in a particular grade (or range of grades) within a school over the course of the academic year. In these cases it was possible to use a delayed-implementation design, provided that the implementation of these programs was delayed for an interval of time at least as long in duration as the program itself. For example, one program featured a series of weekly, hour-long musician residencies. These residences were offered to all students in fourth grade at a series of schools and took place over the course of six weeks in February and March of the academic year. Given that we knew all fourth graders would ultimately participate in the program, we randomly assigned all students to a treatment or control group at the beginning of the academic year. For students assigned to the control group, data were collected six weeks prior to the first residency session and again two days before the residency began. Data for students assigned to the treatment group were collected within two days of the program's first residency and again within two days of its conclusion.

The advantage of this design relative to the quasi-experimental design with a matched comparison group is that selection bias poses no threat to internal validity. The disadvantage is that the effects of time and treatment are conflated. Thus, it is possible that group differences in socioemotional outcomes could be attributed to the different times at which data were collected for both groups of students. This threat can be minimized (but again, not eliminated) by using this design in contexts where: (1) outcomes are fairly stable over short periods of time (e.g., general self-efficacy); and (2) programs are of relatively short duration. It is also important to collect data from the control group as close to program implementation as possible.

Employing an Observational Measure of Quality with Respect to SEL To further strengthen our evaluation design, we incorporated an observational measure of the quality of instruction with respect to SEL. On one hand, this measure served as a manipulation check that allowed us to ensure each program incorporated some practices that could foster SEL. The measure also served a valuable function from the perspective of formative evaluation, in that it allowed us to identify areas of instruction in which most or at least many of the foundation's grantees excelled, as well as any areas of consistent weakness.

To this end we developed a structured observation protocol that drew on existing measures (e.g., the Youth Programming Quality Assessment or YPQA; Smith et al., 2012) as well as research on the practices that may foster young people's socioemotional development (e.g., Benson, Scales, & Syvertsen, 2010; Catalano, Berglund, Ryan, Lonczak, & Hawkins, 2004; Roth, Brooks-Gunn, Murray, & Foster, 1998). The adapted measure was organized into the following broad dimensions:

- **Context:** The physical and interpersonal environment in which the teaching and learning occurs.
- **Challenge:** The degree to which the structure, content, and processes of working offer young people the engagement, high expectations, and scaffolding required to try new materials and skills, make meaning, and identify and develop their own ideas.
- **Belonging:** A young person's sense that they are a welcome and acknowledged member of the classroom or school community, regardless of their identity and current level of skill. Correspondingly, this refers to the ways in which youth, as well as teachers, acknowledge others.
- **Relevance:** The extent to which assignments, materials, ways of working, and models and examples acknowledge who young people are, and the extent to which young people themselves forge connections to their own lives and experiences.
- **Self-Efficacy:** The observable behaviors that index teachers' and students' understanding of and commitment to strategies for setting and reaching goals in specific situations (e.g., drawing, writing a personal narrative, singing, etc.).
- **Growth Mindset:** The extent to which teachers and students emphasize growth mindsets, in which capacity can be expanded with effort, persistence, revision, and risk taking, over fixed mindsets, in which capacity is immutable or innate.

Each of these dimensions comprised a number of scales. These are listed in Table 7.1. For the scales marked with an asterisk, both staff and student behaviors were rated independently. For example, raters assigned

Table 7.1   Scales for the observational measure

Context	Challenge	Belonging
Space	Explanation	Tone
Materials	Appropriate time	Interaction*
Teacher partnership	Higher-order	Collaboration*
	thinking*	
	Larger projects*	
Relevance	*Self-efficacy*	*Growth mindset*
Exchange*	Skill focus*	Challenge*
Connection*	Goal setting*	Persistence*
Choice/generativity*	Improvement*	Growth-oriented response*
	Leadership*	Mindset reflection
	Critical assessment*	

two scores for the scale entitled "Larger Projects"—the staff score asked about the extent to which staff linked the work of one residency session to the prior or subsequent sessions and to the larger process, outcomes, and purpose of the project, while the student scale asked about the extent to which students linked their current work to prior or future activities.

All programs were observed by raters who had been trained to an acceptable degree of reliability; as such, we had a high level of confidence that the scores assigned to a program by one rater would be very similar to the scores assigned by another rater. Shorter programs were observed once at their midpoint, while longer programs were observed twice (halfway and two-thirds through their duration) and the average of the two observations was used as that program's score. Across these observations the average inter-rater reliability was $\alpha = 0.86$ for ratings of the staff dimensions and $\alpha = 0.83$ for the student dimensions.

To inform the reduction of the data, a pair of exploratory factor analyses were performed. The results of these analyses indicated that a one-factor solution in which all subscales loaded onto a single latent variable was the best fit for the data. Based on this result, two scores representing the overall quality of instruction with respect to SEL were calculated: one for staff and another for students. Internal consistency was $\alpha = 0.89$ for the staff score and $\alpha = 0.84$ for the student score. These scores were highly correlated ($r(892) = 0.91$, $p < 0.0001$) and therefore the staff scores were used in all subsequent analyses.

Overcoming the Measurement Challenge

In addition to the design challenge, the evaluation also presented a substantial measurement challenge. In short, we were required to assess socioemotional development in a sample of children ranging in age from 8 to 18 in such a way that responses from children across this age range could be included in a single analysis. To accomplish this, we began by reviewing the literature for measures of our domains of interest that had displayed favorable psychometric properties. Based on this review, we selected the following measures:

- **Perseverance:** The eight-item short grit scale (Duckworth & Quinn, 2009).
- **School Engagement:** The six items from the Identification with School Questionnaire (ISQ; Voelkl, 1996) that previous analyses had revealed to be the most strongly related to the construct of school belonging.
- **Growth Mindset:** The six-item growth mindset scale (Blackwell, Trzesniewski, & Dweck, 2007).
- **Academic Self-Concept:** The pre-adolescent version of Marsh's Self-Description Questionnaire (SDQ-I; Marsh, 1992).
- **Academic Self-Efficacy:** The self-efficacy scale from the revised Patterns of Adaptive Learning Scales (PALS; Midgley et al., 2000).
- **Academic Goal-Orientation:** The mastery goal orientation sub-scale, also from the PALS.

Prior to collecting our pilot data, we made two modifications to these measures. First, we simplified the language of the perseverance and growth mindset measures, given that these instruments had not previously been used with students younger than 11. Second, we created parallel versions of the measures of academic self-concept, self-efficacy, and goal orientation in order to assess these constructs in the context of the artistic discipline(s) in which instruction was offered to students by a particular program. For example, parallel items from measures of academic self-efficacy, artistic self-efficacy in theater, and artistic self-efficacy in the visual arts read as follows:

- Academic self-efficacy: "Even if something in school is hard, I can learn it."
- Artistic self-efficacy in theater: "Even if something in my theater program is hard, I can learn it."
- Artistic self-efficacy in visual arts: "Even if something in my art program is hard, I can learn it."

Table 7.2 Results of the pilot study

Domain	M	SD	Range		Skew		Consistency (α)
			Minimum	Maximum	G_1	SE	
School engagement	3.6	0.72	2.0	5.0	−0.300	0.223	0.62
Growth mindset	3.6	0.83	1.7	5.0	−0.048	0.223	0.77
Perseverance	3.4	0.58	1.8	5.0	−0.145	0.222	0.60
Academic goal Orientation	4.2	0.76	1.4	5.0	−1.23	0.222	0.85
Artistic goal orientation	3.7	1.2	1.0	5.0	−0.751	0.347	0.96
Academic self-concept	3.6	0.72	1.8	5.0	−0.355	0.223	0.80
Artistic self-concept	3.7	0.92	1.2	5.0	−0.626	0.350	0.91
Academic self-efficacy	4.0	0.70	1.2	5.0	−1.04	0.222	0.81
Artistic self-efficacy	3.9	0.92	1.0	5.0	−0.844	0.340	0.90

M = mean, SD = standard deviation, G_1 = Fisher-Pearson standardized moment coefficient, SE = standard error of G_1

Given that younger students might find it difficult to reliably differentiate between their academic and artistic selves, these measures were administered only to students in high school.

Table 7.2 reports descriptives and internal consistency for the pilot measures, which were administered to 122 students (70 students in grades 3 through 8, 52 in grades 9 through 12) drawn from a subset of the schools included in the full study. In general, the measures performed well, though there were two causes for concern: first, the measures of academic goal orientation and self-efficacy exhibited some evidence of skew. Second, while the internal consistency for the perseverance measure was marginally acceptable, it was well below that reported by its authors ($α$ = 0.83). This was true even among the subsample of high-school students. Additional items were added to each of these measures in an effort to combat skew and improve internal consistency.

Data Collection and Analysis

Data were collected from nearly 900 students attending school in a large Northeastern city. These students participated in one of 11 programs that took place either during or after school and collectively represented four major artistic disciplines: visual arts, music, theater, and dance. As can be seen in Table 7.3, the "average" student in our sample was approximately 12 years old and had a three in five chance of being a girl and of identifying as either African American or Latino/Hispanic. Data were also collected from these students' primary in-school teachers, who were asked to complete a three-item measure of each student's school engagement from the Research Assessment Package for Schools (RAPS; Institute for Research and Reform in Education, 1998) and the informant version of the short grit scale as a measure of perseverance (Duckworth & Quinn, 2009). For treatment-group students, both student and teacher data were collected just prior to and immediately following program participation (within a two-day window in all cases). In quasi-experimental designs, data were collected from comparison-group students according to the same schedule

Table 7.3   Distribution of students surveyed by group

	Overall (N = 892)		Treatment (N = 462)		Comparison (N = 430)		Difference	
	M	SD	M	SD	M	SD	t (df)	p
Age (in years)	11.93	2.85	11.54	2.42	12.35	3.21	−4.04 (793)	< 0.001
Gender	n	Percent	n	Percent	n	Percent	X² (df)	p
Female	480	57.9	241	60.9	239	55.2	2.72	0.057
Male	349	42.1	155	39.1	194	44.8	(1)	
Ethnicity	n	Percent	n	Percent	n	Percent	X² (df)	p
African American	264	32.2	139	35.6	125	29.1	19.8	0.003
Latino/Hispanic	238	29.0	103	26.4	135	31.4	(6)	
Asian/Pacific Islander	43	5.2	29	7.4	14	3.3		
Native American	9	1.1	4	1.0	5	1.2		
Caucasian/White	87	10.6	38	9.7	49	11.4		
Mixed*	80	9.8	26	6.7	26	6.7		
Other	99	12.1	51	13.1	51	13.1		

M = mean, SD = standard deviation, n = number of participants in a given cell, t = t-statistic, df = degrees of freedom, X^2 = chi-squared statistic, p = p value
*students selected two or more categories to report their ethnicity

used for treatment-group students. In delayed-implementation designs, data were collected from control-group students prior to their eventual participation in the program: pre- and post-program data collection sessions were separated by an interval of time equal in length to the duration of the program, with the post-program collection occurring as close as possible to the program's start date. This approach is illustrated in Fig. 7.1.

Preliminary analyses indicated that with the exception of the student-reported measure of perseverance, our measures displayed acceptable internal consistency among both younger and older students. The additional items added to the academic self-efficacy measure to combat skew did so, though the measure of academic goal orientation continued to display some evidence of skew. Moreover, the internal consistency for the perseverance measure remained low, and while we report the results obtained using this measure below, they must be interpreted with caution.

All data were analyzed using a series of multilevel models in which post-program scores on each domain of socioemotional development were estimated as a function of pre-program scores. These models accounted for the nested structure of the data (in which students were nested within classrooms, which were nested within schools) and controlled for relevant covariates. Students' age and race/ethnicity differed significantly as a function of group (treatment versus comparison), while group differences

Quasi-Experimental Design

Comparison Group	√			√
Treatment Group	√			√
Events	Pre-Collect	Program Begins	Program Ends	Post-Collect

Delayed-Implementation Design

Control Group	√	Delay Length = X	√	O	Program Length = X	O
Treatment Group	O		O	√		√
Events	Pre-Collect		Post-Collect	Pre-Collect	Program Begins	Program Ends	Post-Collect

Fig. 7.1 Schematic of data collection schedules for quasi-experimental and delayed-implementation designs. Note: Gray bars indicate when the program was in operation. "Pre-Collect" and "Post-Collect" refer to pre- and post-program data collection, respectively. The symbol √ indicates that pre- or post-program data collection occurred for a given group at a particular point in time, while the symbol O indicates that it did not

by gender and prior instruction in the arts in school approached signifi-cance. As such, all models controlled for these factors, while prior and current in-school instruction in the arts were controlled for only when one of these factors was significantly related to post-program scores for a par-ticular domain of socioemotional development.

Our analyses proceeded in three steps: first, we tested for omnibus or main effects of program participation, examining whether post-program scores on each measure of SEL differed as a function of students' designa-tion as members of the treatment or comparison group. Second, we tested for conditional or interaction effects, examining whether there was a rela-tionship between group membership and post-program scores that was dependent on either program factors (e.g., dosage, the quality of instruc-tion with respect to SEL) or student factors (e.g., age, pre-program scores). Finally, we broke the sample into 11 subsamples corresponding to the 11 programs in the study and re-ran our tests of omnibus effects. This final set of analyses was conducted in an exploratory mode: while we had insufficient statistical power to offer a reasonable likelihood of detecting effects, we nevertheless wanted to examine whether trend-level effects might vary by program, as this would raise the possibility that there was an effect of factors that varied by program in addition to dosage and the quality of instruction with respect to SEL. These might include artistic discipline and setting (in- or out-of-school time).

Results of the Evaluation

We began our analyses by looking for omnibus or main effects for pro-gram participation. This allowed us to address our first two guiding questions:

1. Would participation in a program of arts education be associated with higher levels of socioemotional development in the distal domains of perseverance, school engagement, growth mindset, and academic or artistic goal orientation, self-concept, or self-efficacy?
2. Would participation be associated with higher levels of development in the more proximal domains of artistic goal orientation, self-concept, and self-efficacy?

No significant main effects were observed for either distal or proximal socioemotional domains. However, we did find trend-level effects for the

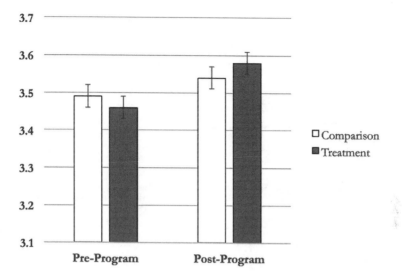

Fig. 7.2a Observed values of growth mindset. Note: Error bars correspond to two standard errors about the mean. Multilevel models indicated a trend-level effect of *group* (1 = treatment) on post-program scores ($B = 0.08$, $p = 0.083$), corresponding to a modest effect size ($d = 0.13$)

distal domains of growth mindset and the proximal domain of artistic goal orientation. In the case of growth mindset, the magnitude of the effect was modest (following Cohen's (1988) guidelines; see Fig. 7.2a), whereas for artistic goal orientation, it was moderate (see Fig. 7.2b).

The scarcity of effects is not surprising when considered in the context of an evaluation featuring such a heterogeneous portfolio of programs working with a diverse set of students. A main effect would mean that across all students in the myriad of programs, participation was associated with higher levels of socioemotional development. However, it may be more likely that the effects of participation were contingent upon the characteristics of students or particular features of programs.

Are Associations Between Arts Education and Socioemotional Development Contingent upon Student Factors?

To investigate this possibility, we added a series of interaction terms that included various student factors to our model. Through these analyses,

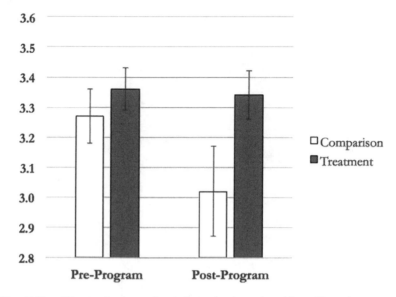

Fig. 7.2b   Observed values of artistic goal orientation. Note: Error bars corre-spond to two standard errors about the mean. Multilevel models indicated a trend-level effect of *group* (1 = treatment) on post-program scores ($B = 0.36$, $p = 0.086$), corresponding to a moderate effect size ($d = 0.46$)

two student factors emerged as moderators of program effects: students' age and their pre-program levels of certain aspects of socioemotional development. For example, an association between program participation and higher levels of growth mindset was observed, but only among younger students. As can be seen in Fig. 7.3, younger students (age approximately 9 years) participating in arts education exhibited an increase in growth mindset over time, whereas students who were not participating exhibited a decrease. At the post-program assessment, the difference in growth mindset between enrolled and unenrolled students corresponded to a moderate effect size. We also observed a similar pattern of results for academic goal orientation, though here the effect of participation only approached, rather than achieved, statistical significance.

For certain domains, we also observed interactions between participation and students' pre-program scores. For example, students who exhibited high levels of school engagement at their initial measurement demonstrated a steep decline in scores over time if they were not participating in a pro-

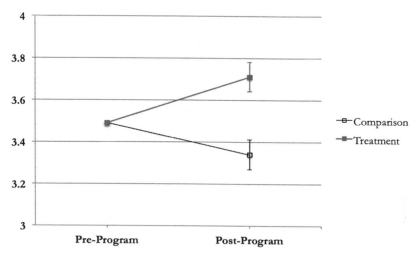

Fig. 7.3 Differences in growth mindset among younger students. Note: Type III test of fixed effects indicated that there was a significant interaction between *age* and *group* in predicting post-program growth mindset scores ($F(1, 462) = 3.73$, $p = 0.038$). Post-hoc probing revealed significant differences in model-implied post-program scores among younger students. For illustrative purposes, model-implied post-program scores for both groups are depicted relative to a common model-implied origin (or intercept) that disregarded group status. The difference in growth mindset scores post-program corresponded to a moderate effect ($d = 0.30$)

gram. Students who were participating exhibited a slight decline, but it was sufficiently small that by the post-program measurement, there was a group difference corresponding to a moderate effect size (see Fig. 7.4). A very similar pattern of results was observed for academic self-efficacy.

Are Associations Between Arts Education and Socioemotional Development Contingent upon Program Factors?

As noted above, the programs included in our sample varied considerably by both discipline and dosage, in that the sample included programs that focused on visual arts, music, dance, or theater and ranged in dosage from approximately 4.5 hours of instruction offered over the course 6 weeks to over 150 hours of instruction offered over most of the academic year. Moreover, programs varied in the observed quality of instruction with

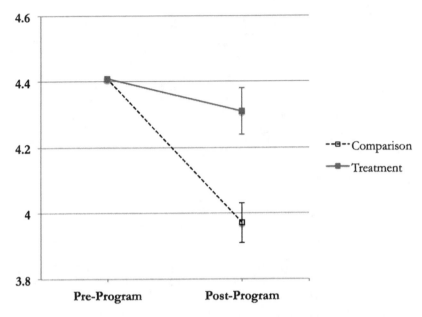

Fig. 7.4 Differences in school engagement among students with high pre-program scores. Note: Type III test of fixed effects indicated that there was a significant interaction between *pre-program engagement scores* and *group* in predicting post-program growth mindset scores ($F (1, 514) = 4.89$, $p = 0.027$). Post hoc probing revealed significant differences in model-implied post-program scores among students with higher pre-program scores. For illustrative purposes, model-implied post-program scores for both groups are depicted relative to a common model-implied origin (or intercept) that disregarded group status. The difference in growth mindset scores post-program corresponded to a moderate effect ($d = 0.46$)

regard to SEL, with some programs earning overall scores of less than 2 (on a scale of 1 to 5, where 1 indicated no evidence of behaviors that promote SEL and 5 indicated high levels of such behaviors) and others earning scores over 4 (see Fig. 7.5).

Given this diversity in dosage and quality of instruction, we were surprised not to observe conditional effects of participation as a function of either of these two factors. On one hand, this may speak to the importance of student factors, such as age and pre-program scores, in promoting or constraining the effects of participation, relative to program factors.

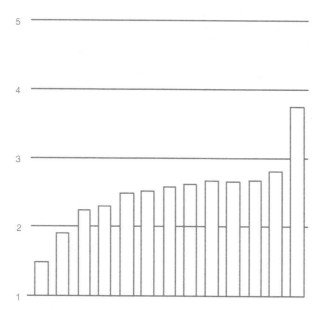

Fig. 7.5 Observed quality of instruction with respect to SEL by program. Note: Each column represents a program. Program names have been removed

However, as we discuss below, it may also suggest that there are program factors other than dosage or quality that are contextualizing the effects of participation, such as the broader context of the host school(s) and the extent to which programs are explicitly designed to foster students' socio-emotional development.

To explore what these factors may be, we examined the main effects for three programs, which were selected because they represent a range of ages served, artistic disciplines, dosages, and quality with respect to SEL. We will refer to these as programs A, B, and C.

- Program A was a music residency offered to students in fourth grade. The program featured a series of six-hour-long visits by professional musicians who performed in students' classrooms and answered questions. The overall quality of instruction with respect to SEL was rated at 2.24.
- Program B was an elective dance program offered to students in grades three through eight that met once a week for 45 minutes over

the course of 36 weeks. Instruction was offered by a teaching artist to a group of approximately 30 students and focused on demonstrating techniques necessary to participate in a dance routine. Overall quality with respect to SEL was rated at 2.18.

- Program C was a theater program offered to high-school seniors in their English language arts classrooms. The program met once or twice per week for 45 minutes over the course of 13 weeks. A pair of teaching artists worked with the class as a whole as they participated in a series of theater activities, including improvising scenes. The overall quality of instruction was the highest observed for any program: 4.41.

We observed a different pattern of significant and sub-threshold effects for each of these programs, as summarized in Table 7.4. "Sub-threshold" effects were defined as effects that were not statistically significant, but for which the effect size exceeded $d = 0.25$, corresponding to Tallmedge's (1977) benchmark for a program to be of "educational significance." We considered both significant and sub-threshold effects given the limits on statistical power imposed by disaggregating our sample by program.

Despite our relative lack of statistical power, a significant effect of program participation on teacher-rated perseverance was observed for stu-

	Student Measures	School Engagement	Growth Mindset	Perseverance	Academic Goal Orientation	Academic Self Efficacy	Academic Self-Concept	Artistic Goal Orientation	Artistic Self Efficacy	Artistic Self-Concept	Teacher Measures	School Engagement	Perseverance
Program A		---	.32	---	.27	---	---					.62*	.28
Program B		---	.29	.56	---	.71*	---					---	---
Program C		---	---	---	---	---	---	.28	.33	---		---	.42*

Table 7.4   Summary of effects for a selection of programs

Note: The number in each box indicates the effect size (d). Asterisks indicate that an effect was statistically significant at $p < 0.05$. The boxes for the artistic domains (artistic goal orientation, artistic self-efficacy, and artistic self-concept) are shaded for Programs A and B because these programs did not serve students in high school, and only these students were judged capable of reliably distinguishing between the contexts of school and program

dents in Program C, while sub-threshold effects were observed for artistic goal orientation and artistic self-efficacy. Sub-threshold effects in these domains were not observed for the other programs serving high-school students that were rated as lower in quality of instruction with respect to SEL. Thus, it may be the case that to achieve effects among older students even in proximal domains of socioemotional development such as artistic goal orientation requires a program of particularly high quality.

In contrast, effects were observed in multiple *distal* domains for the two programs serving younger students, despite the fact that both of these programs were rated below the mean for overall quality of instruction with respect to SEL. Together, these programs achieved significant effects for school engagement as rated by teachers (Program A) and academic goal orientation as rated by students (Program B), as well as sub-threshold effects for growth mindset (both programs), academic goal orientation (Program A), and teacher-rated perseverance (Program A). These results echo the results of our cross-program analyses, which indicated that multiple distal outcomes, including growth mindset, were achieved only among programs serving younger students. While these within-program analyses are not conclusive, they do suggest that these distal outcomes may be achieved even by programs of modest quality when those programs are offered to young students.

Also consistent with our cross-program analyses was the fact that dosage appears to exert little influence on the effects of these programs. Program B offered students nearly 30 hours of instruction over the course of the academic year, while Program A comprised approximately 6 hours of instruction. Despite this, the programs both achieved widespread outcomes.

If dosage and quality of instruction are, at most, loosely coupled with socioemotional outcomes, what other factors may be at work? One potential factor is the quality of the program as *designed* in the broad sense, rather than as implemented with respect to SEL. One common element among Programs A, B, and C was that each had a defined curriculum, in that the program provided teaching artists with lesson plans and activities for each session. Even if this curriculum as implemented did not explicitly emphasize SEL (and it did not in the cases of Programs A and B), its presence may have contributed to an overall sense of order and cohesion that was absent for programs where no curriculum was present.

Another factor is the overall context provided by the school and students, which was not assessed, rather than the specific context for the program sessions and student behaviors in those sessions, which was indexed by our measure. While school and program contexts would be expected to overlap, they are hardly synonymous: some of the sessions for Program B occurred in a space that was ill-equipped for a dance program (thus contributing to a low score on the context dimension of our measure), but the school itself was a high-functioning charter serving students who were, on average, *relatively* more affluent than many of their peers attending other schools in our study. All else being equal, this school context is more amenable to program implementation than one offered by a troubled school serving a high proportion of children in deep poverty.

An Additional Finding with Broader Implications

Though not included in the course of addressing our research questions per se, one additional finding emerged that is worth mentioning. Our analyses addressed whether there was a *unique* association between participation and socioemotional outcomes after accounting for other factors, such as gender and school. One set of factors we controlled for was students' current and prior exposure to the arts in school. In doing so, we observed that there were positive relationships between current and prior arts exposure and a number of socioemotional domains. The question then became: how strong are these relationships and to what extent are they unique?

To answer this question, we estimated a series of models that predicted select socioemotional domains as a function of prior or current arts exposure after accounting for students' age, gender, race/ethnicity, classroom, and school. The results of these models indicated that there were unique relationships between prior in-school arts exposure and students' interest in the arts, awareness of other cultures, academic self-efficacy, academic self-concept, and engagement, with students who had prior exposure to the arts in school reporting higher scores in each of these domains. In each case, the size of the relation between prior exposure to the arts and the socioemotional domain in question was modest. A similar set of relationships was observed between current exposure to the arts and both academic self-concept and school engagement. In both cases, higher levels of current in-school arts instruction were associated with higher levels of socioemotional outcomes in these domains. While the relationship between current arts instruction and academic self-concept was modest, the relationship between instruction and school engagement was moderate, and even a modest effect could have great practical significance. Academic self-efficacy, academic self-concept, and school engagement are known to predict success in school (Zins, Weissberg, Wang, & Walberg, 2004), and the potential for in-school arts education to enhance the likelihood of school success constitutes an opportunity for intervention that is too important to ignore.

WHAT ARE THE IMPLICATIONS FOR OUR UNDERSTANDING OF ARTS EDUCATION IN SCHOOLS?

The results of our evaluation are best suited to address a more refined version of this question: what are the implications for our understanding of arts education programs like those the students in our study attended? This is an important distinction. As noted above, much of the literature on the benefits of arts education cannot be generalized to samples of low-income students of color—precisely the students served by the schools in our study.

Contextualizing Program Effects One implication of our findings for the understanding of arts education in these contexts is that when "arts education" is defined broadly, achieving general or widespread effects may not be likely. This represents a dilemma: in order to accrue a sample size large enough to provide statistical power adequate to detect omnibus effects, multiple programs serving distinct groups of students had to be included in our study. But the resulting diversity of programs and students served necessitated controlling for program and student factors, and reduced the likelihood that omnibus effects would be observed in a given domain if those effects are truly driven, for example, only by high-dosage theater programs (relative to a study that examined only high-dosage theater programs).

On the other hand, examining the effects of arts education programs with a diverse group of students revealed that some program effects were contingent upon student factors. For example, program participation was associated with increased levels of growth mindset, but only among younger students (approximately 9 years of age). One tentative implication of this finding (which awaits replication) is that arts education may be most likely to influence distal socioemotional domains for younger students, among whom these domains are more malleable.

Working with a diverse group of students also enhanced the likelihood that we would observe substantial variability in pre-program levels of socioemotional domains. This variability was observed, and was found to influence program effects. Students with high pre-program scores in school engagement and academic self-efficacy maintained those scores if they were enrolled in an arts education program; students who were not enrolled in a program experienced declines in scores over time. This finding may cause us to question what is meant when we say that a program "achieved" a particular outcome. Achieving an outcome can also mean the preservation of high scores among students who exhibit these scores prior to program participation. While this may seem like a modest goal, preserving high levels of school engagement and academic self-efficacy is a worthy aim for programs to achieve, given the known relationships between these domains of socioemotional development and school success.

Finally, the results of our work suggested only a loose coupling between the observed quality of instruction and outcomes, and no relation between dosage and outcomes. This suggests that program factors other than those measured here may be important to consider in future work. These may include broader contextual factors that impinge upon program implementation and the extent to which a program is designed to foster socioemotional outcomes.

Convening Communities of Practice Another implication of our findings is that it may behoove arts education programs and the organizations that support them to consider convening communities of practice. No program achieved benefits in every socioemotional domain, but benefits were observed for every program in at least one domain. This suggests that promoting an exchange of best practices programs could improve collective practice and thereby increase the likelihood that they would achieve the outcomes they seek. Without wishing to be overly prescriptive, we envisioned that these communities of practice would be organized around a single or small set of socioemotional domains that a group of programs sought to achieve and that the leadership of these programs would attend a series of meetings organized around the following topics:

- A presentation of the literature that speaks to the capacity of arts education to influence the selected domain or domains. Special emphasis would be placed on: (1) whether the findings presented in the extant literature can be generalized to the populations served by the programs and (2) the specific features of programs that may have promoted the achievement of a particular domain.

• How the design of each program might foster students' learning in that domain, as presented by program leadership. Crucial elements of design would include their methods for hiring and training teaching artists, selecting or designing curricula and instructional materials, and strategies for forming fruitful partnerships with schools and teachers.

• Reflections on the extent to which programs, as implemented, realized their designs. This session could feature data collected using the observational measure developed for the present study, as well as the exchange of videos that capture the practice of teaching artists employed by programs.

• Reports of the results of student-reported data pre- and post-program. While supporting organizations may have to facilitate the analyses and presentation of these data, both program and supporting organization staff could be trained to collect and collate the data using the measures developed for this study.

CONCLUSION

This study made three contributions to the field of arts education. First, it contributed new knowledge to the field. The results presented here indicate that arts education programs can foster SEL in certain domains, but that these effects are most likely to be observed among subsets of students, including younger students and students exhibiting high levels of socioemotional development prior to program participation. Second, the project has contributed new tools to the field that can be used to continue to generate knowledge in the future. The measures administered to students and teachers in this study produced reliable data across an array of socioemotional domains, and can be expected to do so again in the future, while the observational measure will allow researchers to assess program practices designed to achieve outcomes across multiple domains of socioemotional development. Third, it highlighted how these measures can be situated within evaluation designs that can be employed when conducting a conventional randomized-control design is not viable.

However, it is the context in which these contributions were made that is perhaps the most important benefit of this study to the field. As noted above, our understanding of the effects of arts education on socioemotional development is based largely on evidence collected from children who are more affluent and demographically homogenous than those served by the schools included in this study. With some exceptions, the measures available to assess socioemotional development were also created with less diverse groups of students. It is only by investing in the creation of knowledge about more diverse samples of students—as well as the measures necessary to generate this knowledge—that we may begin to address the inequitable distribution in our understanding of how the arts may improve their lives.

NOTES

1. This study was funded by the William Penn Foundation. The opinions expressed in this report are those of the authors and do not necessarily reflect the views of the Foundation.
2. Unlike the other studies reported in this paragraph, Walker et al. (2011) examined the effects of a theater-integrated ELA (English language arts) curriculum, rather than a general program of arts education.

REFERENCES

Ames, C. (1992). Classrooms: Goals, structures, and student motivation. *Journal of Educational Psychology, 84,* 261–271.

Anderman, E. M., & Maehr, M. L. (1994). Motivation and schooling in the middle grades. *Review of Educational Research, 64,* 287–309.

Aronson, J., Fried, C. B., & Good, C. (2002). Reducing the effects of stereotype threat on African American college students by shaping their theories of intelligence. *Journal of Experimental Social Psychology, 38,* 113–125.

Bandura, A. (1986). *Social foundations of thought and action: A social cognitive theory.* Englewood Cliffs, NJ: Prentice-Hall.

Barnett, S. M., & Ceci, S. J. (2002). When and where do we apply what we learn? A taxonomy for transfer. *Psychological Bulletin, 128,* 612–637.

Benson, P. L., Scales, P. C., & Syvertsen, A. K. (2010). The contribution of the developmental assets framework to positive youth development theory and practice. *Advances in Child Development and Behavior, 41,* 197–230.

Bertalanffy, L. (1969). *General system theory: Foundations, development, applications.* New York: George Braziller.

Blackwell, L. S., Trzesniewski, K. H., & Dweck, C. S. (2007). Implicit theories of intelligence predict achievement across an adolescent transition: A longitudinal study and an intervention. *Child Development, 78,* 246–263.

Bournot-Trites, M., Belliveau, G., Spiliotopoulos, V., & Séror, J. (2007). The role of drama on cultural sensitivity, motivation and literacy in a second language context. *Journal for Learning Through the Arts, 3*(1), 1–33.

Burton, J., Horowitz, R., & Abeles, H. (2000). Learning in and through the arts: The question of transfer. *Studies in Art Education, 41,* 228–257.

Carter, C. S. (2005). Effects of formal dance training and education on student performance, perceived wellness, and self-concept in high school students. *Dissertation Abstracts International Section A, 65,* 2906.

Catalano, R. F., Berglund, M. L., Ryan, J. A., Lonczak, H. S., & Hawkins, J. D. (2004). Positive youth development in the United States: Research findings on evaluations of positive youth development programs. *The Annals of the American Academy of Political and Social Science, 591,* 98–124.

Catterall, J. S. (1998). Involvement in the arts and success in secondary school. *Americans for the Arts Monographs, 1,* 1–10.

Catterall, J. S. (2007). Enhancing peer conflict resolution skills through drama: An experimental study. *Research in Drama Education, 12,* 163–178.

Catterall, J. S., & Peppler, K. A. (2007). Learning in the visual arts and the world-views of young children. *Cambridge Journal of Education, 37,* 543–560.

Cohen, J. (1988). *Statistical power analysis for the behavioral sciences.* London: Routledge.

Connell, J. P. (1990). Context, self, and action: A motivational analysis of self-system processes across the life-span. In D. Cicchetti (Ed.), *The self in transition: Infancy to childhood.* Chicago, IL: University of Chicago Press.

Costa-Giomi, E. (1999). The effects of three years of piano instruction on children's cognitive development. *Journal of Research in Music Education, 47,* 198–212.

Degé, F., Wehrum, S., Stark, R., & Schwarzer, G. (2009). *Music training, cognitive abilities and self-concept of ability in children.* Proceedings of the 7th Triennial Conference of European Society for the Cognitive Sciences of Music, Jyvaskyla, Finland.

Devroop, K. (2012). The social-emotional impact of instrumental music performance on economically disadvantaged South African students. *Music Education Research, 14,* 407–416.

DICE Consortium. (2010). The DICE has been cast. Research findings and recommendations on educational theatre and drama.

Duckworth, A. L., & Quinn, P. D. (2009). Development and validation of the short Grit Scale (Grit-S). *Journal of Personality Assessment, 91,* 166–174.

Dweck, C. S. (2000). *Self-theories: Their role in motivation, personality, and development.* Philadelphia, PA: Taylor & Francis.

Eisner, E. W. (1998). Does experience in the arts boost academic achievement? *Arts Education Policy Review, 100,* 32–40.

Elpus, K. (2013). *Arts education and positive youth development: Cognitive, behavioral, and social outcomes of adolescents who study the arts.* Washington, DC: National Endowment for the Arts.

Finn, J. D., & Voelkl, K. E. (1993). School characteristics related to school engagement. *The Journal of Negro Education, 62,* 249–268.

Fredricks, J. A., Blumenfeld, P. C., & Paris, A. (2004). School engagement: Potential of the concept: State of the evidence. *Review of Educational Research, 74,* 59–119.

Heath, S. (1998). Living the arts through language and learning: A report on community-based youth organizations. *Americans for the Arts Monographs, 2,* 1–20.

Holochwost, S. J., Propper, C. B., Wolf, D. P., Willoughby, M. T., Fisher, K. R., Kolacz, J., et al. (2017). Music education, academic achievement, and executive functions. *Psychology of Aesthetics, Creativity, and the Arts, 11*(2), 147–166.

Horn, J. (1992). *An exploration into the writing of original scripts by inner-city high school drama students.* Washington, DC: National Arts Education Research Center.

Institute for Research and Reform in Education. (1998). *Research Assessment Package for Schools (RAPS).* Adelphia, NJ: Institute for Research and Reform in Education.

Kaplan, A., & Maehr, M. L. (2007). The contributions and prospects of goal orientation theory. *Educational Psychology Review, 19,* 141–184.

Kennedy, J. R. (1998). *The effects of musical performance, rational emotive therapy and vicarious experience on the self-efficacy and self-esteem of juvenile delinquents and disadvantaged children.* Doctoral Dissertation, University of Kansas.

King, A. (1983). Agency, achievement, and self-concept of young adolescent art students. *Studies in Art Education, 24,* 187–194.

Lee, K. (2007). The effects of dance class on educational self-efficacy and social skills for middle school students. *Korean Association of Arts Education, 5,* 61–70.

Lee, S. O. (2006). The effects of dance education on self-concept formation of high school girl students. *Korean Association of Arts Education, 4,* 55–62.

Marks, H. M. (2000). Student engagement in instructional activity: Patterns in the elementary, middle, and high school years. *American Educational Research Journal, 37,* 153–184.

Marsh, H. W. (1992). *Self Description Questionnaire (SDQ) I: A theoretical and empirical basis for the measurement of multiple dimensions of preadolescent self-concept. An interim test manual and research monograph.* Macarthur, New South Wales, Australia: University of Western Sydney, Faculty of Education.

McPherson, G. E., Osborne, M. S., Barrett, M. S., Davidson, J. W., & Faulkner, R. (2015). Motivation to study music in Australian schools: The impact of music learning, gender, and socio-economic status. *Research Studies in Music Education, 37,* 141–160.

Metsäpelto, R., & Pulkkinen, L. (2012). Socioemotional behavior and school achievement in relation to extracurricular activity participation in middle childhood. *Scandinavian Journal of Educational Research, 56,* 167–182.

Midgley, C., Maehr, M. L., Hruda, L. Z., Anderman, E., Anderman, L., Freeman, K. E., et al. (2000). *Manual for the patterns of adaptive learning scales.* Ann Arbor, MI: University of Michigan.

Peterson, C., & Seligman, M. P. (2004). Persistence [perseverance, industriousness]. In *Character strengths and virtues: A handbook and classification.* Washington, DC: American Psychological Association.

Rapp-Paglicci, L., Stewart, C., & Rowe, W. (2011). Can a self-regulation skills and cultural arts program promote positive outcomes in mental health symptoms and academic achievement for at-risk youth? *Journal of Social Service Research, 37,* 309–319.

Rickard, N. S., Appelman, P., James, R., Murphy, F., Gill, A., & Bambrick, C. (2013). Orchestrating life skills: The effect of increased school-based music classes on children's social competence and self-esteem. *International Journal of Music Education, 31,* 292–309.

Roth, J., Brooks-Gunn, J., Murray, L., & Foster, W. (1998). Promoting healthy adolescents: Synthesis of youth development program evaluations. *Journal of Research on Adolescence, 8,* 423–459.

Scott, L. (1992). Attention and perseverance behaviors of preschool children enrolled in Suzuki violin lessons and other activities. *Journal of Research in Music Education, 40,* 225–235.

Shields, C. (2001). Music education and mentoring as intervention for at-risk urban adolescents: Their self-perceptions, opinions, and attitudes. *Journal of Research in Music Education, 49,* 273–286.

Shin, J. (2011). An investigation of participation in weekly music workshops and its relationship to academic self-concept and self-esteem of middle school students in low-income communities. *Contributions to Music Education, 38,* 29–42.

Smith, C., Akiva, T., Sugar, S., Lo, Y. J., Frank, K. A., Peck, S. C., et al. (2012). *Continuous quality improvement in afterschool settings: Impact findings from the Youth Program Quality Intervention study.* Ypsilanti, MI: David P. Weikart Center for Youth Program Quality at the Forum for Youth Investment.

Smithrim, K., & Upitis, R. (2005). Learning through the arts: Lessons of engagement. *Canadian Journal of Education, 28,* 109–127.

Tallmedge, G. K. (1977). *The joint dissemination review panel IDEABOOK.* Washington, DC: U.S. Department of Education.

Voelkl, K. E. (1996). Measuring students' identification with school. *Educational and Psychological Measurement, 56,* 760–770.

Walker, E., Tabone, C., & Weltsek, G. (2011). When achievement data meet drama and arts integration. *Language Arts, 88,* 365–372.

Winner, E., & Cooper, M. (2000). Mute those claims: No evidence (yet) for a causal link between arts study and academic achievement. *Journal of Aesthetic Education, 34,* 11–75.

Winner, E., Goldstein, T., & Vincent-Lancrin, S. (2013). *Art for art's sake?* Paris: OECD Publishing.

Winner, E., & Hetland, L. (2008). Art for our sake. School arts classes matter more than ever – But not for the reasons you think. *Arts Education Policy Review, 109,* 29–31.

Zelenak, M. S. (2015). Measuring the sources of self-efficacy among secondary school music students. *Journal of Research in Music Education, 62,* 389–404.

Zins, J. E., Weissberg, R. P., Wang, M. C., & Walberg, H. J. (2004). *Building academic success on social and emotional learning: What does the research say?* New York, NY: Teachers College Press.

CHAPTER 8

AP Research and the Arts: Evaluating a New Approach to College Preparation

Ivonne Chand O'Neal, Serena Magrogan, Lynnette Overby, and Greg Taylor

College readiness is becoming a topic of critical concern throughout the United States. The Educational Policy Improvement Center defines college readiness as the ability of a student to enter a college classroom, without remediation, and successfully complete entry-level college requirements (Dougherty, Mellor, & Jian, 2005). Studies conducted by the National Assessment of Educational Progress (NAEP) examining college readiness demonstrate that while math and reading scores have improved in elementary and middle school over the past 40 years, there is still a "disturbing" lack of improvement among the nation's high school students that may

I.C. O'Neal (✉)
MUSE Research, LLC, Kensington, MD, USA

S. Magrogan
The College Board, Duluth, GA, USA

L. Overby
University of Delaware, Newark, DE, USA

G. Taylor
Purchase College, SUNY, Purchase, NY, USA

© The Author(s) 2018
R.S. Rajan, I.C. O'Neal (eds.), *Arts Evaluation and Assessment*,
https://doi.org/10.1007/978-3-319-64116-4_8

very well inhibit their college success (Camera, 2017). Explanations for this lack of improvement have been offered by studies that focus on arts education and arts integration, suggesting that students participating in the arts are more engaged in their schoolwork, spend more time on task (Martin, Anderson, Gibson, Liem & Sudemalis, 2013), have higher idea generation, and are evaluated by their teachers as being more creative than students who are not in arts-integrated programs (Chand O'Neal, Paek, & Runco, 2015). These findings bring into question how we can utilize the "engagement factor" of the arts to improve student performance.

Recent results reported by American College Testing (ACT) revealed that close to one in three high school graduates who took the ACT test is not ready for entry-level college courses in English, reading, math, or science, according to new data released by the testing organization. Additional findings indicate that of the 1.8 million high school graduates who took the ACT in 2013, only 26 percent reached the college readiness benchmarks in all four subjects. Two or three of the benchmarks were met by 27%, and 16% met benchmarks in just one subject (The ACT Profile Report, 2016).

At first glance, these results appear to demonstrate that all groups have shown some gains since the early 1970s; however, the one group that has remained relatively stagnant is 17-year-old students. In fact, ACT data reported in 2017 indicate that taken as a whole, this group has not made a marked improvement in either math or reading over the last 40 years (National Center for Educational Statistics, 2012).

The College Board is one organization dedicated to addressing this stasis by delivering courses focused on improving college readiness. Founded in 1900, The College Board connects students to college success and opportunity. Each year, this organization helps more than seven million students prepare for a successful transition to college through programs and services in college readiness and college success—including the SAT and the Advanced Placement Program. The organization also serves the education community through research and advocacy on behalf of students, educators, and schools. One recent research initiative yielded results that identified skills, content knowledge, and behaviors that must be acquired before leaving high school in order to improve success in college, which include:

- The ability to think critically and problem solve in the context of a continuously changing set of circumstances.

- The advancement of reading, writing, and numeric skills that enable success in all college courses.
- The capacity to communicate effectively with individuals from a variety of cultural, educational, and professional backgrounds (The College Board, 2008).

Each of these skill sets has been examined in the context of the arts, where results demonstrate that participation in the arts increases cognitive flexibility (Chand O'Neal, Schulz Begle, Constantinescu, & Runco, 2015), spatial reasoning (Hetland, 2000; Rauscher & Zupan, 2000), and collaboration (Chand O'Neal, 2014), the very skills high school students are lacking. The College Board recognized the potential of offering AP courses that could focus on research in the arts as a means of engaging students in the excitement of conducting research on a topic that ignites their imaginations and love of learning, including spoken word, film, theater, dance, painting, media arts, and music.

The current chapter will focus on the evaluation methods used by the College Board to examine the impact of the pilot launch of AP Research, the second course in the AP Capstone series. Though this work is still in its early phase and is ongoing, it is being presented in an effort to illustrate how evaluation can be utilized to shape high school curriculum. Starting first with a brief description of both the Formative Evaluation and Phases 1 and 2 of the Process Evaluation, the Impact Evaluation places emphasis on the student outcomes of the pilot AP Research launch, which preceded the worldwide launch in 2015.

FORMATIVE EVALUATION: BACKGROUND LEADING TO THE DEVELOPMENT OF AP CAPSTONE (2014–2016)

In 2012, The College Board began a systematic effort to aggressively improve college readiness skills based on their extensive research on the topic (e.g., The College Board, 2008, 2010, 2011, 2012, 2016). A series of interviews, surveys, and focus groups began in 2014 with a number of constituent groups that influence student learning in high school, including high school teachers, students, administrators, and members of the higher education community. These sessions revealed a number of specific skill sets that were underdeveloped in high school, contributing to the poor performance of incoming freshman on their college-level coursework. Figure 8.1 depicts the timeline of the multigroup Formative Evaluation that took place

Fig. 8.1 Timeline of AP Research Formative Evaluation

from 2014–2016. During this period, constituent groups were surveyed and interviewed to provide recommendations on what skills sets to build in high school student populations to increase college success.

The challenging areas included:

- Most freshman students arrived on campus without adequate writing and research skills. Colleges and universities had to spend students' freshman year teaching these skills
- Colleges and universities wanted students with a passion for learning, a demonstrated interest in a subject that showed their commitment to something larger than themselves.
- Colleges and universities wanted students to arrive on campus with the critical skills necessary to navigate the rigorous college experience—the skills to complete a four-year degree program, no matter what the discipline.

THE ACADEMIC INTERVENTION: AP RESEARCH

Program development began with a theoretical framework based on the Understanding by Design model (Wiggins & McTighe, 2012) used to guide the content design of the AP Capstone sequence, consisting of two courses: AP Seminar and AP Research. AP Seminar provides the knowledge base, critical thinking skills, and research proficiency necessary for students to be prepared to enroll in AP Research. AP Research is a course in which students apply the skills they learned in AP Seminar through a research project on a topic of their choice. The AP Research curriculum framework provides a clear and detailed description of the course requirements necessary for student success. This conceptualization guided the development and organization of learning outcomes from general to specific, resulting in focused statements about content knowledge and skills needed for success in the course. The curriculum framework contains the following structural components (see Fig. 8.2):

AP Research is organized around five big ideas, which are referred to as the QUEST:

- *Question and Explore*: In this step, students are instructed to challenge and expand the boundaries of their current knowledge.
- *Understand and Analyze*: Students contextualize arguments and comprehend authors' claims.

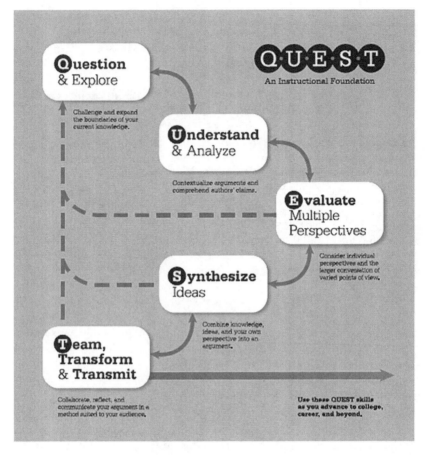

Fig. 8.2 Instructional framework for AP Capstone

- *Evaluate Multiple Perspectives*: Students consider individual perspectives and the larger conversation of varied points of view.
- *Synthesize Ideas*: Students combine knowledge, ideas, and their own perspective into an argument.
- *Team, Transform, and Transmit*: Students consider purpose and audience when developing the written or oral presentation based on their new understanding or conclusion, and engages in peer review to ensure the effectiveness of the communication style.

Each big idea contains several enduring understandings. These are defined as the long-term takeaways related to the big ideas that a student should have after exploring the content and skills. These understandings are expressed as generalizations that specify what students will come to learn about the key concepts in the course.

Linked to each enduring understanding are the corresponding learning objectives. The learning objectives articulate what students need to be able to do in order to develop the enduring understandings. The learning objectives are the targets of assessment for the course, used to assess student achievement. For each of the learning objectives, essential knowledge statements describe the facts and basic concepts that a student should know and be able to recall in order to demonstrate mastery of the learning objective.

The big ideas and learning objectives in the AP Capstone Program reflect the core academic skills needed for college, career, and life readiness identified by leading educational organizations and College Board membership.[1]

PROCESS EVALUATION: PHASES 1 AND 2 (2015–2016)

Upon completion of the first iteration of the AP Research curriculum framework, the Phase 1 Process Evaluation began at strategic intervals (once a quarter for a three-day period) to assess the extent to which the framework reflected college-level expectations independent of discipline. A curriculum review committee consisting of college faculty and expert AP teachers was tasked with assessing this alignment throughout the development of the AP Research curriculum. The results of this phase were embedded in the changes made to the course curriculum.

Phase 2 of the Process Evaluation began with the appointment of the AP Curriculum Development Committee who served dual roles. First, the Development Committee was tasked with conducting ongoing alignment checks between the finer details of the curriculum framework (e.g., defining and constructing a thesis statement to guide a research inquiry) with what students should know and be able to do upon completion of the AP course. These alignment checks were conducted through assessments of student work, with detailed analysis of what components of the curricular framework needed to be clarified, expanded, or divided into smaller units, in order for student learning goals to be reached. Second, the Development Committee was to draw clear and well-articulated connections between the curriculum framework and the performance assessment task—work that included designing and approving the assessment specifications and associated rubrics based on psychometric assessment conducted by The College Board. The Phase 2 Process Evaluation of the AP Research curriculum and assessment was a multiyear endeavor, requiring the curriculum framework and assessment task to undergo extensive review, revision, piloting, and analysis. This process ensured that framework and performance task descriptions were of high quality and fair for equity and access to all students, with an appropriate spread of difficulty across the points assigned by the rubric.

Throughout this multiyear process, the Development Committee made recommendations and suggestions for change that included recommendations for incorporating the arts into professional development examples, and presenting research methods in the arts as viable options to students in AP Research lectures. These recommendations were informed by data collected from a range of colleges and universities on both national and international levels, in order to guarantee that the coursework would reflect current scholarship and advances pertaining to the undergraduate research experience.

A crucial point of emphasis for the Development Committee, and a hallmark of AP Research, was disciplinary agnosticism. That is, it was imperative that students be able to come to the course from anywhere within the full range of academic disciplines, and that the course objectives and rubric be designed to accommodate scientific, humanistic, and artistic modes of research. The very real possibility that budding physicists, sociologists, literary critics, art historians, playwrights, and choreographers might find themselves side by side in the same classroom, benefitting equally from the core skills administered by the Capstone experience, was exciting for the Committee. This possibility raised obvious challenges in overcoming longstanding assumptions and biases regarding the specialized needs and practices of governing disciplines.

At an extreme, the sciences are often associated with highly disciplined research, while the arts are associated with disciplined creativity. This false dichotomy is anathema to the very premise of the AP Research course and ignores both the creative impulse that lies at the heart of scientific inquiry and the highly disciplined research that lies at the heart of the artistic process. Nevertheless, through data collected from high school teacher interviews, the Committee acknowledged that in practice it may be difficult for artistically inclined students and teachers alike to spot immediate points of entry into the course content due to the common assumption that research is for the sciences, not for the arts. Therefore, a particular effort was made to articulate the relevance of Capstone methods to the full scope of academic inquiry, which included the potential of arts-based inquiry. The ease with which a student interested in the arts can navigate their way through the AP Research course is an outcome of critical importance to the Development Committee. This was a central part of the ongoing assessment during the Phase 2 Process Evaluation.

As part of the many aspects of the Phase 2 Process Evaluation, non-arts high school teachers (who would potentially teach AP Research) were asked about their comfort level in mentoring students who were interested in conducting research in the arts. Many non-arts teachers commented on their lack of expertise in the arts, causing them to either explore other domains of inquiry with their student, or perhaps find a mentor who had the required expertise. The following case study developed by members of the Development Committee offers a hypothetical account of how a high school teacher, who does not have arts expertise, may approach working with an AP Research student who is interested in conducting research in the arts, while simultaneously acknowledging their own resistance to this field.

Preparing for Research in the Arts

When a student decides to conduct a research project based on an art form, the non-arts teacher may experience much trepidation. Why? Research and arts seem to portray opposing views of the world—one creative and the other analytical. However, research in the arts, just as in other disciplines, can be both creative and analytical.

When a student expresses interest in conducting research in a performing art (e.g., dance or theater), the following approach may help facilitate a productive research experience for teacher and student alike:

1. Ask the student to search through important databases that include research on the particular art form. For example, in the field of dance, the National Dance Education Organization has established a Dance Education Literature and Research descriptive index (DELRdi).

   The DELRdi includes dance research from 1926 to present. The topics include qualitative, quantitative, and mixed method studies. Studies focused on the artistic processes of creating and performing are also included in the index.

   Similarly in theater, research can be very broad from performance and directing analysis to historical documentations.

The North American Theater Online covers many aspects of Canadian and American Theater with over 40,000 pages of references. For both dance and theater, the International Index to Performing Arts full text indexes more than 210 international journals in the performing arts dating form 1864 to present.

2. Utilize the information from AP Seminar and AP Research in helping students develop an appropriate research question.

Once the student has researched the topic and asked an appropriate research question, the instructor may provide assistance in helping the student design a clearly articulated research methodology.

For example:

- A question regarding a comparison between novice and experienced dancers' body awareness will need an experimental methodology with *quantitative analysis.*
- A question regarding the audience reactions to two types of theatrical performances may require a *survey/interview methodology* with a *qualitative analysis.*
- A question regarding the creation of a new dance work designed to foster greater understanding of a complex problem may utilize a *qualitative approach (movement analysis of the dance, surveys of the audience).*
- A question about the impact of integrating theater and math in a curriculum for third grade students may utilize a *mixed method approach*—quantitative analysis of pre-post knowledge and skill impact and qualitative analysis of journal entries designed to assess affective impact of the curriculum.

3. Contact an expert/mentor

Throughout the process of research in the arts, a mentor or expert, in the art form, will provide important insight. The mentor will also assist in clarifying the research methodology. As the research project progresses, a mentor with deep knowledge of the discipline will be able provide the student with a larger vision of the discipline and information on how this project fits within the discipline. Finally, a good mentor can suggest options for presentation and dissemination of the project.

4. Gain knowledge of the art content/vocabulary

The AP teacher may not have knowledge of the art content, but the Core National Arts Standards are excellent resources for this information. The website includes the five art forms (dance, theater, visual art, theater, media arts) and artistic processes of performing, creating, connecting, and responding. The standards are formatted to allow one to view the similarities and unique qualities of the art forms in preK through 12th grade.

5. Form a partnership with an art teacher

Most schools have arts teachers, who are required to teach a very structured curriculum. These teachers will make excellent partners in the research mentoring process. While these teachers will probably not be traditional researchers, and will need guidance in this process, they will undoubtedly already be employing research methods within their own creative endeavors and may thus benefit from learning more about the confluence of such methods within the broader scope of academic inquiry.

In summary, becoming comfortable with the process of mentoring an AP student in research involving the arts will require collaboration between the student, the teacher, and the mentor.

• The student must consider existing research prior to developing an appropriate research question. Review databases of the art form, select several as potential models.

• The AP teacher may reach out to an artist or arts educator as a potential mentor. This could be a teacher in their building, a working artist in the community, or an arts educator in a university.

• The student, AP teacher, and artist will form a partnership—each with a specific contribution to the project.

At the conclusion of the work (the student successfully presents their research, project, and paper), dissemination may take place in undergraduate research conferences or disciplinary conferences/symposia. The teacher may become an expert facilitator of the creative and analytical research of an art form.

This research process example in dance and theater offers a brief glimpse into a research project timeline that a non-arts high school teacher may follow. Examples such as these provided a clear course of action for teachers during professional development, easing the reluctance of a teacher to encourage their student to conduct a research project in the arts.

Pilot Impact Evaluation (2015–2016)

The pilot Impact Evaluation for the year prior to full-scale launch included data from two groups: (1) teachers of AP Research, and (2) students who had taken both AP Seminar and the pilot AP Research course. The purpose of the pilot Impact Evaluation was two-fold. First, by examining teacher outcomes, we hoped to determine the extent to which the Professional Development sequence was meeting the goal of providing curricular resources and mentorship support to teachers, equipping them to successfully teach the AP Research course. Second, by examining students who had taken both AP Seminar and the pilot AP Research course, we hoped to determine how academically well-prepared students believed they were during their first year of college as a result of their work in the AP Capstone Program. An important aspect of student learning was how well the high school teachers who taught the course understood, and were confident in teaching, the AP Research curriculum.

Teacher Pilot Impact Evaluation Results

At the time of data collection for teachers of AP Research, the first year of the operational AP Capstone Program was underway in 139 schools around the world. In summer 2014, the first operational cohort of AP Seminar teachers and school and district administrators took part in AP Seminar professional development (PD) sessions in Miami, FL; Dallas, TX; and Spokane, WA. Attendees completed a confidential on-site paper-and-pencil assessment with feedback on the PD ($n = 227$). In addition, in the weeks following the third PD event, 160 of the 217 AP Seminar teachers completed an online survey, which focused on specific areas of the PD and the teachers' preparation for teaching the course. As it pertains to AP Research (which would not be launched worldwide until the following year, 2015), some of the questions asked helped the Development Committee further refine the curriculum framework during the Phase 2 Process Evaluation. The teacher results were also instrumental in refining assessment tasks, rubrics, and the development of future professional development.

Teachers were administered a six-question survey to rate their confidence in their understanding of the Capstone Program. Results demonstrated that teachers were "confident" or "very confident" that they understood the purpose of the Capstone Program (97%), the QUEST model of inquiry (97%), what students need to do to earn the Capstone Diploma (95%), the assessment structure of the program (91%), what students need to do to earn the AP Seminar and Research Certificate (91%), and how to use the online teacher community (75%).

Group 2 Pilot Impact Evaluation Results

Students who had taken the complete AP Capstone sequence and were in their first year of college were administered an online survey in March 2015 (n = 90). Student respondents were now attending college and answered a series of 14 questions assessing their perceptions of the extent to which their participation in the AP Capstone Program impacted particular interests, skills, and decisions, as well as confidence in certain contexts. For each item, respondents indicated the level of impact on a five-point scale with "1" meaning "No impact at all" and "5" meaning "Strong impact." Respondents indicated the strongest program impacts on their ability to find credible information on a particular topic, followed by the ability to communicate an argument in writing and in an oral presentation; confidence to give a presentation in class and the ability to collaborate on projects with other students; interest in local, national, and/or world news; ability to manage time effectively; and confidence to seek help when needed from professors and teaching assistants also ranked highly in terms of perceived impacts. Over 50% of respondents selected a "4" or "5" on the five-point scale. In this set of 14 items, impacts were perceived to be lowest on interest in volunteering, interest in leading a student organization on campus, confidence to get involved in a student organization, thinking about a college major, and decisions making a course selection.

Summary survey findings suggested that the students saw value in the Capstone courses, particularly in terms of the research, writing, argumentation, presentation, and time management skills they gained. Furthermore, they anticipated that these skills did indeed benefit them in college as indicated by their qualitative responses. The following sample comments reflecting students' academic experience are related to the construct of *finding credible information*:

> I also think my research skills were greatly improved, which was useful in my first year writing/research class this year in college, where I found primary documents that surprised even my professor.

I am currently working on a paper where our professor wants us to use credible sources. When she went over the steps to find credible sources, it was like clockwork for me, just because of this program.

Finding credible information on a particular topic is also something that I've found really helpful in terms of the classes that I've taken first semester in college. I was able to find the information that I needed and not waste my time on information that isn't useful, and because now that I'm a research assistant, this skill really does help me a lot.

When asked if AP Research helped them in their college research work, students responded Yes, for the following reasons:

We have to write a scientific paper where we have to cite sources and find credible sources. AP Capstone helped me develop not only the writing skills needed for an assignment like this but also the ability to find credible sources.

It has taught me the correct way to go about starting and organizing any type of project. For example, when we were given the constraints on what we could conduct research on with the survey, I was able to immediately identify and organize potential ideas, which helped my group get started on narrowing it down, etc.

I find the research process much more second nature and less frustrating. I understand how to find good, relevant sources easily.

It made me better at reading scientific papers and looking for the information I need. Also I know how to write in the style required by the [academic] community. I also know how to argue my points well and how to structure the paper.

It definitely did. It gave me the basis of my attack plans to attack scholarly articles. Also, it made me familiar with the way research articles are set up and how exactly I should evaluate them (for validity, credibility, logical reasoning, etc.).

Students were asked to describe two to three ways in which the AP Capstone helped them with their first year of college. Sample responses included:

The research process that we underwent in the seminar and research courses have fully prepared me for the type of work that has and will be presented to me in my college level courses. The ability to formulate and communicate arguments orally and in written form has given me a confidence in essay writing and presenting that now seems second nature.

Working through the various aspects of argumentative writing in both the seminar and research portions have helped me both plan and develop effective academic papers I've had to write in university. Having gone through the process of gathering credible resources to use in an academic paper has helped me in that regard as well. Participating in this program certainly gave me a good idea of how.

Confidence to seek help: We were given a lot of freedom and often went to teachers for guidance. This contrasts with classes where if we didn't know the answer, it'd be because we didn't do the reading and so going to the teacher would be letting them know you weren't trying. Here, going to get help meant we were trying, and we got practice at seeking help at a fairly high level.

Confidence to give a presentation in class: Most classes didn't take the time to have us give a full on presentation. This one did, and it smoothed out a lot of beginner mistakes.

Discussion

It might be noted that these findings, like the courses themselves, are broad-based and stress the acquisition of larger skills and competencies rather than disciplinary expertise per se. Again, while increased disciplinary expertise will certainly be an important outcome for students, the governing ethos of AP Capstone reflects a more fundamental desire for enhanced college readiness as outlined at the beginning of this chapter. According to David Conley (2017), founder and CEO of the Educational Policy Improvement Center (EPIC), "High schools are designed to get students to graduate ... They are not necessarily designed to enable students to succeed in college ... The time has come to think past admission to academic success." For the high school student interested in the arts, the opportunity has now been presented to combine a deep interest with a rigorous skill set that will prepare the student for a successful college career. Students with a deep love of the arts, or even a passing intellectual curiosity, will have the research skills to intellectually explore these domains using rigorous methods. They will discover their own connections between the arts and the sciences, reflecting on similarities and differences in approach. This critical thinking process increases their lexicon of strategies for approaching multiple college-level tasks, including test taking, analysis, divergent thinking, and deductive reasoning.

The intersection of such broader skills and competencies, and their applicability across disciplines, further underscores the equal relevance of arts, sciences, and humanities within the course framework. In addition, this intersection may encourage (one hopes) the softening of traditional barriers separating such disciplines and modes of study within the secondary school environment, as all become granted equal legitimacy as confluent forms of research-based inquiry. Certainly the course provides a vital and timely opportunity for students and teachers alike to come together to explore the creativity of mathematics but also the rigorous problem-solving of filmmaking, painting, or theatrical staging. In a world increasingly marked by the sheer ubiquity of aesthetic engagement within every facet of daily life, an "age of look and feel" (Postrel, 2003) where the plating of restaurant entrees is appreciated alongside popular fashions, furniture and appliance design, and films and videos played on handheld devices, such exploration has the added benefit of nurturing a more engaged, knowledgeable, and enlightened citizen spectator. In addition, in this age of vast amounts of information, our students are constantly seeking methods to discern quality, truth, and the inspiration for their next best idea. In the words of Richard Riley, former U.S. Secretary of Education, "We are currently preparing students for jobs that don't yet exist ... using technologies that haven't been invented ... in order to solve problems we don't even know are problems yet" (2016, World Economic Forum). The potential of the AP Research course to increase high school student skills in areas of greatest deficit is promising. More importantly, it teaches students how to ask good questions, where to look for the most promising answers, and determine the quality and validity of answers they find. These are life skills they will use in college and well beyond.

LIMITATIONS

The intent of the evaluation was to examine the impact of the pilot launch of the AP Research course. However, student responses indicated that they viewed each course as an integral component of learning research skills along a continuum where the AP Seminar course introduced them to the skills that they would eventually master as an independent researcher in the AP Research course. What became evident was that specific questions about the practice of research needed to be posed as they were conducting their research project to document when they ran into difficulty.

To further refine either professional development or curricular materials, it would be important to pose questions to professors of students who had taken the AP Capstone sequence to determine how research skill sets, and accompanying cognitive skills improved, examining differences between incoming freshmen who took AP Research and those who did not. The results of such an examination would be another way to conduct an assessment from the perspective of the educator.

Additional alignment between high school teachers and college professors on material taught in high school with explicit connections made to expectations in college would help to facilitate a clear pathway for students to obtain support if their skills were less than optimal. This alignment will also provide a better understanding of how skill sets can sometimes build upon each other, requiring the need to master a certain level before moving on to the next.

SUMMARY

In the Formative Assessment, educators of high school students and incoming college freshmen offered structured feedback documenting in what ways college freshman are ill-prepared for college success. This information was used to create the AP Capstone Program consisting of a two-course sequence: AP Seminar and AP Research.

Phases 1 and 2 of the Process Evaluation involved the College Board appointment of two committees to oversee the alignment of theoretical frameworks with learning objectives that could be easily translated to the high school classroom. Each iteration of the AP Research curriculum was presented to high school teachers in professional development forums to determine ease of delivery and developmental and cognitive alignment. As a result of these efforts, high school AP Research teachers reported high levels of comfort with the curricular material and high levels of confidence in their understanding of the AP Capstone Program.

The Impact Evaluation demonstrated that student gains were reported in a number of areas including: ability to find credible information on a particular topic, the ability to communicate an argument in writing and in an oral presentation, confidence to give a presentation in class, and the ability to collaborate on projects with other students. Interest in local, national, and/or world news, ability to manage time effectively, and confidence to seek help when needed from professors and teaching assistants were also reported as key outcomes. An unexpected finding was that student comments reflected improvement in unexpected areas, including persistence, and grit, as they described their process of "working through the various aspects of argumentative writing." Students also reported comfort with asking for help if they got stuck, a skill that is often overlooked as a positive construct.

IMPLICATIONS

The critical skills developed in the AP Capstone Program—analytical thinking, collaboration, and applied research—are certainly crucial for student success within and after college, and can be developed in AP Research at a higher level of intensity than in traditional AP courses. Further, because AP Capstone is skills-based rather than content-based, it focuses on learning how to learn and how to think, and therefore accelerates and expands students' potential for achievement within the broad array of classes and experiences they will face in coming years. In so doing, it additionally downplays disciplinary specialization in favor of a more holistic embracing of commonalities uniting research activities in the arts, sciences, and humanities. For students and teachers in the arts especially, AP Capstone provides an invaluable opportunity to engage their own practice within this larger developmental context, looking within but also beyond their particular media in order to enhance preparedness skills while contributing to the larger intellectual, emotional, and creative maturation of students as they move toward and beyond post-secondary education.

It is the skill set from this course that will prepare students for jobs that have yet to be invented.

NOTES

1. The following organizations have highlighted AP Capstone core academic skills as necessary for college, career, and life readiness: The American Association of Colleges and Universities (AAC&U), College Learning for the New Global Century, Essential Learning Outcomes, The Partnership for 21st Century Skills (P21), A Framework for 21st Century Learning, Association of College and Research Libraries, Information Literacy Competency Standards for Higher Education, Council of Writing Program Administrators, Framework for Success in Postsecondary Writing.

REFERENCES

The ACT Profile Report—National. (2006). Retrieved from URL.

Camera, L. (2017). *Thriving state economies support robust public education systems.* U. S. News and World Report, February 28.

Chand O'Neal, I. (2014). Selected findings from the John F. Kennedy Center's Arts in Education Research Study: An impact evaluation of arts-integrated instruction through the Changing Education Through the Arts (CETA) program. The John F. Kennedy Center for the Performing Arts.

Chand O'Neal, I., Paek, S., & Runco, M. A. (2015). Comparison of competing theories about ideation and creativity. *Creativity: Theories-Research-Applications, 2*(2), 1–20. https://doi.org/10.1515/ctra-2015-0018

Chand O'Neal, I., Schulz Begle, A., Constantinescu, C., & Runco, M. (2015). *The art of character: How the arts improve grit, social emotional learning, and creativity.* For presentation at the Learning and the Brain Conference: The Science of Character: Using Brain-Psychological Sciences to Promote Self-Regulation, Resilience and Respect, Boston, MA.

The College Board. (2008; 2010; 2011; 2012; 2016). AP data – Archived data. Retrieved from https://research.collegeboard.org

Conley, D. (2017). Educational Policy Improvement Center (EPIC). Retrieved from https://www.epiconline.org/

Dougherty, C., Mellor, L., & Jian, S. (2005). *The relationship between advanced placement and college graduation.* National Center for Educational Accountability.

Hetland, L. (2000). Learning to make music enhances spatial reasoning. *Journal of Aesthetic Education, 34,* 179–238. https://doi.org/10.2307/3333643

Martin, A. J., Mansour, M., Anderson, M., Gibson, R., Liem, G. A. D., & Sudmalis, D. (2013). The role of arts participation in students' academic and nonacademic outcomes: A longitudinal study of school, home, and community factors. *Journal of Educational Psychology, 105*(3), 709–727. https://doi.org/10.1037/a0032795

National Center for Education Statistics. (2012). The nation's report card: Trends in academic progress 2012.

Postrel, V. (2003). *The substance of style: How the rise of aesthetic value is remaking commerce, culture, and consciousness.* New York: Harper Collins.

Rauscher, F. H., & Zupan, M. A. (2000). Classroom keyboard instruction improves kindergarten children's spatial-temporal performance: A field experiment. *Early Child Research Quarterly, 15*(2), 215–228. https://doi.org/10.1016/S0885-2006(00)00050-8

Riley, R. (2016). The global risks report 2016, 11th Edition. Retrieved from http://www3.weforum.org/docs/Media/TheGlobalRisksReport2016.pdf

Wiggins, G., & McTighe, J. (2012). *Understanding by design.* Alexandria, VA: Association for Supervision and Curriculum Development.

CHAPTER 9

The Path to "Play the Past": An Evaluation Journey

Wendy Jones and Jennifer Sly

In 2014 the Minnesota Historical Society (MNHS) launched *Play the Past* (mnhs.org/playthepast), a new model for school field trips that integrates mobile and web technologies into the museum experience to capitalize on the natural behaviors and learning styles of twenty-first century learners. *Play the Past* consists of an in-gallery mobile game that provides a new interpretive tool to engage students in the physical exhibit environment; a "teacher app" to facilitate teacher engagement and interaction with students as they play the game and support real-time field trip assessment; a "digital backpack" accessible through a secure website containing items students collected on the field trip, with curated links to primary sources; and curricular activities that employ Web 2.0 tools for classroom educators to guide historical investigations and support students' development of twenty-first century skills.

In 2009, MNHS could not have imagined writing the above paragraph, let alone offering an experience remotely similar as part of its suite of K-12 programs, products, and services. But in 2009, we had questions—lots of questions. A national decline in school field trips to museums and historic sites and the rise of the "digital native" generation of students had prompted us to do some soul searching. Were we a relevant and essential

W. Jones (✉) • J. Sly
Minnesota Historical Society, Saint Paul, MN, USA

© The Author(s) 2018
R.S. Rajan, I.C. O'Neal (eds.), *Arts Evaluation and Assessment*,
https://doi.org/10.1007/978-3-319-64116-4_9

partner in the education of Minnesota's children? Would we still be relevant in ten years? Twenty years? How was the landscape of public education changing, and what role could we play in meeting the needs of twenty-first century learners, their teachers, and their parents? These and other questions set us on an evaluation and assessment path in 2010 that ultimately led to the launch of *Play the Past* in 2014.

Although MNHS serves the K-12 school audience in a variety of ways, we first directed these existential questions at our field trip programs because they comprise the single largest point of contact we have with this audience. With a network of 26 historic sites and museums around the state, MNHS averages an annual total school attendance of 250,000. Other MNHS K-12 programs and services serve substantial audiences, such as National History Day in Minnesota, with nearly 30,000 student participants annually, or *Northern Lights*, MNHS's Minnesota history textbook and curriculum that is used in over 70% of the state's sixth grade classrooms, but none comes close to the number of students who visit our sites and museums. The school field trip is often a child's first museum experience, and educators who may not know about the other diverse educational resources MNHS has to offer know that our museums and historic sites are field trip destinations. If we were going to examine our current and future relevance, field trips seemed like a good place to start.

FRONT-END EVALUATION: WHAT DOES OUR AUDIENCE NEED?

We started our journey with an extensive literature review of twenty-first century learning theory, digital natives, and trends in K-12 education, and then we embarked on a series of focus groups to further identify audience needs and behaviors and inform our next steps. Although we had some ideas in mind for how we could make field trips more engaging and relevant, including integrating technology into students' field trip experiences, we needed to hear from our stakeholders: teachers, parents, and the students themselves. We targeted grades four through eight, the primary audience for most local and state history field trips due to state academic standards at that time, and narrowed participation to teachers who had previously taken their students on a field trip and parents who had served as a field trip chaperone in the past. Students were recruited through the parent chaperone participants, had to be in grades four to eight, and had to have participated in a field trip within the last year. We did not require participants to have visited an MNHS site, but all participants had previously taken a field trip to at least one MNHS site.

In the spring of 2010, we conducted 7 focus groups around the state with 39 teachers, using our historic sites and museums as hubs to pull from geographically and culturally diverse communities. We then followed up in the fall of 2010 with 4 parent and 4 student focus groups, consisting of 23 adult and 23 student participants. Staff from MNHS's Education Department facilitated the focus groups. At this time, MNHS did not have an Evaluation Specialist on staff, although the Education and Exhibits Departments had a strong evaluation culture and had built staff evaluation skills and capacity through a variety of means. The facilitators had recently completed a focus group training conducted by Richard A. Krueger, the author of *Focus Groups: A Practical Guide for Applied Research*. Offered through the Minnesota Evaluation Studies Institute at the University of Minnesota, the training (and Krueger's excellent book) grounded the staff in focus group best practices and provided essential guidelines for the overall process and data analysis (Krueger & Casey, 2015). The objectives of the focus group research were:

- Research the field trip and related classroom support needs of twenty-first century learners and their teachers.
- Assess the value of field trips to teachers, parent chaperones, and students.
- Identify the goals and expectations of teachers, parent chaperones, and students for museum field trips and other informal learning experiences.
- Assess MNHS's service to twenty-first century learners and their teachers and identify strengths, weaknesses, opportunities, and threats.
- Research new technologies and their applications to museum and classroom learning.

We asked teachers 36 questions, which covered the learning preferences and behaviors of their students; challenges and opportunities in the classroom; their evaluation of field trips as learning experiences for their students; and an assessment of their use of technology at their school. Recognizing that we had been overly ambitious with the teacher focus groups (36 questions and a 3-plus hour focus group can overwhelm even the hardiest of participants), we narrowed the parent focus groups to 19 questions. We questioned parents on the topics of their children's learning preferences and behaviors; how well they thought schools were meeting their children's learning needs; their expectations for field trips; and an assessment of their child's use of technology at home and at school.

Students had a harder time answering direct questions, so we used four different activities to prompt their input. We asked each child to draw a picture of his or her favorite field trip and then describe what they liked about the field trip. We then gave each student a stack of cards listing typical things you could do on a field trip, from touching real things to taking a guided tour, and asked the students to sort the cards according to their most favorite through least favorite activities. Students also wrote down all the different types of technology they used in their lives on Post-It Notes and then placed the notes on a Venn diagram to indicate whether they used them in school, at home, or both. Finally, we gave students Polaroid cameras and a ten-pack of film. We invited the students to explore the museum or historic site we were at and asked them to take photos of things they thought were interesting. We used these photos to prompt further discussion with the children about their motivations and learning preferences.

Two primary issues emerged from the literature review and focus groups:

- Traditional interpretive strategies employed by historic sites and museums, such as guided tours, text panels, and object displays, fell short when it came to engaging digital natives. Influenced by the omnipresence of video games, the web, social media, and other digital technologies, twenty-first century learners prefer learning experiences that are networked, nonlinear, and graphical; include frequent feedback; and utilize technology.
- Digital technology is creating an "anytime, anywhere, anyhow" learning paradigm, blurring the boundaries between formal (classroom) and informal (museum) learning environments and enabling personalized learning experiences to flourish. Teachers, students, and parents expect museums to capitalize on the new opportunities afforded by technology, and museums risk becoming irrelevant if they fail to do so.

Digging deeper, the focus groups revealed needs and behaviors specific to each stakeholder group:

Teachers Value Field Trips but Face Challenges, Including Technology Of all the resources teachers used to supplement their classroom instruction, they ranked field trips as having the highest impact on their students' learning. However, they had limited time and resources to prepare students for the field trip and to reflect on their experience upon their return. They also felt that the pressure of standardized testing and budget cuts limited their ability to take field trips or offer other deep learning experiences, such as project-based learning units. They could only offer a few of these each year and selected them very carefully. Field trips that clearly connected to curriculum and academic standards were much more likely to be approved by school administrations. Teachers most liked having their students see/touch a real thing and do hands-on activities on field trips.

Teachers were supportive of the idea of having their students use a mobile device on a field trip, and they wanted more opportunities to model technology as a learning tool with their students. Most felt that they had neither the time nor the resources to integrate technology into their instruction in effective or meaningful ways. If their students used mobile devices on a field trip, they would use the photographs and other digital items students collected in classroom activities. When asked about twenty-first century skills, teachers ranked critical thinking and problem solving as the most important skills students needed to succeed in the future.

Parents also Value Field Trips and Support Positive Examples of Technology Use for Their Children Parents valued field trips as an opportunity to learn more about their children while observing them in a social setting. They also valued field trips as a personal learning experience and would return to the site with their entire family if they enjoyed their experience as a chaperone. When asked about twenty-first century skills, parents felt that adaptability, self-motivation, and social skills were most important for their children to have to be successful in the future.

Most parents were happy with the amount of technology their children had access to at home, and all parents had family policies about how and when their children used technology. However, parents felt that schools were not using technology as effectively as they could be and that too often it was being used for technology's sake rather than as a tool for learning. They supported the idea of having their children use a mobile device on a field trip and were open to using mobile devices in their roles as chaperones. Parents would use the digital items students collected with a device during a field trip as talking points to engage their children in conversation about school activities.

Students Value Personal Choice on Field Trips and Are Discerning Technology Users Children valued the opportunity to explore museums and historic sites with adults and other students. They picked hands-on activities as what they would like to do most on a field trip, and they preferred experiences that gave them opportunities to make personal choices. One student drew a picture of herself selecting the pumpkin she got to take home with her as part of a class field trip to a pumpkin patch—an expression of agency and personalization that characterized most student drawings (Fig. 9.1). While exploring the museum or historic site, students exhibited very personal motivations for what they sought out and demon-

Fig. 9.1 Personal choice, such as getting to select your own pumpkin to take home with you, was a common theme in students' drawings of their favorite field trips (Minnesota Historical Society, 2010)

strated different preferences for how they liked to explore. During their time with the Polaroid camera, for example, students created frameworks for exploration that ranged from looking for interesting shapes and patterns to looking for things that were mechanical or moved.

With their increased exposure to media and technology, today's students are sophisticated content consumers with high standards for how content is presented. "It's more about style than it is about content," reported one teacher when discussing how he engaged his students. Children were extremely comfortable with technology but had significantly less access to technology at school than at home. Although they liked the idea of using a mobile device on a field trip, they were less interested in the technology itself than in what they could do with the technology. Would they use the device to take photos? To play a game? To text their classmates? These and other questions consistently emerged when we asked them if they would like to use a handheld device on a field trip.

FORMATIVE EVALUATION: TESTING AND SHAPING THE CONCEPT

With this information in hand, we knew we wanted to create an experience that capitalized on what our stakeholders valued most about museum field trips—immersive, hands-on learning environments. But we also wanted to capitalize on students' affinity for and proficiency with familiar technology, which teachers and parents agreed was now essential to engaging students in learning, both at home and in school. Furthermore, we knew we needed to leverage technology to create a seamless connection between the museum and the classroom, not only by ensuring that activities aligned with content and skills specified in state academic standards, but by creating a digital space interconnected with the physical experience of exploring an exhibit. We established the following goals for the experience we wanted to create:

- Deepen student engagement with exhibit content through the use of a mobile game application.
- Bridge the gap between classroom and museum learning environments.
- Promote the development of students' twenty-first century skills, primarily critical thinking and collaboration.

Mobile technology was not new to museums. Art museums, such as the San Francisco Museum of Modern Art and the Walker Art Center in Minneapolis, were early adopters of mobile technology and effectively used it to enhance exhibit interpretation with curator insights, artist interviews, and other material. Most institutions were using it as a wayfinding tool or a vehicle to layer on additional content, creating an enhanced version of the traditional audio guide targeted primarily at adults. We decided we wanted to put mobile technology into the hands of students and have them use it to physically interact with the museum, solving problems (individually and collaboratively), using feedback to inform their next move, and collecting digital artifacts and other items for further investigation. Each student would have his or her own "digital backpack" in which to store the virtual personal "souvenirs" of the field trip, and teachers and parents could access the "backpack" for classroom or home activities.

Two factors made it possible for us to start testing this concept. First, MNHS received a state appropriation through the Minnesota Arts and Cultural Heritage Fund to create a permanent 14,000-square-foot exhibit at the Minnesota History Center, MNHS's flagship museum in Saint Paul, on the history of the state's diverse regions and cultures. We decided that the exhibit's primary audience would be students on field trips and families with school-aged children, and that we would create the exhibit and the mobile app simultaneously. Dan Spock, Director of the History Center Museum, ensured we would have access to an empty gallery space for more than a year in which we could build temporary exhibit environments to prototype and test exhibit concepts and the related mobile app. Second, we had turned our extensive front-end evaluation into a grant proposal and received a 2011 National Leadership Grant from the Institute of Museums and Library Services (IMLS). With an exhibit concept, a testing space, and support from IMLS lined up, we assembled a cross-departmental team from MNHS's Education, Exhibits, and Web/IT areas and embarked on the development of what would become the *Then Now Wow* exhibit and *Play the Past* mobile app.

The questions we addressed during the design phase and formative evaluation ranged from the prosaic to the profound and fueled a two-year development process, during which we utilized a design methodology of rapid prototyping and extensive user testing (Table 9.1). The exhibit focused on three regions: the Dakota homeland and agriculture-rich prairies of southern Minnesota; the central metropolitan Twin Cities region of Minneapolis, Saint Paul, and surrounding suburbs; and the north woods

Table 9.1   Questions during the design phase addressed a wide range of issues

Typical formative evaluation questions:

- What devices would students use and on which mobile platform?
- Should students share devices or have their own?
- How much instruction did students need to play the game?
- What motivated students to play the game?
- Should the experience take the students through the whole exhibit or focus on one area?
- Should students be able to take pictures and record audio?
- Should students be able to see what other students were "collecting"? How would that affect the game?
- What role should the teacher or chaperone have during the in-gallery experience?
- What concepts or content did students grasp from playing the game?
- To what extent did students collaborate or use critical thinking skills in the experience?
- How could the mobile experience interact with the physical exhibit?
- What should the "digital backpack" look like? How would it be used in the classroom?
- What could make this a transformative learning experience, something that could only be achieved through the integration of mobile technology with the physical exhibit?

region—Ojibwe homeland and source of Minnesota's logging and iron mining industries. We built a sod house, iron mine, streetcar, Dakota tipi, fur trading post, and other exhibit environments out of temporary materials, including cardboard, and simultaneously tested exhibit components and the mobile application with thousands of users. Since mobile technology changes so quickly, the model of rapid prototyping prevents resources from being invested in big projects that might be out of date by the time the application is created. Although accessible tools like color printers, foam core, and teaching props made it easy to switch out exhibit graphics, text, and hands-on activities for testing, we needed a digital platform in which to test the mobile application.

After evaluating and testing a wide range of available platforms (including SCVNGR, OOKL, TAP, Toura, 7scenes, MITAR, Geobob, and Voicethread), we selected Augmented Reality and Interactive Storytelling (ARIS), an open-source software created by the Games+Learning+Society Center at the University of Wisconsin–Madison.

Since we wanted the exhibit and mobile application to work together to create a narrative, ARIS was a perfect fit as it was built for storytelling, using simple game mechanics to generate a large number of possible interactions and scenarios. To overcome the lack of indoor GPS access, the platform could use location-aware QR codes to initiate interaction with characters and virtual objects, and it had built-in access to both audio and camera. Most importantly, its web-based editor made it easy for all of the team members to create new mobile applications that were instantly available on the iPod through a staging server. Prototypes could be made in a day and changed within minutes for quick mobile application development.

In selecting this platform, we also entered into a long-term partnership with ARIS's developers at the Games+Learning+Society Center to build *Play the Past*. Mutually beneficial partnerships such as this were essential to the formative evaluation and development process. ARIS developers, for example, contributed their extensive experience in the field, using related innovations in mobile development, learning theory, and game design to inform the project throughout. We adopted their methodology for extremely rapid idea generation, prototyping, and testing to quickly narrow to the most engaging activity designs. MNHS, in return, gave the ARIS developers the opportunity to build new software features and test them with thousands of users, a scale previously unavailable to their team. On more than one occasion, we brought down the ARIS servers during days of high-volume testing.

We also partnered with four geographically and demographically diverse schools with varying access to technology resources. Working with these schools enabled us to incorporate in-depth audience feedback on all aspects of the project to ensure a seamless experience for the student and the classroom teacher. Teachers from the partner schools reviewed all project components (from application reading levels to project marketing materials), and their classrooms tested multiple iterations of the in-gallery mobile application, the "digital backpack," and related research materials and classroom projects. In exchange for their time and expertise, both individual teachers and their schools received an honorarium, and MNHS covered their field trip expenses, including busing. Additionally, both the mobile application and the "digital backpack" went through multiple day-long reviews with advisors in the education, museum, and gaming fields.

A Culture of Evaluation

Another key ingredient to the design phase was the culture of evaluation and user testing, which we promoted both internally and externally. Dozens of staff from across multiple departments, with varying connections to the project, participated in the prototyping process. After undergoing a brief training, staff assisted with gallery observations, interviews, surveys, additional focus groups, and more. Our mantra, when we disagreed about design or content, was "let's test it." We also promoted the user testing to our visiting public. We set aside and advertised regular Tuesday nights and weekend days when the general public could try the latest version of the mobile app and give us feedback, and we created a "Testing Lab" experience that school groups could sign up for as part of their field trip. Any school could reserve a time to explore our cardboard exhibit components or try the app—all we asked is that they let us observe and ask questions.

Our scheduling office promoted the Testing Lab when teachers booked their field trips, but we also contacted schools that had already scheduled a visit to the Minnesota History Center and asked if they would be willing to spend part of their visit testing the app. Both the general public and visiting school groups were enthusiastic about being "co-creators" of the new mobile experience and enjoyed the behind-the-scenes access to exhibit development.

With continual feedback from our target audience, we refined and tweaked the mobile app (and sometimes went back to the drawing board to start over completely) until we felt we had something that not only met our goals, but that actually worked from an operational and technical standpoint. At the end of our beta testing, we had tested the app with 4076 students in grades 4 through 8, 150 teachers, and 732 parent chaperones. Student demographics reflected the overall demographic profile of History Center field trip attendance (Table 9.2).

Because we were using an iterative design process, the questions we asked changed frequently, and we adjusted our methodology to collect the data needed to answer the specific question. Early in the design process, our questions focused less on content and experience and more on the technology itself. For example, what kind of mobile device worked best, and did it work better one-to-one or shared among two or more students? Staff observed students and noted behaviors, using a form that prompted them to look for both general and specific behaviors, such as sharing of the device. Observers noted the number of children using the device, the type of device (e.g., a Nexus One, Toughbook, Netbook, etc.), the number of boys versus girls, the age range of students, and the number of adults with the group, and they indicated circumstances that might have affected the experience, such as technical difficulties. We found that after about ten

Table 9.2   Minnesota History Center
field trip student demographics

	%
White	64.8
Black	14.3
Asian/Pacific Islander	10.4
Hispanic	9.1
Native American	1.4
Male	51.2
Female	48.8
Free and reduced lunch eligible	40.7
English language learners	10.8

Note: Data from 2013–2014 school year and provided by Minnesota Department of Education for specific public schools that visited the Minnesota History Center. $N = 39,937$ public school students

observations with approximately 40 students representing the History Center's average field trip demographic profile, a pattern of consistent behavior with a particular device was clear. Based on this testing, we decided that each student would have his or her own device, which would be an iPod Touch.

As we moved deeper into the design process, we used observations combined with oral interviews and written surveys to collect data on each iteration of the experience. Although we asked slightly different questions depending on the version we were testing, they typically aligned with one of the following: How much instruction did students need to use the device and play the game? How did students interact with each other and with their physical environment while using the device? What did students enjoy least and most about the experience? What content and concepts did they learn? How did teachers and parents perceive the students' experience and their role in facilitating the activity? Trained staff observers again used a form to note specific behaviors and then interviewed participants individually or in small groups upon conclusion of the activity. We also observed and interviewed adult chaperones, and teachers completed an additional written survey.

ARIS log data enabled us to analyze broad patterns over the larger experience, such as the average time students spent in a particular section, how deep they went into a particular activity, and how many different sections they typically got to. This data also helped us assess the specific exhibit hubs and associated quests that we had created, pinpointing which hubs were most visited, which quests retained students the longest, and so on. Some students, with consent from teachers and parents, agreed to wear GoPro cameras while they used the mobile app to play the game. The video footage enabled us to get a bird's-eye view of student behaviors, including how they navigated the app, where they got stuck or moved quickly, how they engaged with their peers, and how they moved between using the app and physically interacting with the exhibit.

As we designed the in-gallery experience, we also developed the "digital backpack" and in-classroom experience. The four partner schools were essential for this process. Following each school's field trip and testing of the mobile app, MNHS staff made classroom visits to observe how teachers and students used the "digital backpack," including how they accessed it with available classroom technology, how teachers integrated it into their curriculum and instruction, and how students made connections between the items in their backpacks and their field trip experiences. These teachers also participated in in-depth feedback sessions about the "digital backpack" and shared ideas for activities that could be part of the standard classroom "toolkit" associated with the backpack.

Eventually, we had to yield our prototyping space so that construction of the *Then Now Wow* exhibit could begin. During the exhibit installation, we built a beta version of the app and a web platform for *Play the Past*, continued testing and refining the "digital backpack" and classroom activities, and built a technical infrastructure that connected our group scheduling software (Artifax), public wifi network, and exhibit show controller with the ARIS platform server. We also created a new administration infrastructure that includes a system for the maintenance and distribution of iPods to 30 students every half hour and an online dashboard to manage the experience. After the *Then Now Wow* exhibit opened in November 2012, we spent another year testing and debugging the app within the completed exhibit. We did a soft launch of *Play the Past* with school groups in the fall of 2013, and officially launched the app as a marketed field trip experience in January 2014.

Applying the Evaluation Findings: *Play the Past* Becomes Real

Our iterative design and formative evaluation was a vast and complex process, and it is impossible to summarize all of the moving pieces and results in one chapter. In short, the user testing and evaluation informed every aspect of the final experience. We now distribute iPods to students in grades 4–6 as part of a 50-minute in-gallery experience that schools register for in advance.[1]

Students use the application to assume different roles and pursue historical quests: make a living working in a 1907 Minnesota iron mine; survive life on the prairie in an 1872 sod house; or make smart business trades at an 1804 fur post. The iPod is their tool to help them explore, uncover stories, solve problems, and collect and trade items along the way. Students scan QR codes within three exhibit sections, or hubs. Hands-on exhibit interactives, such as using a drill to mine for iron ore, communicate with the game to create a real-time integration between the physical and mobile experience. As students drill for ore, for example, they receive feedback in their mobile device on the quality of their work and the money they make or lose from their drilling efforts (Fig. 9.2).

To complete some quests, students must collaborate to advance to the next level of the game. In the fur trade hub, for example, students take on the roles of traders and hunters and must find each other to negotiate trades. After a trader and hunter have agreed upon the number of beaver pelts that will buy a particular trade item, such as a blanket or kettle, the

Fig. 9.2 As students drill for ore in the iron mine, they get feedback in their devices on the quality of their work and associated earnings. Charlie Vaughan, photographer (Minnesota Historical Society, 2014)

students exchange virtual items, with the pelts in the hunter's inventory moving into the trader's inventory, and the blanket in the trader's inventory moving into the hunter's inventory. Students get immediate feedback on whether or not they negotiated a profitable trade.

Everything students complete and collect through the game is available in a personal "digital backpack," which provides opportunities for further classroom research and is designed to support teachers and create a strong connection between field trip engagement and classroom learning. Upon the completion of the field trip, teachers are emailed a link to a secure website containing the personal backpacks of every student in his or her class. The items students collected are curated with descriptions and images that add context, as well as with links to MNHS and other vetted web resources that facilitate deeper research. The "digital backpack" is grounded in state academic standards and *Northern Lights*, MNHS's sixth grade Minnesota history textbook and curriculum (Fig. 9.3).

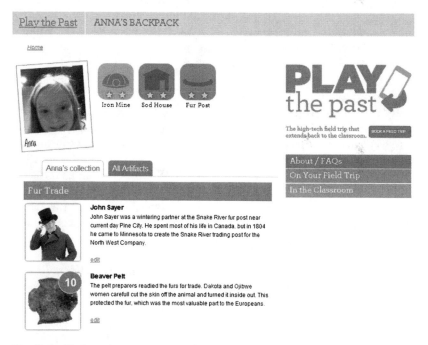

Fig. 9.3 Each student creates an online "digital backpack" as they play the game. It is a repository for the items they collect and the historical characters they meet, and it shows their progress in each hub. (Minnesota Historical Society, 2014)

Summative Evaluation: Did We Get the Outcomes We Were Looking For?

During the spring of 2014, MNHS retained the services of Audience Viewpoints Consulting (AVC) to conduct a summative evaluation to answer the following questions:

- To what extent is *Play the Past* easy to use?
- Do students who experience the exhibition enhanced with the *Play the Past* app show evidence of increased knowledge of and attitudes towards Minnesota history?
- Do students who use *Play the Past* and the "digital backpack" show a greater breadth and depth within their understanding of Minnesota history?
- Do students who experience the exhibition enhanced with the *Play the Past* app demonstrate more communication, collaboration, and problem solving skills (twenty-first century skills)?
- To what extent and in what ways do teachers integrate the "digital backpack" into their post-visit lesson plans?

AVC employed three primary methods within this study: exhibit observations of students combined with post-experience interviews ($n = 89$); post-visit surveys of students who used *Play the Past* on their field trip (treatment $n = 767$) and those who did not (control $n = 107$); and post-visit web surveys of teachers whose students used *Play the Past* during the field trip of *Then Now Wow* ($n = 42$).

AVC developed a protocol and trained MNHS staff and interns to collect data through observations and follow-up interviews. The paired observations and interviews covered how students interact with the exhibits; how they interact with each other, especially communication and problem solving; the types of experiences student groups value most; and the connection between what students do and specific outcomes. For the retrospective post-survey with students, AVC compared differences in learning outcomes between *Play the Past* users and non-users. These paper surveys were administered by teachers back in the classroom, immediately after the completion of the field trip.

Approximately three weeks after the field trip, teachers whose students used *Play the Past* were asked to complete a web-based survey. Areas covered in the survey included teacher memory of the visit experience;

perception of overall themes and messages in the museum; which areas they perceived as most effective for their teaching and why; use of the digital backpack and materials after the field trip; and descriptions of lesson plans and student work related, and completed after the field trip. Key findings for the research questions included the following:

Ease of Use *Play the Past* was, in fact, easy to use. Any technical issues reported never superseded the impact of the app on student outcomes. Although only one-third of students had ever used a QR code before, all students found them easy to use.

Change in Attitudes Towards Minnesota History All students were more interested in history. Over half of the students who used *Play the Past* and half of those who didn't agreed that they liked history more after their field trip. There were no significant differences between *Play the Past* users and non-users in liking history more.

Increased Knowledge and Greater Breadth or Depth Within Understanding of Minnesota History Students who used *Play the Past* learned more about Minnesota history than those who did not. AVC found statistically significant differences not only in what information students recalled, but also in the sophistication of their answers about all three exhibit hubs (sod house, iron mine and fur trade post). After using *Play the Past*, students declared they were more curious about history and asked questions spanning a broad range of topics, including the daily lives of settlers, miners, and fur traders.

Twenty-First Century Skills: Communication, Collaboration, and Problem Solving Students using *Play the Past* showed self-narration, collaboration, and role-playing. A common student behavior was self-narration—students vocalized their progress, what they needed to be doing, when they were confused and when they got it right. AVC saw evidence of high collaboration within each of the hubs, with students helping peers, playing with peers, talking with peers, and trading with peers. Some students internalized the game enough to show evidence of role-playing, embodying the identity of the miners, traders, or sod house inhabitants (Fig. 9.4).

Teachers also felt that *Play the Past* encouraged student collaboration and critical thinking. They were asked to rate how much *Play the Past*

Fig. 9.4 Students collaborate in the fur trade hub and use critical thinking to negotiate profitable trades. Brady Willette, photographer (Minnesota Historical Society, 2014)

encouraged collaboration and critical thinking on a scale of 1 to 7, with 1 representing "did not encourage at all" and 7 representing "completely encouraged." The average rating was 5.79 for collaboration and 5.45 for critical thinking, more than one point above the median for each.

Teachers' Use of the "Digital Backpack" in the Classroom Our testing partners had warned us that it would take a while for any teacher to integrate the "digital backpack" into his or her curriculum and instruction, and we were hoping that 10% of teachers would use the backpack at this stage. AVC found that 30% of teachers used the "digital backpack" after their visit.

Overall Teacher Satisfaction Teachers spoke positively when describing how *Play the Past* impacted their field trip and said that it fulfilled their educational goals. They indicated that they could see the benefits of *Play the Past* and would recommend it, but not overwhelmingly. Their Net

Promoter Score was 32. The Net Promoter Score was determined by subtracting the number of "detractors," or people who would say negative things about the experience (20%) from the number of "promoters," who would actively promote and recommend it to their colleagues (52%). The "passives," or those unlikely to say anything (28%), are not counted when calculating a Net Promoter Score.

The summative evaluation confirmed that *Play the Past* had met its intended goals but also revealed areas that needed additional work, including teacher communications and support, classroom adoption and overall ease of use (Goldman & Montano, 2014).

Next Steps

Shortly after the summative evaluation, we developed a teacher app to help alleviate teacher anxiety and increase their understanding of what students were doing with *Play the Past*. The teacher app had not been part of our original plans, but students tended to learn the mobile app much faster than teachers, who frequently struggled to follow what was happening during the activity. We now provide teachers with an iPad installed with the teacher app, which allows them to see the real-time progress of every student as he or she plays the game and contributes to teachers' feelings of control over the field trip.

In 2016 we expanded *Play the Past* in the *Then Now Wow* exhibit by adding a fourth quest centered on the Dakota tipi. At this hub, students explore art, food and language traditions with contemporary Dakota people. We delayed the launch of this activity to allow adequate time for participation and co-creation with members of the Dakota community.

In 2015 we received an award from the National Endowment for the Humanities (NEH) to extend *Play the Past* into a different exhibit, *Minnesota's Greatest Generation: The Depression, the War, the Boom*, which had opened in 2008 with NEH support. The *Play the Past* quests in *Minnesota's Greatest Generation* will launch in the fall of 2017. We have continued to use a design methodology of rapid prototyping and extensive user testing for all new components.

In fiscal year 2015, the app's first full year, 486 teachers representing 102 schools used *Play the Past*, serving 8036 students, or 12% of all 4th–6th grade students on History Center field trips that year. Over 50% of teachers who tried *Play the Past* during its initial launch in 2014 signed up for it again in 2015. We administered an ongoing survey to the teachers

Table 9.3   Fiscal year 2015 Play the Past (PTP) teacher survey results

	%
Strongly agreed/agreed that PTP supported classroom teaching	83
Felt students were extremely or very engaged using PTP	96
Felt that PTP had positive impact on students' development of critical thinking and collaboration skills	97
Used teacher app while in the gallery	87
Used "digital backpack" in classroom or planned to use in the near future	88
Used "digital backpack" to facilitate classroom discussion	38
Used "digital backpack" for a classroom project	8

Note: $N = 61$, or a 13% response rate

who used *Play the Past* with their students that year, and the overall results showed positive outcomes (Table 9.3). One teacher commented, "[My students] absolutely loved Play the Past. The History Center is definitely the best field trip we've taken in both enhancing classroom learning and in giving the students a fun unique experience."

CHALLENGES AND LESSONS LEARNED

One of the ongoing challenges during the different stages of evaluation and assessment for the *Play the Past* project was, quite simply, adults. Students' familiarity with game mechanics and proficiency in mastering new technology influenced the original concept of *Play the Past* and informed every aspect of the user testing and iterative design. We were creating a unique experience driven by students in the field trip arena, which historically had been tightly controlled by adult "cruise directors": tour guides, teachers and chaperones. As the experience became more and more customized for the student, who ultimately controlled the experience, it was harder for the adults to understand what the student was doing and many were not comfortable ceding control of the experience to the students.

Most adults couldn't keep up with the students, neither if they tried playing the game alongside the students nor if they only attempted to help students as they played the game. Some adults actually interfered, trying to redirect students away from the game. As we refined the experience, we worked on defining the chaperone's role and giving them enough information to feel confident and in control without impeding students' self-exploration. As *Play the Past* is so different from a typical field trip experience, we are continuing to work on communication with teachers that conveys its value, especially the deep learning and engagement value confirmed by the AVC summative evaluation.

We also found it difficult to measure students' use of critical thinking and problem solving during the activity. Although we were able to measure teacher perceptions of student critical thinking and problem solving, we have not yet been able to utilize the log data generated by students themselves to measure their use of these skills. The log data embedded within the game will be a valuable tool to measure student outcomes, but we currently lack the resources and skills to take advantage of this data. We are working with Nic Van Meerten, a doctoral student in Educational Psychology at the University of Minnesota, to develop a system for ongoing assessment and analysis of this data.

Our advice to other organizations who might want to implement a similar evaluation model is simple: just try it. Although *Play the Past* uses a sophisticated technology platform, our evaluation and design process relied on the most basic techniques. We asked questions; threw together something we could test with our target audience; observed; asked more questions; and made changes. And then we repeated this process over and over again. User-centered design requires that you let go of perfection and not be afraid to put something that is rough, clunky or ugly in front of your audience. People like to help, and the audiences you serve as part of your daily operations will be eager participants in your process, especially if your invitation positions them as co-creators. The simplest acts are powerful evaluation tools, and your biggest barrier is the willingness to try.

The front-end, formative and summative evaluation activities not only informed the design and implementation of *Play the Past*, but they challenged our established notions of what "learning" looks like and transformed how we, as a cultural organization, imagine, plan and design for audience engagement. *Play the Past*, and its extensive involvement of stakeholders throughout every aspect of its development, demonstrated that MNHS is a partner with teachers and parents in addressing the challenges of twenty-first century student engagement and is committed to working with them to support student success. *Play the Past* also showed that technology and games, two words that often have negative connotations when associated with children and learning, could be integrated into a museum context and yield positive results.

Biographical Statement Play the Past is the recipient of a 2014 Serious Play Gold Award, a 2014 American Alliance of Museums Muse Award, a 2014 American Association of State and Local History Leadership in History Award, and a 2014 Minnesota Council for Nonprofits Dot.Org Award. *Play the Past* received a 2011 National Leadership Grant from the Institute for Museums and Library Services for its initial development, and a 2015 National Endowment for the Humanities Grant to expand the mobile application into the *Minnesota's Greatest Generation* exhibit.

NOTES

1. We narrowed the grade range to fourth to sixth after new state academic standards banded Minnesota studies in grade six and after we realized that we couldn't accommodate the range of developmental abilities within the fourth to eighth grade experience with our existing resources.

REFERENCES

Goldman, K. H., & Montano, P. A. (2014). *Play the Past: An iPod application to engage middle school students in the exhibition Then Now Wow at the Minnesota History Center.* Unpublished summative evaluation, Minnesota Historical Society, Saint Paul, MN.

Krueger, R. A., & Casey, M. A. (2015). *Focus groups: A practical guide for applied research* (5th ed.). Thousand Oaks, CA: Sage.

CHAPTER 10

The Best of Both Worlds: Using Multiple Evaluation Approaches to Build Capacity and Improve a Museum-Based Arts Program

Don Glass and Patti Saraniero

INTRODUCTION

The Barnes Foundation, like many arts organizations, was interested in evaluating their education programs. While on one hand the purpose of the evaluation was to demonstrate to funders what the program was accomplishing, on the other hand, they wanted feedback on how to improve their work. In this case they hired two evaluators with two different approaches to focus on each of these separate purposes. However, in the course of the work, we discovered how the two approaches could have a complementary and iterative dialog that interlinked design and evaluation. This chapter tells how we arrived at thinking about how to work together more intentionally about the use of evaluative evidence for appraisal and improvement.

D. Glass (✉)
The Kennedy Center, Silver Spring, MD, USA

P. Saraniero
Moxie Research, San Diego, CA, USA

© The Author(s) 2018   223
R.S. Rajan, I.C. O'Neal (eds.), *Arts Evaluation and Assessment*,
https://doi.org/10.1007/978-3-319-64116-4_10

Both evaluation approaches operated under circumstances that are typical to small-scale arts educational program evaluations conducted by independent evaluators. For example:

- the museum staff needed to show program impact to a range of funders;
- the museum staff had a moderate level of experience with evaluation and its use;
- the investment of financial and human resources was modest;
- the time-frame was condensed;
- the travel budget and face-to-face work was limited;
- the local school district had specific conditions and limitations for evaluation by an outside entity (i.e., work with the district schools required Institutional Review Board (IRB) approval and an extensive district review process).

At the forefront, the Barnes Foundation education staff needed an external evaluator to gather evidence of effectiveness, provide programmatic feedback, and report to senior management and funders on the status of their work. To accomplish this, Patti reviewed program documents, interviewed education staff, surveyed participating teachers, observed each aspect of the instructional activities via video recordings, and analyzed a pre- and post-assessment of student knowledge and application.

As the first external evaluation report was being shared, the education staff recruited Don to help with the redesign. Taking cues from the feedback and recommendations from the external evaluation, Don used a more developmental approach. He also analyzed documents and did some participant observations of the program to generate an initial curricular review that would serve as a road map for a collaborative *design study group* comprised of museum staff and district content specialists. In the study group sessions, the team used short surveys, student work samples, discussion protocols, and student feedback to redesign the program to have stronger cross-curricular connections, foster curiosity and wonder, and build knowledge and practices toward clear goals and performance assessment tasks. These sessions were facilitated monthly with the first two sessions on-site at the Barnes Foundation and the remaining three sessions via a conference calling and files-sharing platform.

After the developmental evaluation phase, the education staff asked Patti to return to conduct a follow-up external evaluation on the impact of the program redesign on student learning. In the end, the Barnes

A	B	A
External Program Evaluation (YR1)	Developmental Evaluation (Spring-Summer)	External Program Evaluation (YR2)
	Exploratory Work / Design Study Group	

Fig. 10.1   The A–B–A evaluation design

Foundation needed the credibility and critical distance of an external evaluator to re-evaluate the redesign of the Art of Looking program.

Through each stage, the two evaluators informally conferred and shared their thinking and insights on methods and analysis, as well as gave each other guidance and feedback on how to best support the improvement of the program. Figure 10.1 illustrates the multi-phase external evaluation—developmental evaluation—external evaluation (A–B–A) design that evolved from our process.

EVALUATING THE ART OF LOOKING PROGRAM

The following sections are a narrative explanation of how we arrived at developing this A–B–A evaluation model, with some featured tools and processes and some reflections on challenges and what we learned from the interaction of the components.

Program Background

Science, Technology, Engineering, Arts, and Math (STEAM) is a trend in curriculum design that expands and deepens the practice of arts integration into science and math. Although arts integration has long been a key feature of many arts education programs, cross-curricular design demands that curricular connections across subject areas are conceptually coherent, appropriate and relevant to disciplinary knowledge, as well as scaffolded and flexible enough to support the general transfer of knowledge and practices to other contexts. This complex work could benefit from the use of evaluation, which the Barnes Foundation supported for their Art of Looking STEAM program.

The Goals of Art of Looking

Art of Looking was a multi-visit program for fifth and sixth grade students in the School District of Philadelphia (SDP). The program wove together visual art with science and mathematics to create a richer understanding of these areas. The Barnes Foundation teaching artists worked with students in their classrooms before and after a day-long visit to the Barnes Foundation galleries. The program focused on key works of art from the Barnes collection to investigate math and science concepts. Dolkart (2012) notes about the Barnes method:

> Dr. Barnes thought that there was a scientific way of looking at art ... He wanted us to really look at paintings with the same curiosity and detail that both a scientist and artist look at the world ... the endeavor of both his collecting and his educational ambitions was to develop a rigorous method 'to see how the artist sees.' (p. 10)

Art of Looking had three student-focused goals. The first two goals remained consistent across the two years of the evaluation:

1. Introduce science and mathematics concepts by integrating art from the Barnes collection into scientific and mathematical practices.
2. Students will use scientific and mathematical concepts in creating works of art.

The third goal changed from Year One to Year Two as a result of the developmental evaluation work described in this chapter.

3. Year One: Students will use *scientific and mathematical concepts* in creating works of art.
4. Year Two: Students will use *scientific inquiry* to discover and understand color, light, shape, and space both scientifically and artistically.

Evaluation Questions

The evaluation questions were developed by Patti in collaboration with the Barnes Foundation education staff to guide the external evaluation process. The three questions focused on student learning and experience:

1. To what extent were students engaged during the Barnes activities? How were they engaged?
2. Did the program activities contribute to student learning? If so, in what ways? If not, why not?

3. What did teachers and teaching artists perceive about the students' experience and learning?

Evaluation Methods

A: External Evaluation, Year One

Patti: In the spring and summer prior to the first school year that we studied, the external evaluation was developed collaboratively between the program staff and myself. The program staff brought deep expertise about the program and its stakeholders and I brought the evaluation skills and knowledge. This work was done virtually, as the Barnes Foundation is located in Philadelphia, Pennsylvania, and I am based in California. Later in the chapter, we will describe some of the challenges we encountered and solutions we arrived at to negotiate the 3000 miles between us. Because of the applied needs of the evaluation, a *utilization-focused* approach was the foundation on which the project was designed and built (Patton, 1997). The combined formative and summative purposes of the evaluation required a framework that would be able to support both of these.

As the Barnes staff and I began to work together, two key needs emerged early in the discussions: (1) the first was for the evaluation to identify the program's impact on students in order to provide formative feedback for curriculum development; (2) the second need was to provide cogent and objective data for funder reporting. In addressing the first need, there was an additional intention, which was to assist the program staff in becoming self-sufficient in conducting evaluations of the program beyond this project. There was no guarantee that the evaluation project would extend beyond the school year and the idea was to leave the program staff with tools and processes with which to continue on in the future. Part of this process of building self-sufficiency was to assist staff in recognizing potential data around them, such as student artwork. Using student artwork as a legitimate and important source of data was a relatively new idea in Year One and the developmental evaluation built on this in the curriculum redesign.

The second need, providing data for funders, was addressed through discussions with representatives from each of the funding organizations. The external evaluation plan was reviewed with them and feedback was solicited on how well the plan aligned with their accountability needs.

Table 10.1   Data collection overview

Data source	External program evaluation (Year One)	Developmental evaluation (Spring-Summer)		External program evaluation (Year Two)
		Exploratory work	Design study group	
Document analysis	Curricular materials	Curricular materials (content map, Universal Design for Learning (UDL) review)	Curricular review and peer feedback protocol	Curricular materials
Interviews	–	Program staff	Student interviews by program staff	–
Observations	Structured observation checklist	Participant observation of program activities	Participant observation by program staff	Structured observation checklist
Surveys	Post-program teacher survey with Likert-scale and open-ended questions	Content knowledge	Curricular connections	Post-program teacher survey with Likert-scale and open-ended questions
Teaching artist reflections	Teaching the artist log about engagement and learning aligned with the teacher survey	–	Materials testing notes	Teaching the artist log about engagement and learning aligned with the teacher survey
Student assessment	Pre/post-student assessment Rubric-based student work assessment	–	Student work assessment protocol	Rubric-based student work assessment

This was also an opportunity for program staff to better understand the underpinnings of the reporting expectations.

For the first year of the external evaluation, a variety of methods were utilized to capture data for each stage of the evaluation process, as mapped out in Table 10.1. We deployed a range of tools to triangulate our understanding of the impact on students, including classroom observations, teacher surveys, teaching artist logs, and student quizzes. The evaluation tools were aligned with the program goals and objectives and the collected data would determine to what extent those were met.

Table 10.2   Evaluation use of data

Evaluation use	External evaluation	Exploratory work	Design study group	External evaluation
Product	Progress updates and summative report with recommendations	Provisional report	Formative report with curricular materials	Summative report with recommendations
User	Program staff, administration, funders	Design study group	Design study group	Program staff, administration, funders
Use	Program decisions	Design study group map	Disciplined inquiry for iterative design cycles	Program decisions

In addition, the tools were rooted in the founding tenets of the Barnes Collection, including Dr. Barnes' ensembles, where a collection of art works and objects were connected by the concepts of light, line, space, and color. These concepts underpinned the education team's work and were foundational in developing the evaluation tools. Table 10.2 illustrates how data were used in the evaluation.

B: Developmental Evaluation
Don: When I was first contacted by the Barnes team in the Spring, it was to redesign their Art of Looking program and make it more aligned with exemplary STEAM programs. I was familiar with the art collection and knew some of the history of Dr. Barnes from living in the northeast. I also knew Patti and her involvement with the program evaluation. I had just finished a large STEM project which featured project-based learning (PBL), professional learning communities, and outside-content experts. I was interested by the idea of exploring curricular connections between the arts and science. But rather than act as an external consultant who delivered a new program to be implemented, I suggested that I facilitate a design and evaluation process that invited some content experts from math and science to help us to re-think, adapt, redesign, and test program ideas together. We would have the same goals and output, but the process would be more collaborative, grounded in the disciplines, and tested before full implementation. The staff seemed open to being engaged in evaluation capacity-building, formative feedback, collaborative design, and sharing about the process. Part of the interest of the staff in working

collaboratively with district content experts was to better understand the content and pedagogical content knowledge of the arts, math, and science subject areas.

For this phase of the evaluation, methods and practices were drawn from both teacher professional development and collaborative, utilization-focused evaluation. Over the past 20 years, many practices in professional development—like professional learning communities and coaching—have become more collaborative, inquiry-based, and embedded in practice with aspects of evaluation and feedback on evidence as part of the routine (Elmore, 2002; Smylie, Allensworth, Greenberg, Harris, & Luppescu, 2001). Likewise in evaluation, the field has developed more collaborative, participatory, empowering, and developmental approaches that help build self-determination, as well as evaluation capacity and use at the level of the user (Fetterman & Wandersman, 2005; Gopalakrishnan, Preskill, Gopal, & Lu, 2013; Patton, 2011).

On one level, the group was engaged with a learning design project that had elements of a *community of practice* (Wenger, McDermott, & Snyder, 2002) where the group shared a common interest and potentially intersecting domains of knowledge. Our group had representatives from the Barnes Foundation and the school district, as well as from the subject areas of the arts, science, math, and design. Our small *professional learning community* was purposeful, task-oriented, time-bound, and focused on improvement (DuFour, DuFour, & Eaker, 2008). The group engaged in professional learning as needed to make sure we were familiar enough with the cross-disciplinary content and practices to be able to make valid and strong curricular connections. *Protocols* were used to structure feedback routines (Blythe, Allen, & Powell, 1999; McDonald, Mohr, Dichter, & McDonald, 2003) and *curriculum design frameworks* were used in curricular reviews and development (Meyer, Rose, & Gordon, 2014; Wiggins & McTighe, 1998).

On another level, the group was engaged in evaluation because we made it a routine to gather and review practical data and evidence from self-surveys, student work, student observations, and informal surveys. Student work was periodically used to examine evidence of student understanding of the targeted curricular concepts or practices. The study group iteratively tested various aspects of the program to evaluate its effectiveness and provide formative feedback. As defined by Patton (2015) in the form of principles, our approach was similar to that of *developmental evaluation* because it recognized the problem in its complex context and had a clear purpose to co-create an innovative program. It was utilization-focused with evaluation rigor and opportunities for timely feedback. We also used some analytic tools and routines from *improvement science* to conduct a root cause analysis, as well as use practical measures and practice-based evidence to collaboratively solve problems of practice (Bryk, Gomez, Grunow, & LeMahieu, 2015; Langley et al., 2009).

Using this more developmental approach, the second phase of the evaluation started with an exploratory review of the curricular materials, with participant observations of the program in the schools and during the gallery visits (see Table 10.1). Then five design study group sessions were facilitated over a four-month period: two face-to-face at the Barnes and three online using digital collaboration platforms. Two Barnes education staff, math/science curriculum advisors from the school district and a local education fund, and a practicing arts educator who runs a maker lab participated in the design study groups. The Barnes staff hosted everyone in the galleries, presented their curricular activities, materials, and student work for review and feedback, and piloted the new activities in summer youth workshops. The arts educator and the district math/science coordinator took the lead on writing up the new curricular materials based on our design study group experiences and testing. In the following Fall, the Barnes staff piloted the curriculum with students and drew on those tests to refine the materials. Final piloting and revisions were done independently of the evaluator.

THE OUTCOMES OF THE COLLABORATIVE EVALUATION APPROACH

A: External Evaluation Process

Patti: There were a number of challenges to be addressed in the design of the Year One external evaluation in order to successfully execute it, including navigating the approval process and the long-distance nature of our team.

The Approval Process
Patti: The external evaluation focused on sites within a large urban school district, which, like many of its size, had specific conditions and limitations around evaluation conducted by an outside entity. The evaluation could examine those areas of instruction that were in line with district's goals for

student learning, under which Art of Looking fell. In order to study the students' experience, an extensive application for approval had to first be completed in addition to an IRB review. The district's approval timeline was months long and delayed the start of data collection to the second half of the school year.

Remote Evaluation

Patti: Typically, as an external evaluator, I spend in-person time with the program. This project's resources did not offer this opportunity, so we had to creatively address these limitations in order to execute the external evaluation. The key to unlocking this challenge was video. The Barnes Foundation recorded extensive videos of in-school workshops and gallery tours, allowing me to see the programs in action from my office in California. Meetings were held via videoconferencing and this was particularly useful in talking with the program's teaching artists. That opportunity to see each other and have some sense of each other's space helped build a connection and a sense of trust.

Observation from 3000 Miles Away

Patti: An essential piece of the Year One external evaluation was the structured classroom observation. As this evaluation was to serve multiple purposes, including building staff capacity for evaluation and to identify program impact, classroom observations were a valuable approach. Learning about how to conduct observations presented the museum staff with the opportunity to look closely and think deeply about the students' specific experiences. Classroom observation is recognized as a valuable professional learning experience for educators (Wei, Darling-Hammond, Andree, Richardson, & Orphanos, 2009) as well as an established research method (Spradley, 1980).

Two challenges to conducting observation presented themselves. The first was the long-distance nature of the project and the second was collecting observation in a cost-effective manner. Developing the observation tool and protocol was a multi-step process. We began with the program's goals and objectives and discussed what an in-school workshop or gallery tour would ideally look like if students were meeting the outcomes. What would students be doing and discussing? We made a list of those behaviors and content vocabulary.

Our next step was to record videos of the workshops and gallery tours. The videos were reviewed and field notes were taken about observed student behaviors. The field notes resulted in rich discussions about similarities and differences between the ideal student learning and the observed student learning. Field notes, while rich in qualitative data, would have been time-consuming to produce and analyze across many classrooms and were beyond the budget for data collection. With this in mind, drawing on the program goals and the field notes, a structured observation checklist was drafted. There were several iterations of the checklist before arriving at the version that would be most helpful for internal program development as well as for reporting.

Testing the draft tool was the next step. We used the tool to observe a video of a classroom workshop and then compared results and notes. This exercise provided another round of refinements to the tool (examples are displayed in Table 10.3), but was also a professional learning opportunity for staff as they observed the program session in more specific detail than ever before.

Once we had a tool that we had confidence in, we recruited a former Barnes Foundation education intern who had recently finished her degree to conduct the classroom observation in-person. With an academic background in education and visual art, the observer was somewhat familiar with the program but not in great detail. Her role was to be a complete observer, to observe Art of Looking in action but to take no part in the activities (Spradley, 1980).

Training was conducted online in a similar fashion to the development of the instrument. The observer and I reviewed the timing and structure of the observation protocol, viewed videos of the classroom workshop and the gallery tour online, completed the checklist, and compared results to gauge inter-rater reliability. Once agreement was reached, the observer visited classroom workshops and gallery tours to document the process.

Table 10.3   Examples from the structured observation checklist

Checklist items	Scoring responses				
How many students were on task/ engaged in activity?	All	Most (75%)	Half (50%)	Some (25%)	None
How many students were demonstrating enthusiasm or a positive attitude?	All	Most (75%)	Half (50%)	Some (25%)	None
How many students were volunteering to answer/participate?	All	Most (75%)	Half (50%)	Some (25%)	None

The final element woven into this process was to ask teachers in surveys at the end of the program to record their observations of their students in the classroom and at the Barnes. This allowed us to clarify or challenge the structured observation data during our analysis (Enomoto & Bair, 1999).

A: External Evaluation Year One Findings

Patti: Overall, Art of Looking's Year One results found that student engagement was lower than the other educational offerings by the Barnes Foundation and that student understanding of the program's STEM concepts did not reach the desired levels. In addition, the students' experience of the program was more passive and less experiential, which was also not in line with the Barnes goals for interactive student learning.

Table 10.4 highlights key results from the first external evaluation including differences in the findings from the structured observations and the post-program teacher surveys. As seen in Table 10.4, teachers reported a higher use of STEM vocabulary during program activities than was

Table 10.4 Year One results by program objective

	Year One (%)
Fifth Grade and Sixth Grade	
During in-class workshops and tours, fifth and sixth grade students demonstrated critical thinking skills through scientific practices	23
During in-class workshops and tours, fifth and sixth grade students were actively engaged rather than passively listening	13
During the workshops and gallery tours, students accurately used STEM vocabulary	41
Fifth Grade	
Teachers reported that all or most of their students (75–100%) used science vocabulary during in-class workshops, gallery tours, and workshops	73
During discussions about artwork, students used visual art vocabulary	74
Teachers reported that all or most of their students (75–100%) used visual art vocabulary during in-class workshops, gallery tours, and workshops	74
Sixth Grade	
Teachers reported that all or most of their students (75–100%) used math vocabulary during in-class workshops, gallery tours, and workshops	73
During discussions about artwork, students used visual art vocabulary	70
Teachers reported that all or most of their students (75–100%) used visual art vocabulary during in-class workshops, gallery tours, and workshops	89

captured during the observations. The subsequent analysis and reporting balanced these two data sets by recognizing that while teachers had a higher perception of students' vocabulary use, they reported about this via survey days and sometimes weeks after their students' participation in the program. The structured program observation, however, was collected in real time and was less vulnerable to retrospective survey challenges (Campbell & Stanley, 1963). The differences between the teacher surveys and observations were weighed carefully and examined in contrast with other data, including student assessments. These assessments did not reach the desired levels of achievement, which allowed the external evaluation to triangulate the student outcomes. This analysis resulted in the external evaluation's recommendation to rework the curriculum and instruction. This recommendation kicked off the "B" stage of the evaluation, with Don stepping in to begin the developmental evaluation process and I stepped back.

B: Developmental Evaluation Process and Outcomes

Exploratory Work
Don: The Barnes staff gathered and sent the program materials for review and then invited me to view the art collection in Philadelphia and to observe several gallery sessions taught by docents and classroom-based pre- and post- activities taught by the museum educator. For these two days of participant observation, I wrote field notes, documented samples of student work, and informally conducted interviews with the museum educator and students.

Content Analysis
Don: With this observational data in mind, a curricular document analysis was then conducted. The first was an analysis of the program materials for the frequency of art, math, and science content that was explicitly noted. The program materials included a binder for teachers explaining the program goals and expectations, sections on each set of activities of the Art of Looking program, and some color reproductions of key images from the collection. The main curricular connection being explored between the arts and science was the role of light in the perception of color. The element of color in relation to light was referenced 51 times, making it the most frequently mentioned concept. Artistic effect and art historical background information had less than half that frequency, and only a few references were made to a narrative story.

Table 10.5   Content standards addressed by visual art instructional activities

Pennsylvania core art standards	Assessment evidence	Level of instructional focus (0–none, 1–limited, 2–sustained, 3–extended)
9.1.5.C: Know and use fundamental vocabulary within each of the art forms.	Initial worksheet, survey, discussions	3
9.1.5.A: Know and use elements and principles of each art form to create works in the arts and humanities.	Arts activities, looking at art	3
9.3.5.A: Identify critical processes in the examination of works of arts and humanities.	Discussions	2
9.4.5.D: Explain choices made regarding media, technique, form, subject matter, and themes that communicate the artist's philosophy, within a work in the arts and humanities.	Discussions	2
9.3.5.D: Compare similar and contrasting important aspects of works in the arts and humanities based on a set of guidelines using a comprehensive vocabulary of critical response.	Initial worksheet, discussions	1

Curricular and Assessment Alignment

Don: The next analysis was a simple mapping of the curricular activities and assessment with the stated curricular goals as listed in the program materials, in this case, the Pennsylvania arts and science standards. The curricular materials were reviewed again looking for opportunities where instruction was provided and/or assessment evidence was being elicited either explicitly or implicitly to meet the identified learning standards. This analysis of the curricular alignment and gaps provided some evidence of what content standards were actually being addressed in the original curriculum. In this case, standards for the arts were being addressed by sustained or extended instructional activities, but science content had limited opportunities for instruction. No assessment evidence was available to demonstrate evidence of understanding or ability for any of the standards (see Tables 10.5 and 10.6).

Root Cause Analysis

Don: Based on my exploratory analysis, student work review, qualitative observations, and interviews about the program and its context, a root

Table 10.6   Content standards addressed by science instructional activities

Pennsylvania core science standards	Assessment evidence	Level of instructional focus (0–none, 1–limited, 2–sustained, 3–extended)
S5.A.1.1.1: Explain how certain questions can be answered through scientific inquiry and/or technological design.		1
S5.A.1.1.2 Explain how observations and/or experimental results are used to support inferences and claims about an investigation or relationship.		1
S5.A.1.1.3: Describe how explanations, predictions, and models are developed using evidence.		1
S5.A.2.1.1: Design a simple, controlled experiment (fair test) identifying dependent and independent variables.		0
S5.A.3.2.1: Describe how models are used to better understand the relationships in natural systems.		0
S5.B.3.2.2: Describe the usefulness of Earth's physical resources as raw materials for the human-made world.		0
S5.C.1.1.1: Identify the characteristic properties of matter that are independent of mass and volume.		0

cause analysis was conducted (Langley et al., 2009). The data was displayed in a fishbone diagram to organize the possible root causes of the limited engagement and learning outcomes identified in the external evaluation and to situate them in the more complex system. Figure 10.2 allowed the study group to see the bigger system and to identify what aspects the group could work to improve. The root cause analysis showed how limited student learning may have been caused by weak cross-curricular connections, overly complex activities, and no assessment or feedback.

The fishbone diagram was a visual diagram that helped the selection and focus on a manageable set of improvement areas (e.g., weak curricular connections, overly complex activities, and no assessment feedback), as well as to see where these areas might fit into and possibly influence the rest of the system (e.g., teacher engagement). The district transition to the Next Generation Science Standards also seemed like an opportunity. This visual

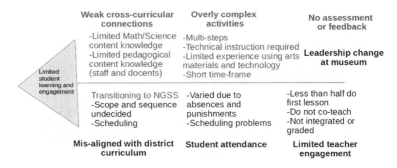

Fig. 10.2 Root cause analysis

display of inter-connected problems and conditions helped us to "see the system" and begin to not only understand why it was producing limited outcomes, but where we might strategically develop and test new approaches.

Provisional Report and Study Group Map
Don: This exploratory analysis was provided to the Barnes Foundation as a report and served to take stock of the current situation, as well as provide a proposed map of actions for our design study group to address in the process of redesign. The report also provided initial data for collaboratively reviewing or generating the desired learning results, assessment evidence, and learning activities for the revised Art of Looking program.

The exploratory work provided data to better understand the complex system that the program inhabits—and then make strategic decisions about how to proceed. Based on the initial external evaluation findings, the exploratory data gathering, and a literature scan of STEAM programs, a series of design group goals emerged to drive our collective design work as a design study group. These recommendations were made by me in response to the Art of Looking curriculum review:

- enhance cross-curricular connections across content and practices;
- align materials with the relevant National Core Arts Standards, Next Generation Science Standards, and Common Core State Standards-Math;
- design authentic performance assessment tasks with opportunities for practice and feedback; and
- ensure accessibility and flexibility of activities and resources to address learning variability and cultural diversity.

The exploratory process and contributions by the study group members also generated a set of design principles to guide our design work:

- start with wonder and be discovery-oriented;
- investigate, plan, make;
- experiment with materials and effects;
- establish and practice looking strategies and routines for making inferences based on evidence (Claim-Evidence-Reasoning);
- scaffold activities with practice and feedback toward a novel performance assessment task or design challenge; and
- pitch content at student developmental and interest level.

The Study Design Group

Don: We began our collective work following our map and using our design principles. We started with the desired results expressed in big ideas, essential questions, and content standards. During the second meeting, we began to develop authentic performance assessments based on specific selected standards that took the form of a design challenge—a common task for STEM project-based learning and assessment. The next three group meetings used a conference call platform and an online collaborative tool to share and comment on the curricular design, student work evidence, and other data from the iterative testing of materials and activities. In the next sections, we will feature three of our developmental evaluation and design strategies: self-surveys, feedback protocols, and iterative testing.

Using Surveys to Jump-Start Design Study Group Discussions
In this section, we will focus on the use of online surveys administered to the design study group members to gather collective ideas, thoughts, and knowledge. The idea was to take stock of knowledge and elicit ratings or rankings on curricular elements prior to our meetings. The surveys would introduce the goal of our study group work and then ask several quick related items. The analysis of the responses was organized in a simple visual display for the group to consider at the beginning of the next session. The aim was to learn more about each other, take stock of our knowledge, surface any areas of great variance, and jump-start our discussions in the limited time that we had together.

Although the design study group included math/science educators as resources and collaborators, we wanted to make sure that we were all on a similar page with some common experiences and familiarity with the vocabulary, concepts, and practices of our respective disciplines. To gain a picture of our levels of content knowledge, a short online survey was administered to the design study group members prior to our first meeting. One of the items on the survey asked that each member self-rate themselves on a scale from 0 to 5 on their level of content expertise for a series of arts, science, and math concepts that had been noted in the program materials (see Table 10.7).

The simply displayed results provided a visual map of our group's content expertise levels in the three subject areas. The arts educators tended to rate themselves more highly for the arts content and at a mid-level for math and science. On the other hand, the math/science educators rated themselves highly for science and math content but low on their arts knowledge. This was the area of greatest variance in the group. Because the math and science folks had less experience with the arts, the design study group started with a common art activity. The group went down into the galleries to experience what students typically do in the galleries—using the Barnes method of close looking and analysis. The group then returned to reflect on the experience in relation to the program redesign. This experience allowed us to have an experience-based discussion on the process of art looking and the potential relationships between science content and practices. The discussion also surfaced an issue around

Table 10.7 Frequency distribution of content knowledge of science, math, and arts ($n = 6$)

Curricular concept	0	1 Novice	2	3	4	5 Expert	SUM	VAR
Energy			1	3	1	1	20	1.1
Physical sciences			1	4		1	19	1.0
Electromagnetic radiation			2	3	1		17	0.6
Measurement, ratio, and scale				3	3		21	0.3
Geometry			1	4	1		18	0.4
Polygons			1	4	1		18	0.4
Visual perception		2		1	1	2	19	3.4
Neuroscience			4	1	1		15	0.7
Painting		1	1		1	3	22	3.1
Scale and perspective			2		2	2	22	1.9
Color theory			2		2	2	22	1.9
Visual arts		2			1	3	21	3.9
Impressionism		2			1	3	21	3.9

using figurative words like "magic" to explain artistic effects. One of the science educators asked that docents not use that type of language because they are talking about real science: visual perception and the physics of light (see Table 10.8).

Another item on the survey asked the group members to rank curricular connections of the visual arts to the Next Generation Science Standards and then rate the curricular strength of the connections on a five-point scale. The idea was to introduce the standards and move quickly to selecting the most relevant standards for the program revision. The discussion around the data table helped the group make a key transition in the program design from focusing on science content, to focusing on scientific processes, with one science/math educator observing:

> ...it might be wise for us to really focus on incorporating the science and engineering practices (SEP) and cross-cutting concepts (CCC) more than spending a lot of time on the physical science concepts. The practices and CCC are more timeless and universal and will be something that students are covering throughout each grade. I'm not suggesting to completely cut out physical science connections (because I think there is still a lot to be learned about light, etc. through looking at visual art) but maybe they are just not the emphasis.

Another survey was administered before our second meeting that gathered ratings on aspects of our initial design decisions. Each item helped us to give collective feedback on the key learning outcomes, big ideas, and

Table 10.8 Ranking of the most relevant Next Generation Science Standards (NGSS) with the strength of curricular connections to the visual arts

Most relevant NGSS (N = 4)	Average ranking	Strength of art connection (0–5)
1. Engaging in argument from evidence	16.0	3.5
2. Planning and carrying out investigations	15.0	3.5
3. Analyzing and interpreting data	14.4	3.0
4. Scale, proportion, and quantity	13.8	4.5
5. Using mathematics and computational thinking	13.4	3.5
6. Asking questions and defining problems	12.6	4.0
7. Patterns	12.4	4.7
8. Developing and using models	12.2	3.3
9. Constructing explanations and designing solutions	11.6	3.8
10. Physical sciences	11.0	4.0

essential questions. Our iterative design decisions on our desired results were then reported in a basic curriculum mapping tool (see Table 10.9). During this study group, the arts educator, who runs a maker's lab, invited us to experience a design challenge. The group did the task together to help us think about how to design our performance assessment task so that it fostered curiosity, fun, collaboration, and rich evidence of evidence-based thinking. The study group also examined student work samples from the original program using a discussion protocol. The assessment analysis helped the group to identify common misunderstandings of the concepts and recognize challenges with the tools or technology.

Facilitating Design and Evaluation Routines Remotely
The self-surveys served to set up routines in the initial face-to-face study group sessions to focus on practical data and iterative testing. After the group settled on a provisional set of desired outcomes in the form of a few targeted standards, big ideas, and essential questions, it was time to move on to designing the aligned performance assessments and learning activities. At this point, the evaluator played more of a facilitator role by providing documentation tools, discussion protocols, and guidelines for interview and observation for the Barnes educators to use.

Table 10.9   Basic curriculum map

Desired results		*Assessment evidence*	*Learning activities*
Big idea:	Artists and scientists use disciplined inquiry, observation, and classification		
Essential question:	How can we act like scientists when we look at art?		
Driving/guiding question(s):	How are things organized and classified?		
Standards:	NGSS/Science and Engineering Practices: Engaging in argument from evidence		
	Visual Arts/Responding (VA:Re8.1): Interpret art by analyzing the characteristics of form and structure, contextual information, subject matter, visual elements, and the use of media to identify ideas and mood conveyed		
	Visual Arts/Creating (VA:Cr2.1): Experiment and develop skills in multiple art-making techniques and approaches		

The final three study groups were conducted using a conference call system and Google Docs. The activities between the group sessions included designing assessments and activities and testing out the arts materials and processes by the group members and then with students during a summer program. The curriculum designers organized their materials in a curriculum map, wrote the assessment and activity descriptions, took photos of resulting artwork, and conducted informal interviews with students about the experience. Many of these items were shared in Google Drive and available for ongoing peer and evaluator comment and questions.

A key strategy for our remote design study group was to use protocols to guide our review, analysis, and feedback on program elements. The protocols provided the steps to guide a purpose-driven, structured, and time-bound discussion. This provided the group with a way to have focused sharing, discussion, and feedback in a safe, facilitated space. The protocols were used to share iterations of activities for formative peer feedback, share student work samples to assess for student understanding of the concepts and student ability to use the materials, and share observations and student feedback. After several iterations, the assessment tasks and activities evolved into a fully scaffolded program design, and the work of the design study group came to an end. The Barnes education staff then pilot-tested the curriculum in the Fall and decided to bring back the external evaluator to see how the program revision worked.

A: External Evaluation Year Two Findings

Patti: As the developmental evaluation concluded, I stepped back in to conduct a second round of external evaluation. We found during Year Two that students engaged in more critical thinking behaviors, spent less time passively listening and more time in hands-on learning, and used more STEM and visual art vocabulary in class discussions and project work.

Table 10.10 highlights the growth in the program's objectives between Years One and Two.

Some objectives had modest growth, whereas others changed significantly. In addition to some new learning objectives, there was an adjustment made to the data collection methods between Years One and Two. Year One included a pre-/post-program assessment or quiz of student learning of the key program concepts. This tool was dropped in the second

Table 10.10   External evaluation findings, comparing Years One and Two

	Year One	*Year Two*
Fifth Grade and Sixth Grade		
During in-class workshops and tours, fifth and sixth grade students demonstrated critical thinking skills through scientific practices	23%	85%
During in-class workshops and tours, fifth and sixth grade students were actively engaged rather than passively listening	13%	32%
During the workshops and gallery tours, students accurately used STEM vocabulary	41%	82%
Fifth Grade		
Teachers reported that all or most of their students (75–100%) used science vocabulary during in-class workshops, gallery tours, and workshops	73%	75%
Teachers reported that all or most of their students (75–100%) used visual arts vocabulary during in-class workshops, gallery tours, and workshops	74%	84%
During discussions about artwork, students used visual arts vocabulary	74% of observations	47% of observations
Students incorporated scientific observations into their artwork	Developed for Year Two	90%
Students completed the claim, evidence, reasoning worksheet to demonstrate their understanding	Developed for Year Two	93%
During Art of Looking gallery tours and workshops, students conducted scientific experiments to investigate conservation problems	Developed for Year Two	100%
During activities, students demonstrated visual arts concepts	Developed for Year Two	72% of observations
Sixth Grade		
Teachers reported that all or most of their students (75–100%) used math vocabulary during in-class workshops, gallery tours, and workshops	73%	83%
During discussions about artwork, students used visual arts vocabulary	70%	78% of observations
Teachers reported that all or most of their students (75–100%) used visual arts vocabulary during in-class workshops, gallery tours, and workshops	89%	92%
Students incorporated mathematical principles into their elevation drawings	Developed for Year Two	78%
Students incorporated mathematical principles into their gallery videos	Developed for Year Two	90%
Students reconstructed a three-dimensional configuration based on a two-dimensional image	Developed for Year Two	78%

year after the developmental evaluation process. Rather than use a traditional quiz, the change was made to use embedded assessments, which Don championed during the design process as useful measures and data for Year Two. The new embedded assessments solved our conundrum of finding data that reflected authentic student learning. The removal of pre/post quizzes to fully focus on embedded assessments was a compromise that was worth making. The Barnes Foundation staff had a more accurate picture of student learning, even if it could not be compared to the first year's data.

Nearly all of the Year Two results demonstrated progress over Year One. The one area of student learning where we did not see improvement was in fifth graders' use of visual art vocabulary. We posited this was due to the increased focus on STEM vocabulary in the revised curriculum, reducing the opportunities to use visual art vocabulary.

CONCLUSION

Upon reflection, we came to understand that our concurrent approaches were collectively contributing to the evaluation in three main ways:

- Building relationships, gaining entry, and managing expectations: We clarified with staff over time as to what was possible and manageable to measure within the contextual constraints. We were able to encourage sharing and integrating of the external evaluation data with the design study group work and vice versa;
- Building design and evaluation capacity: Patti developed instruments to gather program data and peer-score observations. The study group process developed a series of design tools and protocols for supporting reflection and feedback routines, as well as led to an embedded assessment that was then used in the external evaluation; and
- Using digital documentation with remote sharing and collaboration: Technology was an instrumental solution to fostering a coherent collaboration. Student artifacts such as artwork were digitally imaged and stored online for sharing. Video recording was heavily used to document the program sessions and collaborators frequently met via video conferencing and used online collaboration tools.

The process we described in this chapter emerged organically and resulted in an A–B–A design. Each step informed the next, building on each other toward concrete program improvements. The intermingling of external and developmental evaluation offers potential for programs examining growth in their practice. The selection of evaluators, whose expertise was complementary but not redundant, created more opportunity for idea generation and problem-solving as the process developed. In addition to our unique evaluation perspectives, we both were grounded in different art forms. Don's education and artistic practice in visual art was fundamental in thinking about students' arts learning. Patti's background in the performing arts brought an informed distance, being close enough to understand but not so close as to make assumptions.

Patti: Collaborating with Don was a valuable bridge to the Barnes as well. He knew the galleries and had boots-on-the-ground experiences with staff and the space. Our discussions after the summer design work added additional perspective and insight into the programs and organization. Working with Don to unpack what was learned during the developmental evaluation informed the changes we subsequently made to the Year Two external evaluation.

Don: Being able to collaborate with Patti on this A–B–A improvement process was a valuable and initially unplanned opportunity. Patti had the museum education experience to set up an external evaluation to get at student learning and engagement—but with the added challenge of having to do it remotely. Talking with her provided me with the context and initial findings that I may not have had access to if we had not tried to collaborate. It also helped me to set up an embedded assessment of student learning that could be used by program staff and then was picked up by Patti in the follow-up evaluation. I can imagine how a more formal collaboration that uses a developmental evaluation approach in between two external program evaluations would get us even further if was intentionally planned!

Don and Patti: Future projects that take on this A–B–A design would be well-served to integrate the evaluators as early as possible in the process. The reciprocity between us enriched the work that either would have done alone. Because neither the developmental evaluation nor the external evaluation's second year had been part of the initial plan, the opportunity was truncated to better pool our expertise and align our processes. While we did not have the advantage of an early start in our work together, we did make good use of it in Year Two of the external evaluation. Having a more formalized evaluation team that conducts an A–B–A type of evaluation would make for even better alignment, coherence, and quality of evaluation measurement throughout the development and improvement process.

Ultimately, the collective work between museum staff, evaluators, and curriculum consultants resulted in a stronger overall project. Over the course of this collaborative work, staff capacity grew significantly in program development and implementation. Their ownership of the evaluation process and outcomes was positively impacted by this effort. We were also heartened that the process of involving content expertise teams in iterative design and testing seemed to be a routine that would be adopted for future education program work.

REFERENCES

Blythe, T., Allen, D., & Powell, B. S. (1999). *Looking together at student work: A companion guide to assessing student learning.* New York, NY: Teachers College Press.

Bryk, A. S., Gomez, L. M., Grunow, A., & LeMahieu, P. G. (2015). *Learning to improve: How America's schools can get better at getting better.* Cambridge, MA: Harvard Education Press.

Campbell, D. T., & Stanley, J. C. (1963). *Experimental and quasi-experimental designs for research.* Chicago, IL: Rand McNally.

Dolkart, J. F. (2012). To see how the artist sees: Albert C. Barnes and the experiment in education. In *Masterworks: The Barnes Foundation.* New York, NY and Philadelphia, PA: Skira Rizzoli Publications, Inc., and The Barnes Foundation.

DuFour, R., DuFour, R., & Eaker, R. (2008). *Revisiting professional learning communities at work: New insights for improving schools.* Bloomington, IN: Solution Tree Press.

Elmore, R. F. (2002). *Bridging the gap between standards and achievement: The imperative for professional development in education.* Washington, DC: Albert Shankar Institute.

Enomoto, E., & Bair, M. (1999). The role of the school in the assimilation of immigrant children: A case study of Arab Americans. *International Journal of Curriculum and Instruction, 1,* 45–66.

Fetterman, D., & Wandersman, A. (2005). *Empowerment evaluation principles in practice.* New York, NY: The Guilford Press.

Gopalakrishnan, S., Preskill, H., Gopal, S., & Lu, S. (2013). *Next generation evaluation: Embracing complexity, connectivity, and change, a learning brief.* FSG.

Langley, G. J., Moen, R. D., Nolan, K. M., Nolan, T. W., Norman, C. L., & Provost, L. P. (2009). *The improvement guide: A practical approach to enhancing organizational performance* (2nd ed.). San Francisco, CA: Jossey-Bass.

McDonald, J. P., Mohr, N., Dichter, A., & McDonald, E. C. (2003). *The power of protocols: An educators guide to better practice.* New York, NY: Teachers College Press.

Meyer, A., Rose, D. H., & Gordon, D. (2014). *Universal design for learning: Theory and practice.* Wakefield, MA: CAST Professional Publishing.

Patton, M. Q. (1997). *Utilization-focused evaluation* (3rd ed.). Thousand Oaks, CA: Sage.

Patton, M. Q. (2011). *Developmental evaluation: Applying complexity concepts to enhance innovation and use.* New York, NY: The Guilford Press.

Patton, M. Q. (2015). State of the art and practice of developmental evaluation: Answers to common and recurring questions. In M. Patton, K. McKegg, & N. Wehipeihana (Eds.), *Developmental evaluation exemplars: Principles in practice* (pp. 1–24). New York, NY: Guilford Press.

Smylie, M. A., Allensworth, E., Greenberg, R. C., Harris, R., & Luppescu, S. (2001). *Teacher professional development in Chicago: Supporting effective practice.* Chicago, IL: Consortium on Chicago School Research.

Spradley, J. (1980). *Participant observation.* Belmont, CA: Wadsworth.

Wei, R., Darling-Hammond, L., Andree, A., Richardson, N., & Orphanos, S. (2009). *Professional learning in the learning profession: A status report on teacher development in the United States and abroad.* Dallas, TX: National Staff Development Council.

Wenger, E., McDermott, R., & Snyder, W. M. (2002). *A guide to managing knowledge: Cultivating communities of practice.* Cambridge, MA: Harvard Business School.

Wiggins, G., & McTighe, J. (1998). *Understanding by design.* Alexandria, VA: Association of Supervision and Curriculum Development.

CHAPTER 11

Stages, Sights & Sounds: Evaluating Student Engagement with Live, Multimedia Arts Performance

Rekha S. Rajan and Jeanette E. Goddard

The experience of seeing a live performance for the first time can be life-changing. Lights dim, music swells, and the audience is no longer in a performance hall but is experiencing the decorated stage, adorned backdrop, scenery, accessories, and props strategically placed as the actors bring the story to life.

What makes live performance so unique? Its earliest influences on society can be traced to the informal artistic performances—music, theater, dance—of nearly every culture. The importance of understanding audience response to live performance has been partially documented in the literature, most recently noting how a unique relationship exists between the performers and audience members (Barker, 2003; Pitts, 2005a). Pitts (2005b) found that adults who attended chamber music festivals in the UK felt strengthened through artistic bonds and social communities. Reason (2004) examined the "liveness" of audience response and participation,

R.S. Rajan (✉)
PANCH RESEARCH, LLC, Chicago, IL, USA

J.E. Goddard
Trine University, Angola, IN, USA

© The Author(s) 2018
R.S. Rajan, I.C. O'Neal (eds.), *Arts Evaluation and Assessment*,
https://doi.org/10.1007/978-3-319-64116-4_11

inviting students from the University of Edinburgh to attend, reflect, and discuss live theater. He found that audience members have specific perceptions and expectations of the performance, regardless of their prior knowledge or interest in the content of the show, including what it will be like to be in the audience (context).

Performance attendance traditionally takes place outside of the school, within communities or large-scale performance halls. Distinctions between the types of performances students see and where the performances occur are important. Typically, students' engagement with the arts and the development of arts partnerships focus on students' experiences in school instead of the performance venues that are available to them within their communities.

In this chapter, we (the lead evaluator and the program manager for the pilot program) present the process of evaluating student engagement with live, multimedia performance. By collaborating in this chapter, we are able to present the development of the evaluation and the views and goals that the Chicago Humanities Festival put forth. By utilizing an Outcomes-Based Evaluation (OBE) model, we focused on conducting interviews, distributing surveys, and analyzing data from journals, artwork, multimedia, and videos. We sought to capture the essence of experiencing live performance for these students, many of whom were seeing a theatrical show for the first time, and tried to define "student engagement" with live performance. Over the course of two months, students participated in an arts-integrated program, beginning within their classrooms, extending into their community, and concluding with their own school-based performances and reflections. We examined the collected data to identify how the interactions among teachers, students, and visiting artists can contribute to student learning, and to examine the impact of live performance in their lives.

CONTEXT

Since its inception over 25 years ago, the Chicago Humanities Festival (CHF) has provided high-quality public programming in the humanities for the greater Chicago area. Opportunities for students in grades K-12 to experience the humanities through CHF include a range of experiences from interviews with authors to theater performances. For 15 years, one of these opportunities was the annual youth performance festival, Stages, Sights & Sounds. This festival was the centerpiece of CHF's educational programming, featuring innovative international performances presented in theatrical venues across the city every spring.

In looking at the current data-driven trend of artist residencies in the classroom, CHF wanted to see what might be the combined impact of a field trip paired with a short-term teaching artist residency integrated into the classrooms' curriculum. Because CHF is primarily a public presentation organization, the field trip to the matinee would remain the focal point of the Stages Engagement Pilot Program and of the evaluation.

The Stages Education Engagement Pilot Program (SEPP) was developed as an extension of the First Time for a Lifetime initiative of the Chicago Humanities Festival. The goal of the pilot program was to examine student learning around, and appreciation for, live theater by including in-class activities to support students' experiences at a Stages performance of *The Adventures of Alvin Sputnik: Deep Sea Explorer*, a multimedia show created by Australian, Tim Watts. This unique approach to arts education and engagement brought teaching artists into the classroom, and also brought the students into their community to watch this performance at a local theater. The reciprocal experience was important, allowing students both to gain an appreciation for the arts within their classroom and to realize that these experiences are accessible to them at their own leisure.

A 2013 research report by Chicago Arts Partnerships in Education (CAPE), an organization that services the same geographic area as CHF, detailed academic gains made by low achieving students in classrooms that participated in a program where teaching artists were paired with their classroom (Burnaford & Scripp, 2013). While more assessment has been done on teaching artist residency programs, the impact of arts and culture field trips has a relatively shallow research pool. In fact, research from the University of Arkansas on the educational value of cultural field trips, undertaken because of the creation of a museum where students previously had no access to artwork, was published shortly before the Stages Education Engagement Pilot began (Kisida, Bowen, & Greene, 2014). Specifically, their research found that a one-hour field trip to a museum has long-term impacts on student learning. While more work needs to be done, this research provides promising initial data that cultural field trips are an important component of student learning.

METHODS

By 2014, CHF had engaged students as audience members for years but had not formally evaluated the impact of these programs. Since securing funding for arts-related education programs often requires demonstrating a measurable impact on the students that participate in the program, analyzing students' experiences at Stages became a priority.

The goal of the pilot program was to examine student learning and appreciation for live theater. To reach this goal, CHF selected an innovative multimedia performance entitled *The Adventures of Alvin Sputnik: Deep Sea Explorer* from May 5 to 10, 2014, around which to focus the Stages Engagement Pilot Program (see Fig. 11.1).

This particular show, developed and presented by one performer from Australia, embedded the use of video, sound, lights, puppetry, and audience interaction. While, there were five international performances around which the program might have been developed, the ultimate decision to focus on *Alvin Sputnik* was based on the multimedia aspect of the show, the lack of dependence on language for understanding (since one of the classrooms was bilingual), and on the availability of a full-length preview DVD for teachers. Teachers were much more comfortable agreeing to

Fig. 11.1 Photo from the production *The Adventures of Alvin Sputnik*. Pictured Tim Watts. Photo credit to Michelle Robin Anderson. Photo provided courtesy of Laura Colby of Elsie Management

participate in the program when given an opportunity to preview the full performance in advance. This also helped the teaching artists to create meaningful and authentic tie-ins for the performance.

Two school sites located in Chicago, Illinois, were pre-selected for collaboration in this pilot program. A total of four classrooms—two fifth-grade (one of which was a Spanish-speaking, bilingual classroom) and two ninth-grade—three classroom teachers, and two teaching artists (one visual artist and one theater artist) participated in the evaluation.

Once the participating classes were selected, the program provided an opportunity for the teaching artist and classroom teachers to co-plan the in-class activities. They were required to have a pre- and post-activity that was developed independently of the other classrooms and projects. The collaborations resulted in fifth graders making a puppet (similar to the one they would see in the show—see Fig. 11.1) and the ninth graders making a reflective work that focused on a personal fear (similar to the struggles of the protagonist in the show).

Prior to the teaching artists' first visit, each teacher was given information about the teaching artist, the goals and requirements of the program, and a full DVD of the performance of *Alvin Sputnik* to preview. The teaching artists were also provided with the goals and requirements of the program, the detailed information about the school and class with which they would be working, and the full-length DVD of the performance.

In the selected elementary school, one teaching artist worked with two different fifth-grade classrooms. Those teachers and the teaching artist, who focused on theater, planned together in a day-long session. The program provided funding for substitute teachers, as well as paying the teaching artist for her planning time. For the high school teacher and the teaching artist, who focused on visual arts, it was easier to plan in shorter increments over a series of weeks at the school. Despite the differences in planning logistics, in both instances, the goal was to help facilitate the work between teacher and teaching artist in order to create a curriculum-integrated learning experience for students around the matinee performance. In both cases, the in-person joint planning time was approximately six hours.

THE EVALUATION PLAN

Developing an evaluation plan for this pilot program provided a unique set of tasks. First, there were two different age groups (fifth and ninth grades), one fifth-grade classroom that was bilingual, two different schools (an elementary and a secondary school), and two different teaching artists, both using different artistic mediums (theater and visual arts).

Second, because of the short time frame during which the performances ran (one week), and the minimal two visits from teaching artists, this program evaluation focused on examining the impact of two activities on student engagement. The main activity was the experience of attending a live performance. The supporting activities were a short-term, in-classroom artist residency that included two class visits—one prior to the performance and one after. This embedded framework provided us with an outline for establishing data collection, including pre- and post-surveys that were distributed to all students (see Fig. 11.2).

Assessments included a pre-program survey, a post-performance survey, and a post-program survey. The pre-program and post-program surveys posed nearly identical questions to capture changes in attitude over time. Based on the goals of the program, the principal objectives of the evaluation were to investigate:

1. The process of implementing a pilot program focused on attending live performance
2. The program's impact on defining and extending students' engagement before and after a multimedia, theatrical performance
3. The program's impact on students' understanding of a multimedia theatrical performance

Data were collected during three time points, pre-program activities, a post-performance survey, and post-program activities. In order to investigate student learning and to include multiple perspectives to best understand the impact of this program on student engagement, data were collected from surveys, observations, and interviews with students. Although it was not a focus of the evaluation, teacher and teaching artist perspectives were also explored to provide additional perspectives:

- Pre-program, post-performance, and post-program surveys of classroom teachers ($N = 3$), teaching artists ($N = 2$), and students ($N = 72$).
- Interviews with SEPP participants, including classroom teachers ($N = 3$), teaching artists ($N = 2$), and students ($N = 16$).

Date _____ School _____ Age ____

Circle a number from 1 to 5, indicating how much you agree with each sentence.

If you circle a "5" that means you really agree with the sentence.

If you circle a "1" that means you really do not agree with the sentence.

	1	2	3	4	5
1. I enjoy watching live, theater shows	1	2	3	4	5
2. It was exciting to attend a live performance	1	2	3	4	5
3. I learned something new from the live performance	1	2	3	4	5
4. I enjoy working with my classmates	1	2	3	4	5
5. I enjoyed the show the Adventures of Alvin Sputnik	1	2	3	4	5
6. I would like to see another live performance	1	2	3	4	5
7. I would like to perform on stage	1	2	3	4	5
8. I prefer to learn about the arts than other academic subjects	1	2	3	4	5
9. I learned something new from the teaching artist who visited our class	1	2	3	4	5
10. I think the arts are very interesting	1	2	3	4	5

How did you feel while watching the show *The Adventures of Alvin Sputnik?*

Did you learn anything new after attending the show, The Adventures of Alvin Sputnik?

Are you interested in attending more live, multimedia shows?

Fig. 11.2 Student post-program survey template

- Descriptive observations of the SEPP planning meetings, pre-performance and post-performance activities, and collaborative meetings between classroom teachers and teaching artists from both schools.
- Student work samples gathered from the pre-performance and post-performance activities in each of the classrooms (selected samples from the classroom teachers).

The interview data were recorded using a digital recorder and were transcribed and coded for emerging and recurring themes representative of student learning and engagement.

RESULTS

The following sections contain findings of the key constructs related to student engagement with live, multimedia performance. These include (1) Interest in Attending a Live Performance, (2) Interest in the Show's Content, (3) Learning about the Arts, (4) Engagement with Live, Multimedia Performance, (5) Learning about Theater and Multimedia Arts, and (6) Making Connections.

Each of these six constructs is presented in accordance with our time-line of data collection—pre-program activities, post-performance survey, and post-program activities. We also weave our conclusions throughout these sections before moving into a brief discussion on teacher and teaching artist collaborations.

PRE-PROGRAM

The fifth-grade students (versus the ninth-grade students) were particularly excited to have the chance to see *The Adventures of Alvin Sputnik*. Many of the students had never attended a live theatrical show prior to this experience, while some students had attended an opera or a play with their class near the beginning of the school year. In the first survey distributed to students by the classroom teacher and completed prior to their performance attendance, students were asked to describe how they felt about attending the show, *The Adventures of Alvin Sputnik*, and if they were interested in attending live theatrical performances. Their responses revealed that the content of the show was an important aspect of what the students found appealing. As demonstrated by the following quotes, the concepts of "adventure" and use of puppets were interesting components for students. They also hoped to learn more about controlling puppets, performing on stage, and live theater through their experience at the show. Additionally, the opportunity to see live theater made students feel lucky, honored, and excited:

- I'm kind of excited since in the title it says the Adventures of Alvin sputnik and I like adventures.
- I feel very excited about attending this show because I want to find out what is it about. Also try to figure out how they control all the puppets at the same time. I am very excited to see how the puppets look and move.
- I feel very excited because I always loved shows and because the "adventures of Alvin Sputnik" I never heard it before and I'd love to see and learn new things about it.
- I feel excited because I want to know more about different kinds of arts and how they are showed.

In addition to excitement regarding the content, some students were apprehensive about attending a show and wanted more information in advance about the content and length of the performance. This concern arose in the following responses:

- I am excited about attending the show Alvin Sputnik but I would be even more excited about it if I had some background knowledge on the subject. I assume that it will be very entertaining.
- I feel like nervous because I never go to a theater show.

In the pre-program survey, students were also asked if they were interested in attending live theatrical shows. The concept of puppetry was particularly interesting to students, as many expressed a desire to learn about and use puppets. Students also shared that they enjoyed the experience of live theater as it afforded them the chance to see performers on stage and get "drawn into" the show. For many of these students, they were going to see a show for the first time. Finally, students also hoped to learn more about the arts through their experience:

- I am since I have never gone to one so I'm not sure how it really works.

- I am interested in live theatrical shows because I have never went to a live theatrical show.
- I am interested because this is going to be my first live theatrical show. I want to go this when was little. I think it going to be a lot of cool.
- I feel very lucky to be chosen to watch this play. Because I love puppets and plays.

Learning About the Arts

Students were interested in learning more about the performing arts as audience members and as artists. Through this experience, they described their own aspirations for being on stage, dancing, acting, or manipulating their own puppets. A few students noted their experience performing, and others highlighted the ability to learn from and enjoy others' performances. The students also knew that the show involved puppetry, and they were interested in what they would learn about puppets through attending the show:

- I think it would be a fun and great experience, and I am a dancer so I am used to being on stage and people looking at me.
- I could … learn different kinds of things that I haven't learned.
- I am interested in attending live theatrical shows because it's a cool way to see how performers act on stage.
- I've grown up performing and that involves seeing many shows that vary from play to musical.

In the fifth-grade classrooms, students created a puppet that was made of the same basic materials as Alvin—a Styrofoam ball and a white glove. In the activity pre-performance, students decorated their puppet, gave it a name, and created a backstory, which they wrote about in their "puppet journal"; they also worked on basic manipulations of the puppet, which included walking, greeting, and talking. The classroom teachers extended the activity further by having students reflect on the activity in their puppet journal after the teaching artist's visit.

In the ninth-grade classrooms, students prepared to attend the matinee by creating "fear landscapes." Through the use of various materials, the students created three-layered visual pieces that depicted themselves in a location, an overlay that made the location frightening for them, and a final layer that depicted themselves taking control of the environment and dispelling their fear. This project drew on the fear of the unknown that the main character in the performance, Alvin, has in venturing to the bottom of the sea, and how he ultimately masters that fear.

POST-PERFORMANCE

Students were surveyed at two separate points after watching the show. One survey was given to students immediately after they watched the performance. This allowed us to capture their immediate reflections rather than only collect data on their thoughts several days after the performance concluded. Upon exiting the theater, but before leaving the building, students were asked to reflect on their feelings and understanding of the performance, of attending a live show, and on the content of the production.

Students' emotions right after seeing the show were reflective and poignant. While students were happy to see the show and found some of the plot to be funny, others were sad because of the main character's search for his wife and his death at the end of the show. The show had many lighter moments within it, but the main character, Alvin, dies while successfully saving the world in the show's conclusion. In the survey, many students reflected on their mixed emotions about the show, though they appreciated and valued the plot:

- Sad because it was entertaining and I did not want it to end.
- I have mixed emotions I feel happy yet sad.
- Amazed and sad because when Alvin and Alina died. I felt amazed because I have never actually seen a play before.

In addition to enjoying the show, the character of Alvin, and the adventurous plot, students were also drawn to the technology and animation used to support the story. *The Adventures of Alvin Sputnik: Deep Sea Explorer* draws upon a variety of technology and multimedia tools in order to tell the story. While there is only one actor on stage, he uses light, sound, music, puppets, animation, and live action, in addition to several props in the course of the performance. At the end of the performance, there was also a Q & A with the student audience, during which the actor showed students many of the pieces of technology and demonstrated how they worked together to create specific effects for the show. He also emphasized that many of the materials could be purchased cheaply at local hardware stores, and it was creativity that turned these basic materials into a theater piece. In the process of demystifying the multimedia aspect of the show, students were even more impressed with how the show used a variety of components to create a coherent and moving story:

- I like when Alvin started to dance and I like the song they were playing.
- I enjoy the puppets and how the show was animated too.
- I mostly enjoyed when the man did the puppetry.
- The way it was thought out and how it was written also how it was very unique.

POST-PROGRAM

After completing the pre-program activity (i.e., creating their puppet or completing their artwork) and seeing *The Adventures of Alvin Sputnik*, many students' attitudes towards live theater changed. We tested and found statistically significant differences in students' attitudes (see Fig. 11.3) from before they watched the show to after seeing *The Adventures of Alvin Sputnik*. In their responses to the pre-program surveys, students were generally less interested in attending a live performance (particularly the ninth graders). When presented with the same survey questions during post-program activities, students' responses were increasingly positive in their attitudes towards enjoying and attending live performance. This was supplemented by data from student interviews. While some students had not seen any theatrical performance before, for all students this was a new type of theater given its multimedia dimension. Additionally, while several students were initially reserved or disinterested, they described changed perceptions of live theatrical shows and multimedia performances.

Engagement with Live Theater

Students demonstrated an interest in continuing to attend live theatrical shows because they felt shows were exciting, entertaining, and inspiring. After attending the show, students wanted to pursue similar activities, both as audience members and as performers. More specifically, students wanted to extend their own engagement with the performance. *Alvin*

PRE: I am excited to see the show the Adventures of Alvin Sputnik

GRADE	Number of Responses	Mean (Average)
FIFTH	52	4.73
NINTH	21	2.38

POST: I enjoyed the show the Adventures of Alvin Sputnik

GRADE	Number of Responses	Mean (Average)
FIFTH	48	4.88
NINTH	16	3.63

PRE: I enjoy watching live, theater shows

GRADE	Number of Responses	Mean (Average)
FIFTH	52	4.33
NINTH	21	2.62

POST: I enjoy watching live, theater shows

GRADE	Number of Responses	Mean (Average)
FIFTH	48	4.92
NINTH	16	3.44

Fig. 11.3 Student attitudes towards live performance (pre-program and post-program)

Sputnik was an hour-long show, and many students wrote that they felt the performance was too short.

Students also demonstrated changed perceptions after attending the performance. Many students were expecting the show to be a more traditional theatrical play and were surprised with their own enthusiasm:

- I didn't think I liked plays, I was not into it, but now I've seen it and I like it—the story got me.
- It was very different. The interactions with the crowd get you involved.
- Amazing sound effects, I would like to go see another play. Other plays are usually not as interesting, this was interesting.
- It was a one-person play, he was dedicated and you have to think about it more.
- I thought it would be a waste of time but I really liked it.

- I thought the play was going to be like Shakespeare but after seeing it I like it, it had interesting concepts.
- I thought it was going to have a lot of actors and be on a big set, but it was on a simple set that makes it more original.

The teachers and the teaching artists also reflected on students' experiences after attending the live show. All of the teachers and teaching artists combined ($N = 5$) reported that students demonstrated an increased interest in theater after the performance. They also believed that attending a show was a unique part of this experience and, importantly, afforded students the chance to see a performance that was not a traditional theatrical show. Having a one-man show in a more intimate, black box setting was a unique experience.

One teacher had a classroom that had visited a large theatrical venue in Chicago in the past and noted, "when they got to the small theater, none of them compared it to the Lyric, it was like a whole new experience." A teaching artist also noted the unique quality of the play and reflected, "I think it was eye-opening walking away from this kind of performance, and all the different elements that go into a performance like this, and performances like this are not the norm. And not something you have access to regularly—many different ways to tell a story."

In addition to the uniqueness of the show, seeing the show and talking with the actor afterward in the Q & A was an important part of the experience. One teacher asked her students if they were interested in seeing other plays and a larger variety of plays after this experience, to which her students responded, "Yeah!" Another teacher noted the effectiveness of the Q & A after the show, reflecting,

> the Q&A was one of the most spectacular parts of the show—showing the audience how accessible making art really is. Have to see that art and mediums happen in a lot of venues and forms. So, you learn what your tastes are by experiencing a lot of different things.

Attending the show was not only an important part of this experience, but according to the teachers it also increased their students' engagement during class time. One teacher in particular noted how students who were dreading the performance, expecting it to be like an opera they saw, loved *The Adventures of Alvin Sputnik*. She even gave an example of a student who had a track record of disliking school and exhibiting difficult behavior but "was so excited about the show and the performance and he said 'I would go do that again.'" Another teacher highlighted that this experience changed students' perceptions:

> they saw they can go to this type of thing, it is open and available to them. I'm not sure in this economic group, how many of these students go downtown and do this.

According to one teacher, what was additionally important for this student audience was that the show was friendly to non-native English speakers. She emphasized,

> They were picking things out of the play, little details, they were coming up with things—there was a miniature puppet that they loved, another student talked about the disco ball that Alvin found, they thought that was hilarious, there was a whale in the story that they found interesting. They also really enjoyed the love story—they talked about how sad it was. They noticed that—because English was not their first language so it was important that they understood the whole thing.

Learning About Multimedia Arts

One of the unique aspects of the performance was how heavily it drew on multimedia tools and effects as opposed to a traditional classical music concert or play. Given the construction of the show and the Q & A which highlighted the materials used to create these effects, it is not surprising that students demonstrated an interest in continuing to learn more about multimedia shows and to further understand how artists can use their own materials and props to perform and create new things:

- I learned interacting with markers, tools, and creating a masterpiece.
- It was amazing, I always wanted to be an artist and use new materials.
- I learned you can make something new with the materials you have.
- I never thought puppets could be so exciting and now I will use them in my house.
- I learned that you can explore anything.

Teachers and teaching artists also felt that the multimedia aspects of the show provided students with new ways of experiencing theater and the arts. One teaching artist noted how a lot of productions for children are expensive, elaborate, and require specialized training:

> shows like this that uses elements of technology that they have at home, a cell phone can be a camera, a glove—its homemade in a way but also spectacular. Do[ing] a little with a lot makes art more accessible.

Students were also excited to work with the teaching artist after having seen the play. The fifth-grade students performed with their puppet as part of the in-class activity after watching the performance. Each student had the opportunity to introduce their puppet, have their puppet do a dance that was digitally recorded and projected onto a big screen in the classroom. The teaching artist noticed:

> The students, despite moments of shyness or uncertainty, were all extremely eager to take part in the showing of their puppets via the live streaming video projections. Almost every single student in both classes eagerly took part in the exercise and were attentive and celebratory of their classmates taking part as well.

Students showed an appreciation for the time, effort, and practice that were required to create and perform a complete show:

- I am interested in attending multimedia because you are creative with your own things.
- I did like it the technology of the shows.
- I like the way the sounds go and lights and how puppets moved.
- I really want to learn the movement and how it is made.
- Because I want to be creative. I want to feel like part of a show and I did. It would be fun if you are part of the show it really would.
- I would like attending multimedia often because it would be fun and so interesting and I would like to make the puppet with the one who invented Alvin.

In their final art projects, the students further reflected on the entire experience. While they expressed being nervous about presenting their puppets, they were also motivated by performing in front of their peers:

> My experience of today was really cool and funny because we were moving dances and funny things. I was really nervous because it was in a big screen.

My puppet and I could not even talk but I had to say about my puppet—but it was really great and fun and we had fun moving.—Fifth-Grader

My favorite part is that when we decorate the gloves it was really fun to decorate and we have fun with it. I was really nervous because I don't want to [mis]represent my puppet and we needed to dance with the puppet but my favorite part is that the students [were] having fun with their puppets and that is the coolest.—Fifth-Grader

Making Connections

Teachers and teaching artists also observed students making connections between the show and the academic subjects in the classroom and reported that students made connections between multimedia performance and other academic areas. One of the teachers noted that the art project students did post-performance was pre-writing that helped them to take a different approach to close-reading and analysis:

Some kids who would previously struggle were able to flourish, or some who struggled with the deeper meaning, exploring it first artistically they were able to articulate better in their writing.

The teaching artist who worked with her class echoed this sentiment, in comparing the pre-performance activity with the post-performance activity:

they were able to do it in a fun safe way the first time, but the second time they were able to think critically about the performance and the book. They didn't struggle about how do we do this, it was how will I represent this aspect of what I saw in the show. In this instance, the art became a vehicle for furthering learning in other academic areas.

The classroom teachers also noted the continued engagement of students even after the project was finished. One emphasized the multiple ways in which the project encouraged student learning in literacy while also appealing to their creativity and imagination; she suggested that it was this combination that "fully engaged" the students. Another noted that students continued to talk about the puppets and experience after the teaching artist left. She also highlighted that the puppets that students created were tangible and gave them ownership over their work.

In making connections, the teachers and teaching artists noted that having a post-performance follow-up activity helped students to engage with the material in a more meaningful way. One teacher specifically mentioned that given the results of this program, she was going to plan field trips differently in coming years—with a pre-activity, field trip, and post-activity.

TEACHER AND TEACHING ARTIST COLLABORATION

There were several aspects of the collaborative process that the teachers and teaching artists found helpful in this program. Teaching artists and classroom teachers noted the uniqueness in this program of having co-planning time with one another prior to beginning the program. As one teaching artist stated:

> I've never had the luxury of having such dedicated time set aside to coordinate with the classroom teacher. It was invaluable to have their insight going into the classroom and to be on a good working relationship even before setting foot in the school.

In addition to the co-planning time built into the program, the teaching artists, in particular, appreciated the professionalism with which the teachers treated them. They noted the experience of the teachers, how their expectations for students helped the program to succeed, as well as the respect that the teacher showed them as experts in their field.

The collaborative nature of this program facilitated opportunities for professional educators to learn, as well as students. One teaching artist noted that "it was eye-opening walking away from this kind of performance, and all the different elements that go into a performance like this, and performances like this are not the norm. And not something you have access to regularly." In some instances, it also encouraged thinking about new artistic mediums as one said:

> I haven't done anything like this, in my own practice that involved going to see a performance. That was very different and new and cool for me. I usually am just very visual—I thought it was very cool, it was brand new. It was a really fun new, different challenge—it was a new media for me, to use performance as a text.

For the classroom teachers, the experience sparked a desire to risk more collaborative and creative work in the classroom. One teacher concluded,

"I was reintroduced to how much I love the collaborative process." Another teacher also described how it encouraged and empowered her to be more creative in her pedagogy:

> I think for next year this was an eye opener for me, because things have gotten so monotonous. It brought me back to my first year of teaching, I used to do these huge projects and wonderful activities, and it took me back! This is my eleventh year—I felt like a first-year teacher. I think for next year I'm more likely to do things like this on my own.

LIMITATIONS

There is still a lot of work to be done to examine the optimal time teaching artists would be in the classroom, the kinds of theater best suited to impact student learning, and whether student learning from field trips in other artistic mediums would benefit from the pre-program, performance, and post-program format. One of the main limitations of this evaluation is that the site and sample selections were already determined prior to developing an evaluation plan. Although a strong working relationship with CHF had already been established, the teachers' ability to attend a matinee with students and a willingness to adapt their curriculum were the primary criteria for their selection to participate in the program. While this in some ways may be viewed as a strength (teachers already had a buy-in to collaborating with CHF), this restricted the small sample size and nearly assumed a positive outcome in teacher and teaching artist responses.

Additionally, the small-scale of the program and short timeframe for data collection (six weeks) limited our ability to explore the alignment between the arts-integrated program and the organizational goals of the Stages, Sights & Sounds Festival. All of this presented logistical challenges for data collection itself, given the fact that teaching artists only made a total of two visits to the classrooms (as opposed to longer residencies), the students attended only one live performance, and the show itself was a part of the CHF festival for the month of May.

IMPLICATIONS

For CHF, this evaluation demonstrated the impact of attending a multimedia performance on students' engagement with this art form. It suggested that providing access to a variety of theatrical performances, and not simply the more traditional performances, is important in growing students' appreciation for, and expansive understanding of, the arts. While there are compelling reasons to invest in long-term arts residencies in classrooms, and extended partnerships with organizations, it is possible that the impact of their outreach to school-aged children can be amplified by careful, strategic activities that build out from attending a single performance. Additionally, providing time for teachers and teaching artists to work together within the structure of the program benefitted everyone involved and highlighted the need for establishing a strong partnership among teacher, teaching artist, and non-profit organization.

In addition to the many programmatic challenges (including staffing and program development that were neither explored nor were the focus of this evaluation), the limited funding and scheduling challenges related to bringing international theater performances for youth to Chicago led to the ultimate suspension of the Stages, Sights & Sounds Festival and this program. Although most arts organizations want to maximize the impact of arts and culture experiences for students, not all programs are large enough to maintain long-term teaching artist residencies. For 15 years Stages, Sights & Sounds provided hundreds of Chicago students with their first live theater experience.

The evaluation presented in this chapter was an attempt to explore student engagement with live performance in the Stages Engagement Pilot Program. The focus was not to determine the feasibility of developing an education program or measuring the sustainability or scalability of the current project. As such, it is important that we note that CHF's decision to end the Stages, Sights & Sounds Festival was completely independent of our findings. Rather than informing or influencing CHF, this evaluation now stands as an example of an independent, small-scaled exploration of how students engage with live performances and how teacher and teaching artist collaboration can be strengthened when appropriately planned.

CONCLUSION

Student learning and engagement in this program was heightened because of the opportunity to interact with the performer after the performance. This gave students an opportunity to ask questions and learn about the show. In addition, the content of the show, the puppets, the adventure theme, as well as the use of multimedia and technology enabled students to appreciate and learn about the arts through a different lens. As a result of seeing this multimedia performance, students realized that they can access the arts within their own communities.

In addition, the artistic activities in class provided students with a venue for expressing themselves, which was particularly valuable for English language learners. Finally, students learned that they have the capacity and tools to be artists—whether by expressing themselves through puppetry or different visual arts mediums.

The recommendations from the participants emphasized both what they felt was helpful and what they would like more of in future programming. Teachers recognized the value of exposing their students to a variety of performances rather than exclusively seeing traditional theater, and in turn asked CHF for access to different types of theater and performing arts experiences. In addition, they would have liked the program to be more robust, including longer residencies of the teaching artist and beginning the program earlier in the school year. They also requested longer performances, as well as an opportunity after the program is completed to share and disseminate ideas with one another.

The aspects of the program that were most valuable were the significant (and unique) planning times between teachers and teaching artists, as well as the structure of the program with a pre-activity, performance, and post-activity. This structure allowed teachers and teaching artists to follow-up with students so that they could reinforce concepts and reflect on the experience.

The promising information regarding student learning about and engagement in the arts as a result of their participation in the Stages Education Engagement Pilot is detailed in this evaluation and hopefully provides evidence for the necessity of providing access to live performances for students of all ages.

References

Barker, M. (2003). Crash, theatre audiences, and the idea of "liveness". *Studies in Theatre and Performance, 23*(1), 21–39.

Burnaford, G., & Scripp, L. (2013). PAIR research summary. Retrieved from http://capechicago.org/wp-content/uploads/2016/11/PAIR-Research-Summary-CAPE.pdf

Kisida, B., Bowen, D. H., & Greene, J. P. (2014). The educational value of field trips. *Education Next, 14*(1), 78–86.

Reason, M. (2004). Theatre audiences and perceptions of 'liveness' in performance. *Particip@tions, 1*(2), 1–24.

Pitts, S. E. (2005a). What makes an audience? Investigating the roles and experiences of listeners at a chamber music festival. *Music and Letters, 86*(2), 257–269.

Pitts, S. E. (2005b). *Valuing musical participation.* Aldershot: Ashgate.

CHAPTER 12

Accounting for Taste: Using Propensity Score Methods to Evaluate the Documentary Film, *Waiting for "Superman"*

Johanna Blakley and Sheena Nahm

INTRODUCTION

In 2014, the National Endowment for the Arts (NEA) and the UK's Cultural Value Project co-sponsored a symposium that brought together researchers—including demographers, cognitive scientists, arts policy wonks, and "recovering" academics—to discuss how participation in arts and culture ought to be measured on the local, regional, national, and global scale. The *Measuring Cultural Engagement* meeting framed some

The authors would like to thank Heesung Shin for her considerable contributions to this research project, as well as Grace Huang for her assistance in its earliest phase. The authors would also like to thank Veronica Jauriqui and Adam Amel Rogers for graphic design support and editorial and formatting assistance during the final phases of this work.

J. Blakley (✉)
Annenberg School for Communication and Journalism, University of Southern California, Los Angeles, CA, USA

S. Nahm
Anthropology & Sociology, The New School for Public Engagement, New York, NY, USA

© The Author(s) 2018
R.S. Rajan, I.C. O'Neal (eds.), *Arts Evaluation and Assessment*,
https://doi.org/10.1007/978-3-319-64116-4_12

271

of the key problems facing those whose task it is to evaluate the effectiveness of arts programming, and more specifically, arts participation. Construed as a "reality check," the symposium sought to understand how participation metrics might evolve in order to better capture the effects of the arts on individuals and communities. One particular concern was establishing rigorous measurement techniques that would account for the arts' contribution to people's sense of well-being. Survey costs and sustainability were identified as key problems to be addressed (pg. 3) and the keynoter, Robert Groves, identified five challenges to sample surveys of culture and arts engagement, including increasing cost, increasing demand, and declining budgets. He also argued that new technology and digitization complicated efforts to measure engagement because they were generating large, organic datasets that traditional survey researchers are not equipped to link to standard sample survey data. Throughout the proceedings, new technology was frequently situated as a problem to be addressed rather than a tool to be harnessed to solve some of the intractable problems that have bedeviled arts evaluators since the field was formed (pg. 14).

A recent impact evaluation conducted at the Norman Lear Center, a research and public policy center at the University of Southern California's Annenberg School for Communication and Journalism, offers a method for conducting survey research focused on audience engagement and social impact, bringing together classic statistical principles of controlling for selection bias and matching control and intervention groups with the affordances of new technology. The Lear Center, through its Hollywood, Health & Society (HH&S) program, a partnership with the Centers for Disease Control and Prevention (CDC), has developed a body of research demonstrating the efficacy of using entertainment-education (EE) methods for public health messaging (Marcus, Huang, Beck, & Miller, 2010; Morgan, Movius, & Cody, 2009; Murphy, Hether, Felt, & Buffington, 2012; Nahm et al., 2010). Since the 1970s, academics and social activists have developed and implemented the entertainment-education strategy, which often harnesses the power and reach of mass media storytelling to affect social change.

Albert Bandura's influential work on Social Learning (1977) has been tremendously influential in efforts to understand the social impact of storytelling. Bandura determined that individuals adopt behavior changes based on the observation and imitation of other individuals, including fictional characters appearing in mass media. Building on the foundational principles of Bandura and others in the field of entertainment-education, the HH&S group consulted on 855 TV health storylines that originated in the United States, but aired all around the world between 2009 and 2015. Impact evaluations of these storylines have found plentiful evidence of knowledge gains as well as attitude and behavior change among viewers, as cited above.

While the Lear Center has concentrated on using EE methods to evaluate the impact of creative storytelling in media, there is a long history of the use of live theater and other performing arts to educate the public (Singhal & Rogers, 1999). Studies of international EE campaigns that have used live theater have demonstrated success in affecting audience members' awareness, knowledge, attitudes, and behaviors, as well as influencing social and cultural norms, often around health issues (Conquergood, 1988; Singhal, 2004; Singhal & Rogers, 1989, 1999). And, as Bandura's work has demonstrated, the content of entertainment does not need to be engineered to educate audiences in order for it to impact behavior (Bandura, Ross, & Ross, 1963).

Propensity Score Matching (PSM)

Given the logistic and cost-related challenges that arise in designing arts evaluation studies, most researchers rely on convenience samples. This can include cross-sectional surveys of people who are exposed to the art in question (though this limits results without a comparison group). It can also include matched pair analysis by respondents who complete surveys before and after exposure to the arts program being evaluated (Brown & Novak, 2007). Survey respondents in the aforementioned study serve as their own control. While this method allows for impact evaluation, it can require resources to follow up with audience members and also does not account for the fact that people who attend the play, concert, or exhibition may be more receptive to messages even if they are new viewers who exhibit change as a result of the performance.

First proposed in a 1983 publication by Paul Rosenbaum and Donald Rubin, PSM has become a useful method of working with observational (non-randomized) studies. The propensity score is defined as the probability that a subject would be assigned to a particular treatment group given a vector of covariates. PSM refers to the pairing of units with different group assignments (treatment and control in clinical literature but sometimes referred to as exposed and unexposed in health communication literature) but similar scores. In non-randomized studies there is no single formula for the propensity score model; each logit model can be estimated using unique observed data.[1]

In clinical studies, randomized trials or pre-post studies are often utilized to avoid selection bias. However, random assignment or pre-post data collection is not always practical. In such cases, PSM has become a useful method of controlling for selection bias when analyzing cross-sectional data. For example, PSM has been used in studying causal effects of ambulatory cardiology care on mortality (Landrum & Ayanian, 2001). It has also been used to study the effect of mammography on the stage of diagnosis (Posner, Ash, Freund, Moskowitz, & Shwartz, 2001). PSM has been applied in clinical as well as non-clinical settings.

In non-clinical studies, randomized trials or pre-post studies may also be impractical. Limitations such as time, money, and access to participants can make studying the real-world impact of media difficult to align with gold standards of laboratory research design. PSM ought to be considered a useful way of studying the effects of arts programming on the public by controlling for selection bias when using cross-sectional data. PSM is also a good option for dealing with adjustments for Web bias in online surveys (Danielsson, 2004). Online surveys are useful because they are timely and cost-efficient, but there can be differences between the target population and the frame population because not everyone in the general population has access to the Web. This is similar to the limitation of cross-sectional samples of TV viewers since viewers as a group are self-selected and different from non-viewers; they are usually predisposed to respond differently to a program than non-viewers (Do & Kincaid, 2006, pg. 301).

Since the publication of the first paper in 1983, PSM methods have emerged in various fields of study including economics and communication studies. PSM methods "provide a natural weighting scheme that yields unbiased estimates of the treatment impact" (Dehejia & Wahba, 2002, pg. 151). In multimedia evaluations, there are often many variables influencing outcomes, making simple weighting schemes difficult to determine. PSM allows for control of multiple variables so that the impact of an intervention can be examined more specifically.

The process of PSM follows a few basic steps. The first phase entails finding the predicted probability of a subject being in one group or another. This means asking how likely a person is to be exposed or not exposed to an intervention. The propensity score is obtained using logit or probit regression to build a model that predicts the probability that a person will be part of the treatment group rather than the control group.[2] In

EE research, treatment could refer to someone's probability or propensity to be exposed to a particular film, television show episode, play, or musical performance.

In conducting the logistic regression to determine propensity scores, one needs to select a tentative list of covariates for adjustment. A tentative list can be determined by findings from literature or knowledge from the field. For example, several basic demographic characteristics of a film genre's typical audience could be considered. The final list of covariates should be determined carefully because the propensity model needs to include any important reason why a subject would be "selected" for the treatment or control group. A propensity score is assigned to each individual; the score is a single number representing probability from 0.0 to 1.0. The score is the weighted sum of the individual's values for all the characteristics included in the logit model.

In the second phase, subjects with the same propensity but different exposure categories are matched with one another to study the impact of exposure. Do and Kincaid (2006) suggest first stratifying respondents into five groups across ranges in propensity scores. Quintile subclassification is sufficient in removing at least 90% of the bias (Cochran, 1968). Statistical tests can be conducted for each quintile to determine if the average score for the exposed is equivalent to the average score for the unexposed. If there is a significant difference between the two, then the quintile is divided into even smaller subgroups. When there is no significant difference between the average score of the exposed and unexposed, the groups are balanced enough for comparison. Statistical analyses of the relationship between exposure and outcome variables are conducted separately for each balanced subgroup. Then the overall result can be obtained by computing the average of the differences in outcomes of the balanced subgroups, weighted by the proportion of viewers (exposed) within each group.

PSM allows for reducing confounding effects by creating equal groups between exposed and unexposed (matched pairs) while also allowing for causal inference even without pre- and post-test data from subjects. In order to match, the sample size needs to be large enough to ensure overlapping propensity scores (Winkelmayer & Kurth, 2004, Dehejia & Wahba, 2002, pg. 153).[3] At least a one-to-one match is needed for making any inference, but one can also match one-to-many. Scores without overlap (that is, scores that do not have a counterpart for comparison) are excluded and explained separately.

Dehejia and Wahba (2002) describe several key issues involved in matching. It has been suggested that treatment units be matched to the closest comparison unit even if a comparison unit gets matched more than once (i.e., nearest neighbor method).[4] This is a way to "match with replacement" when there is not as much overlap. One can "match without replacement" if there is enough overlap in the distribution of propensity scores. Using a single comparison unit for a treatment unit ensures less distance in propensity scores. On the other hand, multiple comparison units matched to each treatment unit increases precision (as well as bias). Ideally, the data will have enough overlap in the distribution of propensity score such that the need for matching using neighbors as replacements will not be needed. Also, in cases where there is a lot of overlap, different matching methods will produce similar results.

Applications and Examples Related to Studying Media Impact
Bertrand, O'Reilly, Denison, Anhang, and Sweat (2006) conducted a review of 24 mass media interventions that aimed to change knowledge, attitudes, and behaviors related to HIV/AIDS. Findings from these interventions were published between 1990 and 2004. In their review, they point out that there were no studies of full coverage media programs that used random allocation of subjects to treatment areas. Given that controlled group assignments are difficult if not impossible in media programs that reach the masses, alternative methods to study arts impact need to be explored.

An evaluation of *Tsha Tsha*, a dramatic television series using entertainment-education approaches to deal with HIV/AIDS and youth, did exactly this by combining traditional evaluation methods like focus groups and a panel study with PSM analysis (CADRE, 2005). In discussing PSM, researchers state that this method "effectively overcomes the problem of confounding variables that influence exposure being associated with outcome variables—an issue that has been one of the most vexing challenges in establishing equivalent exposed and unexposed groups for evaluation of mass media interventions" (pg. 17). Variables related to propensity for watching *Tsha Tsha* included gender, age, education, income, languages spoken, TV and radio consumption habits, knowing someone who is HIV positive, and condom usage (pg. 19). In this study, multiple logistic regression analysis of data at the end of the third wave of episodes showed that the variables above predicted who watched the drama. These variables were then used to create a model for predicted probability of exposure. Every study has a unique combination of variables that are related to propensity, but this study suggests that basic demographics, frequency of exposure to media formats involved in the EE intervention, exposure to similar shows (such as *Soul City* for *Tsha Tsha*), personal connection to the issue, and behaviors that reflect awareness of the issue are variables to keep in mind. This study also emphasizes why PSM can be useful in researching the impact of media-related interventions; there is no way to restrict viewing of public campaigns that are part of mass media interventions, and differences in outcomes may be related to essentially different groups rather than to the impact of the intervention itself. In the *Tsha Tsha* study, researchers analyzed recall of the drama to find which variables contributed to differences between exposed and unexposed. Then, using these 15 variables, a "virtual" control group of non-viewers were matched with viewers.[5] Although PSM is explicitly for non-random experimental designs, the results can be the same as long as respondents are matched on variables that influence exposure and expected outcomes (pg. 19).

Evaluating the Impact of a Documentary Film Given the applications of PSM to evaluate media campaigns and formats which are often asking similar questions (with similar cost constraints and questions of sustainability) as arts evaluation, the Lear Center applied PSM to better understand the impact of several films. We focus on a case study involving the evaluation of the documentary film *Waiting for "Superman"* (WFS). The goal of this study was to determine (1) variables that influence someone's likelihood of watching this film and (2) whether exposure to this film impacted viewers' knowledge, attitudes, and behavior.

Participant Media approached the Lear Center to help them answer these questions about their film, *Waiting for "Superman."* Participant Media is a production company whose goal is to make films that change society; they have made dozens of critically acclaimed films, both documentaries and fictional feature films, that deal with serious social issues in entertaining and engaging ways. Participant Media wanted the Lear Center's help figuring out whether their films were having the impact they had hoped for. Lear Center researchers began to answer these questions by developing an online survey methodology that could evaluate the impact of Participant Media's films and associated social action campaigns on the general public.

Waiting for "Superman" is a 2010 documentary directed by Davis Guggenheim, who also directed *An Inconvenient Truth*. The film looks at the failures of the American public education system through the stories of students and their families who strive for better educational opportunities. The film received the Audience Award for best documentary at the 2010 Sundance Film Festival and, since its release, has directed donations to over 2.8 million children (TakePart, 2010). The film's release ignited a heated debate about the challenges facing public education to provide adequate education and opportunities for students, parents, and teachers.

METHODS[6]

Although *Waiting for "Superman"* was quite successful for a documentary—grossing $6.5 million during its theatrical release and winning 16 awards—a very small proportion of Americans saw it. Therefore, answering questions about the impact of the film on a nationally representative sample of viewers would have been very expensive to do and probably ill-advised. The main problem is that people who decide to see a social issue documentary are highly "self-selected"—that is, the vast majority of the film's viewers are probably biased toward the perspective of the film, and probably more likely than an average non-viewer to take the actions recommended in the film. In short, niche films attract niche audiences and so trying to construct national representative samples is neither cost-effective nor helpful if the goal is to understand what kind of impact niche programming has had on its viewers. One could say the same about a wide variety of arts programming, including ballet, opera, and jazz and classical music.

When researchers at the Lear Center pivoted to measuring the impact of documentary and feature films, they experimented with new survey research methods that allowed them to better navigate the problem of self-selection bias, which is also one of the biggest obstacles for arts and culture impact evaluation research. For evaluators studying a cultural program that does not have "blockbuster" status, it is extremely difficult (and expensive) to create a broad nationally representative sample of people who have encountered it. This is a problem of all research design in that it asks sample groups to be representative of the population in question. Because many arts programs have limited geographical reach in ways that mass media do not, recruitment into the study may be difficult in order to determine national impact. However, with careful sampling that matches questions about the locally specific population (i.e., not over-reaching in generalizing results beyond the population represented by the sample), the risks can be mitigated.

In addition to geographic access and convenience, research design in arts evaluation must also account for taste and self-selection. People who attend specific plays, operas, concerts, and museum exhibitions, or tune into various arts programming, are likely to be predisposed to the form and to the "message," making a control group highly advisable. Researchers at the Lear Center developed an innovative survey instrument that leverages digital social networks to create matched comparison groups at low cost. The Lear Center has only applied this method to media—a feature film, two documentaries, and an international news site—but it can be adapted easily to a wide variety of artistic events and installations. The research team used propensity score matching (PSM) to help determine whether the difference in results between exposed and unexposed survey respondents was associated with exposure to the programming in question, controlling for any confounding factors that might influence the type of individual who would be more likely to opt in to the exposed group versus the control group. In the case of arts programming, the treatment or intervention may be a book, a concert series, a PBS documentary, a museum exhibition, or any kind of theatrical production.

The Lear Center developed a survey instrument that could assess the impact of *Waiting for "Superman"* on its viewers by comparing their responses to very similar people who had not seen the film. Propensity score matching was used to help determine whether the different results that we see between viewers and non-viewers are associated with watching WFS, rather than pre-existing differences between these two groups (see Fig. 12.1).

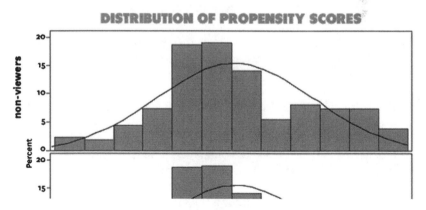

Fig. 12.1 PSM survey flow

This research began with a link to a survey about Participant Media films that was posted on various Participant Media sites and an email newsletter. The invitation to take the survey did not mention the survey was specifically for *Waiting for "Superman"* because the goal was to attract respondents who had not seen the film as well as those who had. The survey contained many traditional questions: demographic questions, questions about their political affiliations and their attitudes toward the issues depicted in the film (see Table 12.1). However, survey respondents were also asked if they had taken specific actions recommended in the film regardless of whether they had seen the film or not. Action questions included the following: (1) look for information about improving public education; (2) encourage my friends, family, and colleagues to demand better schools; (3) ask my elected official to improve public education; (4) donate books or classroom materials to schools; (5) volunteer or mentor a student; (6) join a local education organization.

The Lear Center's impact evaluation of *Waiting for "Superman"* and its campaign began over a year after its release, beginning in November 2011 and concluding in September 2012. The year between the release of the film and data collection allowed for the population of viewers to grow well beyond moviegoers to those who were exposed to the film through television, video/DVD rental, or online media in their homes, classrooms, and communities. Additionally, waiting a year made it possible to capture sustained changes in knowledge, attitudes, and behavior, as opposed to the short-lived or aspirational changes that might register in a survey taken immediately after a screening of a film.

The research began with a 5–10-minute online survey designed by the Lear Center. The survey was disseminated through a link placed in a Participant Media email blast. The survey was also posted on the film's promotional website and newsletter, the Participant Media website, the TakePart website, and the Facebook and Twitter accounts associated with the film.

The first phase of PSM entailed finding the factors that would predict the likelihood of a subject being exposed to the film. These factors might include some combination of personal taste, ideology, media preferences, past behavior patterns, and demographics. Using logistic regression, a model was created based upon those predictors (see Fig. 12.2).

In the second phase, subjects were assigned propensity scores based on the propensity model created during the first phase: subjects who did not

Table 12.1   Sample questions from the *Waiting for "Superman"* survey instrument

	PROPENSITY
Demographics	*Do you have any children?*
Media Habits	*How often do you watch documentary films that focus on a social issue?*
Media Attitudes	*How much of an impact do you think a film can have on a person's attitudes?*
Politics/Activism	*I would describe myself as someone who is sick of politics. (yes/no/don't know)*
Organizational Affiliations	*Did you hear about Waiting for 'Superman' through any of the following organizations?*
Awareness of Subject	*In the last year, do you recall seeing or hearing anything about the crisis in public education in the US in any of the following...?*
Marketing Campaign Exposure	*Have you encountered any of the following aspects of Waiting for 'Superman' outreach campaign?*
	OUTCOMES
Knowledge	*Overall, US schools lead the world in academic excellence. (yes/no)*
Behaviors	*When did you join a local education organization?*
	When did you participate in your PTA? (parents only)
	EXPOSURE
Exposure Details	*Where did you first see Waiting for 'Superman'?*
Knowledge	*How much about the following topics do you feel you learned from watching Waiting for 'Superman'?*
Attitudes	*After seeing Waiting for 'Superman,' do you feel like US public education is going to get better or worse?*

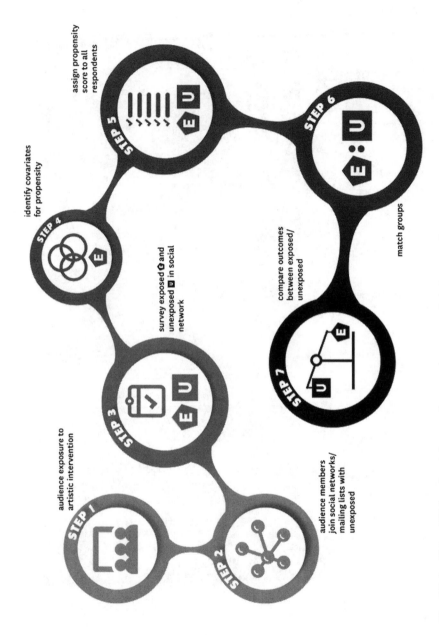

Fig. 12.2 Using PSM and social networks to evaluate an artistic intervention

view *Waiting for "Superman"* were matched and compared with subjects with the same propensity score who did view WFS. In EE studies of this type, researchers typically assess impact of the intervention on awareness, knowledge, attitudes, and behavior based upon exposure to the film.

Using this methodology allowed the Lear Center's researchers to create a detailed profile of likely viewers of the film and to compare viewers who saw the film with very similar people who did not. Unlike typical survey research, this method allowed researchers to construct something similar to a classic study design where individuals assigned to a treatment group and a control group could be compared.

Data Collected

A total of 2726 surveys were started and 78% of respondents completed the survey. Of the respondents, 1527 said they had seen *Waiting for "Superman"* (exposed group) whereas 596 responded that they had not seen the film. All surveys were completed online; participation was voluntary and all survey items were in English.

Results

Propensity score modeling was based on a subset of 1568 respondents who answered all of the propensity questions. All of these survey respondents were assigned a propensity score indicating the likelihood that they would view *Waiting for "Superman."* The scores were based on 27 variables such as demographics, prior viewership of social issue films, and exposure to WFS promotional materials. After performing one-to-one matching, both the exposed and the control groups were composed of respondents with the same range of propensity scores. There were 311 people in each of these groups and there was a standard distribution of scores in the exposed and the control group (see Fig. 12.3). The salient difference between the two groups was whether or not they had viewed *Waiting for "Superman."*

Creating the Control Group A statistical analysis of survey responses from all the respondents who watched *Waiting for "Superman"* determined what personal characteristics increased their likelihood—or propensity—to see the film. Viewers with a high propensity to watch *Waiting for*

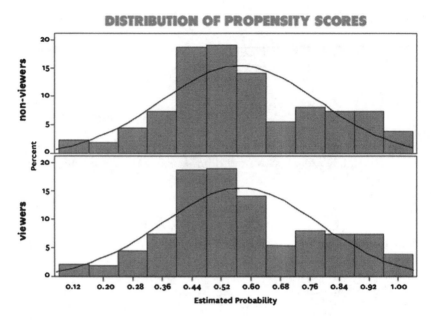

Fig. 12.3 Distribution of propensity scores between viewers and non-viewers of *Waiting for "Superman"*

"Superman" shared various combinations of 27 characteristics categorized by personal taste, ideology, media exposure, and demographics (see Table 12.2).

The variables above were used to generate a propensity score for survey respondents who had seen the film, and those who had not. People with most of these characteristics received the higher scores and those with the fewest received the lowest. In short, the vector created by this model predicted someone's propensity for viewing this film. However, just because someone had a high score did not mean that they had actually seen the film—it just made it more likely that they had seen it. Therefore, a person with a very high score may not have seen the film yet, and a person with a very low score may have seen it despite themselves (for instance, a teacher may have screened the film in a class where students with low scores happened to see it and thus landed in the exposed group).

Once scores were assigned, two groups were created: people who had watched *Waiting for "Superman"* and those who had not. Next, the range

Table 12.2   The PSM model for viewers of *Waiting for "Superman"*

Demographics:	White
	High income
	Work in K-12 education
	Have children
Media exposure:	Heard about crisis in public education from:
	Radio
	Conversations with friends, family, or colleagues
	Exposure to *Waiting for "Superman"* through:
	Preview
	Waiting for "Superman" website
	Waiting for "Superman" Facebook page
	John Legend's song "Shine"
	Media coverage
	Invitation to house parties/special screenings
	Discussion guides
	Film viewing:
	Watches three or more social issue documentaries per year
	Saw *Food, Inc.*
	Saw *Countdown to Zero*
	Saw *The Kite Runner*
Ideology & taste:	Online engagement:
	Joined *Waiting for "Superman"* mailing list
	Signed up for Participant Media Newsletter
	Joined TakePart Social Action Network
	Took the pledge to see *Waiting for "Superman"*
	Organizational affiliations:
	America's Promise
	Donors Choose
	Get Schooled
	Other organization
	Republican party affiliation
	Green party affiliation

of scores in each group (exposed/treatment and unexposed/control) was compared. One-to-one matching was performed using an automated method to remove people from each group until both groups were composed of the same number of respondents with the same range of propensity scores (e.g., each person who saw the film was paired with a person who did not see the film, but was equally likely to see the film based on their propensity scores).

Use of this method approximated the creation of an experimental study design where subjects are randomly assigned to a control group and a treatment group. Here, the treatment or intervention group was comprised of those who had seen *Waiting for "Superman,"* and the control group was comprised of those who had not seen the film but were equally likely to. By making these groups parallel and matching by propensity scores, the researchers were able to examine whether differences in knowledge and behavior were attributable to the film while controlling for any pre-existing factors that contribute to self-selection bias.

Sample and Recruitment Given the propensity of some respondents to see the film, what did the sample look like as a whole? *Waiting for "Superman"* viewers were exposed to the film's outreach primarily through the WFS website (61%), related media coverage (43%), or film previews (37%). Half of viewers first saw the film through online streaming or download. Viewers demonstrated some key demographic characteristics (see Table 12.3).

Viewers exhibited the following pattern of media exposure and preferences. *Waiting for "Superman"* viewers had some previous exposure to other Participant Media films—67% had watched *Food, Inc.* and 59% had watched *An Inconvenient Truth.* Viewers frequently watched social issue documentaries and feature films, with 62% reporting that they watched social issue documentaries at least three times a year. Even more people (72%) reported watching social issue scripted films at least three times a year. These statistics underscore the importance of controlling for selection bias when it comes to evaluating arts programming whose consumption is determined by taste and personal preferences.

Table 12.3 Demographics of viewers of *Waiting for "Superman"*

Variable	Viewers in sample (%)
Female	73
White	68
Did not have children	52
Completed some college	26
College graduates	36
Graduate school	28
Work in education	36
Income of $75K or more	30
Over age of 30	56

A large majority of viewers reported believing that a film can have an impact on individual attitudes, public opinion, and media coverage with 95% of viewers saying a film can impact individual attitudes. On a more macro scale, 87% of viewers said a film could impact public opinion and 82% said a film could impact media coverage.

Finally, one might assume that viewers of social issue films like *Waiting for "Superman"* would be engaged in politics, but the results suggested that a majority of these viewers were skeptical about political engagement.

- Over half (56%) said they were "sick of politics" and 27% claimed no political affiliation.
- Almost half of viewers (49%) said they were not politically active, and another 10% said they were "not sure."
- While 47% of viewers said that they were strong supporters of social and economic causes, only 18% reported strong support for political causes. Another 18% said they had never donated any money or time to any political cause.

Political attitudes, personal taste, media exposure, and demographic characteristics contributed to the propensity score via logit model. Once propensity scores were matched across exposed and unexposed groups, differences in knowledge and behavior could be assessed for the film's impact.

Knowledge In order to determine whether WFS viewers learned anything from the film, viewers and non-viewers were asked four questions—one easy, two medium, and one harder—about education topics covered in the film. WFS viewers demonstrated increased knowledge about education topics after watching the film. Subjects who watched the film were more likely to get all the questions correct while very similar non-viewers did not. This finding is especially significant since this survey was administered over a year after the film was released—not as people exited a screening of the film.

Behaviors In addition to increasing knowledge, the film was optimized to instigate social change by encouraging people to take a range of actions. We found that, after comparing people with the same propensity to have seen the film, watching the film increased the odds for taking four of the six actions that were recommended.

Individual action. Watching WFS increased the odds of taking the following actions, none of which required joining a group:

- Look for information about improving public education
- Encourage friends, family, and colleagues to demand better schools
- Donate books or classroom material to schools
- Volunteer or mentor a student

Organized action. Watching WFS did not increase the odds that viewers would perform either of the following actions, which indicate political or organizational engagement:

- Ask elected officials to improve public education
- Join a local education organization

All respondents were also asked a more general question: "Have you supported any organized efforts to improve public education in your own community?" The following explanation was included in the survey: "'Supporting' an effort can include making a financial donation or volunteering time." Consistent with the previous two findings, watching the film did not increase the odds that viewers had supported any organized efforts to improve public education in their own communities. These three findings may demonstrate the difficulty of encouraging individuals to join an organized effort through a documentary film intervention.

Activating the choir. Documentary filmmakers are often accused of "preaching to the choir," that is, creating messages for people who already believe them. One goal of this research study was to explore whether this film was effective at encouraging people who had been engaged in relevant activities in the past to be engaged in them again after they saw the film. In short, "members of the choir" who had not seen the film were less likely to be involved in these education-related activities by the time they took the survey. This suggests that WFS successfully re-activated former activists to take more action. However, consistent with the rest of the survey sample, "members of the choir" who saw the film were no more likely than similar non-viewers to have taken actions that indicate political or organizational affiliation (i.e., asking an elected official to improve public education or joining a local education organization).

Parents. The film encouraged parents to take four specific actions. For viewers who had one or more children, we found that watching WFS significantly increased the odds that they would take three of them:

- Look up ratings for their schools
- Read with their children 30 minutes a day
- Participate in their PTA

Parents were not more likely to take the fourth recommended action, "get to know their school board and what it does." However, parents' increased involvement in their PTA may demonstrate this film's success at encouraging viewers who may have much at stake in this arena to join an organized effort. The rest of the behavioral findings about all viewers—whether they have a history of supporting education reform or not—suggested that it might be easier for a documentary film campaign to increase individual engagement rather than organized action or political engagement, especially given this population's skepticism about politics and political institutions.

DISCUSSION

In order to survive, the arts community must develop reliable scientific methods to measure the benefits of arts and culture for individuals, communities, and society at large. Digital media, and social networks in particular, offer arts evaluators an unprecedented opportunity to do their work more cheaply and more rigorously than they have been able to do it in the past. Armed with the kind of evidence that this type of survey research offers, arts administrators and policymakers are on firmer ground when they ask for precious resources—particularly public funds—to be spent on the arts. If the power of arts and culture to educate and enlighten can be clearly demonstrated, there should be no shortage of funders who are looking for proven tools to accomplish exactly that.

Belfiore and Bennett (2010) are correct when they assert that it is "not possible to develop a rigorous protocol for the assessment of the impacts of the aesthetic experience that can be boiled down to a handful of bullet-points and a user-friendly 'evaluation toolkit,' to be easily applied to any art form in any setting and replicated whenever the need for impact evaluation arises" (pg. 263). Unfortunately, both public and private funders of the arts (including storytelling on various media platforms) would prefer to see simple, straightforward metrics of success that are easily compared across programs. The availability of quantitative digital data about audience responses to arts programming also encourages arts funders to believe that answers to questions about the social impact of a program should be simple to answer. However, explaining how "hearts and minds" have been affected by an aesthetic experience remains a difficult but certainly not insurmountable task, made more feasible through the thoughtful use of interdisciplinary expertise and research methods.

Challenges

There are some challenges to using PSM as a method that should be kept in mind. One challenge with PSM is to recruit a large enough sample to have enough respondents with similar propensities to be matched across exposed and unexposed groups. Some key strategies to addressing this challenge are to (1) partner with an organization that has a broad social network and (2) recruit respondents via several platforms and allow enough time to collect a large enough sample. Also, long surveys can be problematic: one of the limitations of PSM is that the model must have a limited number of factors before the model becomes too large to be useful. However, all four PSM surveys that the Lear Center has administered to various social media networks have been quite short, typically taking 5–10 minutes to complete, depending on whether a respondent has been exposed or not. Members of social networks are unlikely to tolerate long surveys—especially if they do not expect any form of compensation. Surveys for restless online audiences must be thoughtfully constructed to engage and retain participants to complete as many of the questions as possible. This is less of a challenge for media and arts evaluators since questions about personal taste (i.e., media and aesthetic preferences) are generally more appealing to people than questions about difficult or obscure topics, which respondents may feel they are answering incorrectly.

Other limitations include the fact that PSM can only adjust for observed confounding covariates and not "hidden" or unobserved ones. Treatment and outcomes must be independent and not influenced by hidden factors. Even with these limitations, PSM provides a unique alternative method for addressing selection bias while comparing exposed and unexposed groups in evaluating arts programming, whether delivered through media or in live events.

Biased samples can also be a limitation of online survey research. Because specific social media networks (e.g., LA Opera's Facebook followers) are more homogeneous than the general population, it is a perfect place to generate a matched comparison group wherein people of equally high propensities or low propensities can still be matched with one another and evaluated based on exposure to specific artistic programming. The goal is not to create a representative sample of the entire population of Los Angeles (in the case of LA Opera), but to discover what arts program is effective among a high priority audience segment. Even if the survey population is homogeneous relative to the rest of the world, self-selection bias can be controlled by matching propensity scores and testing for the impact of exposure, including differences in awareness, knowledge, attitudes, and behavior.

Data Application and Implications

PSM has grown in popularity among researchers and evaluators over the past two to three decades. It has been applied to research design in both clinical and non-clinical settings. In non-clinical evaluations like those conducted to study the impact of mass media on the public, cross-sectional data is often the only available data. When pre and post matching of respondents or randomized control designs are not feasible in these contexts, or too costly, a useful alternative is PSM. PSM allows for rigorous analysis of cross-sectional data through the control of selection biases. It also provides a more streamlined approach to dealing with multiple covariates by using a single scalar, the propensity score, to represent any influence of selection bias on outcomes.

In proposing PSM as a useful, cost-efficient, and effective method for those interested in assessing arts programs, we are offering a powerful tool that can be added to the existing evaluation toolkit. A mixed-methods approach that pairs quantitative analysis via methods such as PSM with qualitative analysis that captures recurring themes in more open-ended formats is recommended. Particularly in a growing and developing field of evaluation, mixed-methods evaluation can be a useful means of gleaning quantitative insights about specific programmatic outcomes while also gathering qualitative data about audience responses that can generate new hypotheses about social impact. Big data analysis can also be included in evaluation design, enhancing insights about audience response, and potentially clarifying connections between exposure and specific outcomes.

Social network datasets can be extremely rich, including different types of user generated content (e.g., comments, tweets, Facebook posts), as well as behavioral metrics (e.g., shares, likes, retweets, page visits, scroll depth, time on page, video views). With the use of site intercept technology, which allows researchers to deliver surveys based on the visitor's past activity on the site, survey data (which may include information about offline activities) can be integrated with online behavior data, effectively connecting the dots between an audience member's offline experiences (e.g., performances they attended) and their online engagement. Access to social networks also provides arts evaluators with the opportunity to monitor longer term effects of arts interventions quite economically, which has long been an important criticism of the evidence base for the social impact of the arts (Galloway, 2009, p. 127).

As illustrated in this case study of *Waiting for "Superman,"* the impact of a film in changing knowledge and behavior can be evaluated using PSM. Extrapolating to application in arts evaluation, PSM can be used to control for self-selection bias and address issues of propensity and taste when "opting in" to exposure to the arts. This can be especially useful for evaluating arts that are open to the general public. Arts programs specifically geared for a consistent group—such as youth enrolled in an at-risk program or students in after-school programming—can be surveyed with pre- and post-intervention questionnaires.

As arts programming melts away in cash-strapped public schools, the evaluation community must acknowledge the awful truth—that it is up to them to convince the general public and arts funders that arts and culture is not a luxury, but a necessity, and to provide evidence of their value to society. This has been a particularly daunting problem for people in cultural diplomacy, where the stakes could not be higher (e.g., countering terrorism and genocide), but where the instrumental possibilities of art and culture are typically demonstrated through anecdote rather than rigorous evaluation. For people who frequently attend arts and culture events, the intrinsic value of art may seem obvious: doesn't everyone realize that humans are hard-wired to respond to compelling stories and visuals, whether they manifest themselves as sculpture, video games, concerts, or novels? Isn't it clear that music and movies can bridge the most profound political divides and move hearts and minds? Sadly, the answer is no, and that is why the most important issue in the arts these days is how to justify funding (particularly public funding) for the arts. However, the research methods and strategies presented here should empower arts and culture organizations to measure the social impact of their work, which will help them with fundraising while arming them with insights to guide the crucial course-corrections that all creative enterprises must make when they are committed to achieving complex goals.

NOTES

1. "To a Bayesian, estimates of this probability are posterior predictive probability of assignment to treatment 1 for a unit with vector x of covariates" (Rosenbaum & Rubin, 1983).
2. The binary dependent variable is 1 for exposed and 0 for not exposed.
3. Sensitivity analyses can be conducted to test for the possibility that unobserved characteristics of the subjects independently affect the likelihood of treatment. For example, in the Landrum 2001 study, they hypothesized the existence of an unobserved binary variable related to propensity score and updated estimates of the effect of treatment after adjusting for the hypothetical confounder. They used sensitivity analysis to show that their actual conclusions were mildly sensitive to unobserved effects that are extreme but within range of the observed effects.
4. An alternative to the nearest neighbor method is to use a "caliper" or radius of score standard deviations to find a match (Rubin, 2001, p. 177).
5. "The propensity score was created by regressing high exposure to *Tsha Tsha* (versus none and low) on the identified variables, and then using the resulting probability of watching predicted by those 15 variables for purposes of matching. The probability (propensity score) in the present case varied between 0.03 and 0.97, with an average value of 0.50, which is the same as the percentage of those above the median with a high level of recall of the drama. The lower a respondent scored on the 15 variables, the lower the propensity score, and conversely, the higher a respondent scored on the 15 variables, the higher their propensity score. The sample of respondents was divided into six groups across the range of propensity scores. The first group consisted of all respondents with propensity scores below 0.20. The groups ranged from 0.20 to 0.40; 0.40 to 0.60; 0.60 to 0.80; 0.80 to 0.90, and those with scores above 0.90. Within each of these strata or blocks there was no statistically significant difference between the average propensity score of respondents who watched *Tsha Tsha* and those who did not watch. There was also no statistically significant difference for each of the 15 variables used to construct the score. Thus, within each of these six groups, viewers and non-viewers were statistically equivalent in the same way they would be if they had been randomly assigned to each group" (CADRE, 2005, pg. 20).
6. Funding for this study, which was independently designed, conducted, and released by the Norman Lear Center, was provided by Participant Media, who also co-financed the making of *Waiting for "Superman."*

REFERENCES

Bandura, A. (1977). *Social learning theory*. Englewood Cliffs, NJ: Prentice Hall.
Bandura, A., Ross, D., & Ross, S. A. (1963). Imitation of film-mediated aggressive models. *Journal of Abnormal and Social Psychology, 66*, 3–11.
Belfiore, E., & Bennett, O. (2010). *The social impact of the arts: An intellectual history*. New York: Palgrave Macmillan.
Bertrand, J. T., O'Reilly, K., Denison, J., Anhang, R., & Sweat, M. (2006). Systematic review of the effectiveness of mass communication programs to change HIV/AIDS-related behaviors in developing countries. *Health Education Research, 21*(4), 567–597.
Brown, A. S., & Novak, J. L. (2007). *Assessing the intrinsic impacts of a live performance*. San Francisco, CA: WolfBrown.
Centre for AIDS Development, Research and Evaluation. (2005). Tsha Tsha: Key findings of the evaluation of episodes 1–26. Retrieved January 18, 2011, from http://www.m-mc.org/spotlight/southafrica_tshatsha/CADREeval.pdf
Cochran, W. G. (1968). The effectiveness of adjustment by subclassification in removing bias in observational studies. *Biometrics, 24*, 295–313.
Conquergood, D. (1988). Health theater in a Hmong refugee camp: Performance, communication and culture. *TDR: Journal of Performance Studies, 32*, 174–208.
Danielsson, S. (2004). The propensity score and estimation in nonrandom surveys: An overview. Retrieved January 18, 2011, from http://www.statistics.su.se/modernsurveys/publ/11.pdf
Dehejia, R. H., & Wahba, S. (2002). Propensity score-matching methods for non-experimental causal studies. *The Review of Economics and Statistics, 84*(1), 151–161.
Do, M. P., & Kincaid, D. L. (2006). Impact of an entertainment-education television drama on health knowledge and behavior in Bangladesh: An application of propensity score matching. *Journal of Health Communication, 11*, 301–325.
Galloway, S. (2009). Theory-based evaluation and the social impact of the arts. *Cultural Trends, 18*(2), 125–148.
Landrum, M. B., & Ayanian, J. Z. (2001). Causal effect on ambulatory specialty care on mortality following myocardial infarction: A comparison of propensity score and instrumental variable analyses. *Health Services & Outcomes Research Methodology, 2*, 221–245.
Marcus, P. M., Huang, G. C., Beck, V., & Miller, M. J. (2010). The impact of a primetime cancer storyline: From individual knowledge and behavioral intentions to policy-level changes. *Journal of Cancer Education, 25*(4), 484–489.
Morgan, S. E., Movius, L., & Cody, M. J. (2009). The power of narratives: The effect of entertainment television organ donation storylines on the attitudes, knowledge, and behaviors of donors and nondonors. *Journal of Communication, 59*(1), 135–151.

Murphy, S. T., Hether, H. J., Felt, L. J., & Buffington, S. C. (2012). Public diplomacy in prime time: Exploring the potential of entertainment education in international diplomacy. *American Journal of Media Psychology, 5,* 5–32.

Nahm, S., Le, K., Buffington, S., Schiman, N., Raider, S., & Resko, S. (2010). Engaging youth through entertainment education through partnership and collaboration. *Cases in Public Health Communication & Marketing, 4*(2), 57–78.

National Endowment for the Arts and Arts & Humanities Research Council. (2014). Measuring cultural engagement: A quest for new terms, tools, and techniques.

Posner, M. A., Ash, A. S., Freund, K. M., Moskowitz, M. A., & Shwartz, M. (2001). Comparing standard regression, propensity score matching, and instrumental variables methods for determining the influence of mammography on stage of diagnosis. *Health Services & Outcomes Research Methodology, 2,* 279–290.

Rosenbaum, P. R., & Rubin, D. B. (1983). The central role of the propensity score in observational studies for causal effects. *Biometrika, 70*(1), 41–55.

Rubin, D. B. (2001). Using propensity scores to help design observational studies: Application to the tobacco litigation. *Health Services & Outcomes Research Methodology, 2,* 169–188.

Singhal, A. (2004). Empowering the oppressed through participatory theater. *Investigacion y Desarrollo, 12*(1), 138–163.

Singhal, A., & Rogers, E. M. (1989). Prosocial television for development in India. In R. E. Rice & C. K. Atkin (Eds.), *Public communication campaigns* (2nd ed., p. 331). Newbury Park, CA: Sage.

Singhal, A., & Rogers, E. M. (1999). *Entertainment-education: A communication strategy for social change.* Mahwah, NJ: Lawrence Erlbaum Associates.

TakePart. (2010). Waiting for Superman impact. Retrieved September 12, 2016, from http://www.takepart.com/waiting-for-superman/impact

Winkelmayer, W. C., & Kurth, T. (2004). Propensity scores: Help or hype? *Nephrology, Dialysis, Transplantation, 19,* 1671–1673.

CHAPTER 13

A Ship with Two Prows: Evaluating Professional Development for Contemporary Art Educators

Jessica C. Hamlin and Lois Hetland

Lois: *The Art21 Educators' "evaluation"—I don't know why I put it in quotations—I guess because it seems like it's both more than that and not that—but, at the same time, it really was an evaluation, just not in the way I—or maybe a lot of people in the field—usually think of that term or enterprise.*

Jess: *When we first embarked on discussing your role in helping us evaluate the Art21 Educators program, there was an interesting negotiation which I think set the tone for our work together during the years that you served as a "critical friend" and "participatory evaluator." Initially, I heard your interest in supporting the program's development and working collaboratively rather than as a passive or "objective" observer in the traditional sense of*

J.C. Hamlin
New York University, New York, NY, USA

L. Hetland (✉)
Art Education Department, Massachusetts College of Art and Design, Boston, MA, USA

© The Author(s) 2018
R.S. Rajan, I.C. O'Neal (eds.), *Arts Evaluation and Assessment*,
https://doi.org/10.1007/978-3-319-64116-4_13

297

an evaluator. This synched perfectly with what I was hoping for, as we were continuing to build the program model, working closely with participating teachers to shape the program design and outcomes as we went along.

Lois: *What surprised me most was how my own learning was informed by this evaluation. In previous work in professional development, I had looked at qualities of effective professional development such as keeping the focus of teacher development on student learning (Newmann, 1996; Newmann & Wehlage, 1995; Bruner, 1974, 1977, 1996), but evaluation was not a primary research focus of mine. I was initially reluctant, because of what I thought an evaluation was—I was supposed to judge you? But Jess, your idea of a multi-directional flow of influences among the staff, the participants, and the evaluator really transformed this experience into one of genuine learning for all of us. Sure, the evaluation process benefited Art21. The process supported refinement of the program as you conducted it, and the reports I wrote rigorously evidenced the quality of the program, which the Art21 organization needed. But, for me, I learned directly about a quality program, and that allowed me to use my own background in the field to describe a general process that might, I think, contribute more broadly to the field of professional development in education. Time will tell—we've educed a hypothesis. But for me, this experience was one of those win, win, win, win, win, win situations!*

INTRODUCTION

From 2010 to 2012, the authors worked to co-evaluate an arts education program called Art21 Educators. This program began in July of 2009 with six pairs of art teachers from across the USA who spent a week in New York City. Following that intensive orientation, the educators continued professional development by working together virtually throughout the 2009–2010 academic year. The group participated in monthly class meetings in real time on the Safari Live platform, and another asynchronous online networking platform allowed anytime-anywhere participation. Jessica Hamlin was the co-founder and director of the program, and Lois Hetland came on as the collaborative evaluator in the second summer, July of 2010. We have chosen to mirror in this chapter the conversational approach that Jess and Lois used in conducting the evaluation, an informal, iterative dialogue between us as we tried to understand and describe the program and its evolving pieces.

In many ways, conducting this evaluation was like building a ship while already at sea—it was always exciting, but it also felt dangerous at times (would we fall overboard? would the ship sink?). The nature of this challenge wasn't entirely clear to us initially, but over time, we came to realize that the evaluation had to meet the needs of multiple stakeholders: the program staff, the program participants, and the organization's leadership. We came to think of the evaluation as a ship with two prows—in many ways, we needed to head in two directions at once.

These two prows were built concurrently, informing our dialogic process and the ongoing work of the professional development program. One prow pointed toward the program itself. Jess and the Art21 staff intended to build that collaboratively among staff and participants. When Lois came on, she began participant observation and sought to systematically describe the messy, dynamic process as it unfolded. The second prow aimed toward the organization, Art21. The primary product of the organization, the Art21 video series, was created by curators, and they needed to understand and explain the value of this education program to their Board and build support with funders. That spawned the formal evaluation, in which Jess and Lois developed surveys, administered them to participants longitudinally to gather five waves of data, and analyzed and interpreted data from them to demonstrate why the program was valuable.

Jess sat at the center of a maelstrom, sailing the program with her staff and the participants while studying the charts and navigating a course with Lois toward the destination needed by the organization. The two prows of the evaluation were built in turbulent seas, and at first, we didn't see them as distinct. In practice, they were not clearly differentiated; we only began to recognize them as we sought a process that would satisfy several pilots and their navigational needs and assumptions. The purposes were not well-aligned, and we felt that a single evaluation couldn't address them all. The complexity of purposes led us to a multi-methods approach that emerged from confusion, moments of clarity, and constant revision in both evaluation and program development. In the end, somehow, the directions merged, the prows came together, and we learned through them both.

But perhaps we've gotten ahead of ourselves. Let's go back to the beginning to set up some background framing for the program: its importance, how it began, and the form it took.

Jess: In many ways, the nonprofit arts organization Art21 led an important revolution in expanding access to the voices, working methods, and motivations of visual artists today. Through the vision of its founder, independent curator Susan Sollins, Art21 began producing documentary films about contemporary visual artists for PBS in 2001, centered around seeing directly into artists' studios and working lives and hearing about their processes and motivations without a curator or critic as intermediary. Over the years, Art21's mission and programming expanded to include additional film series, a robust online and social media presence, and educational resources and programs. Art21 Educators was one of these programs.

Art21 Educators was designed to go beyond traditional one-off professional development experiences. The program grew from several years of providing one-day workshops and other short-term professional development to art educators where I would come in as an "expert," present my knowledge and expertise about contemporary art and teaching with Art21 films, and leave with a very limited understanding of who our audience was and what kind of impact we made, or could make. We collected workshop evaluations and distributed surveys to teacher audiences to find out how they rated our workshops and used the materials, but as a staff we wanted to do more to support innovative and meaningful teacher practice with the rich resources we knew we had at Art21.

My colleagues and I wanted to know how contemporary artists, speaking directly to teachers and their students through the films, might inspire innovative classroom methods and change classroom cultures. How might contemporary artists serve as creative role models for classrooms? What tools and resources did Art21 have to support innovative teaching in art education and other disciplines? We needed an infrastructure to build our organizational understanding of best practices and to work more closely and over longer periods of time with educators in ways that allowed us to better understand their teaching contexts and their day to day experiences.

These initial curiosities and commitments led the Art21 staff to collect examples of other program models for professional development with teachers; we culled these to respond to our specific needs and capacities as a small staff with a very small budget. Because we were interested in building a responsive model directly with educators, we didn't conceive of a formal evaluation as an external element to the program design. Rather, we wanted an evaluation process that mirrored how we wanted to work with teachers as they shared their work and we shared ours in a mutually responsive learning environment.

With colleagues Joe Fusaro and Marc Mayer, we outlined the general structure of the first intensive, year-long experience for twelve teachers that combined in-person and virtual or long-distance programming. This format allowed us to include educators from across the United States. The experience began with a six-day summer institute in New York City to build community, to provide access to Art21 resources, and to offer supports for teaching with contemporary artists and Art21 films. The program continued throughout the first year with monthly online sessions and the use of a private social networking space where participants posted videos, blogs, and photos to share their teaching and their students' learning. Video was an obvious medium for us, given that Art21's product is video, and without too much thought to what it might catalyze, we gave every participant a small digital camera to record and share teaching practices and use as a tool for self-reflection.

But the needs of the organization seemed to diverge from the organic needs of the program leadership who was developing the model. During the first year, we attempted to address what Art21 needed as an organization by creating a basic survey of participant feedback at the year's end. We used open-ended prompts like "Art21 is..." and "Art21 Educators is..." and more directed questions like "Do you currently teach with contemporary art and artists? If so, name specific artists and describe how you incorporate them within your class," and "This year, how many times did you use video in the classroom? Which videos did you show?" We also had an extensive collection of video footage that participants had shared with us and each other, documenting their efforts to apply new strategies and content in their teaching.

This footage and enthusiastic responses from the teachers to the first survey convinced us that we had launched a unique program that addressed some of our initial intentions. But we also realized that, as a staff, we lacked the specific expertise and objectivity to collect useful and focused information that would help us better understand what was happening in the program and continue improving it as a refined model. We needed someone with outside perspective and experience in professional development, research, and evaluation who could help us gain perspective on what we were doing, support our work within and outside our organization, and respond to organizational pressure to raise funds and brand the program. We needed a set of outside eyes to help sort through our tacit knowledge and the many moving parts, needs of various stakeholders, modes of engagement, and reflective practices embedded in the program. The evaluation needed to address all these expectations while also being responsive to the spirit of inclusiveness and responsiveness of the program's design and facilitation, which positioned participating teachers as co-learners and developers.

We didn't conduct a formal search process to find someone to carry this outside perspective; we just stayed alert to opportunities for a good match. That came when I attended a conference at the Guggenheim Museum on Learning in the Arts near the end of the first year of the program. I was in the audience because the Art21 artist Janine Antoni was presenting her work. But before she spoke, Lois, you shared your research methods for developing the Studio Thinking framework. I remember noting the way you described your approach as being iterative and process-driven. Many things you said that day resonated with what we were looking at and trying to foster in the Art21 Educators program, and I worked up the courage to introduce myself to you. Using the word evaluator to describe what we were looking for seemed like the closest term to describe the work, and so that was where we started. But I think we both quickly realized that we had to examine our assumptions and expectations about that term.

Lois: I remember being cautious about signing on to do this work with you—did I have the time? Did I really want to be an *evaluator*? That was not my area of expertise. But I left that first meeting intrigued about the program and agreed that we should get to know one another and feel our way forward toward possibly working together on an evaluation. I was really curious about the pedagogy you were using and wanted to understand it. At the time, you were preparing for your second summer institute. It seemed like the only way to understand how to work with the group was to experience it directly, so I asked if I could shadow the incoming cohort of teachers at their institute.

Jess: Your interest in jumping in and getting involved with the program generated a great synchronicity right from the beginning. Working collaboratively meshed with our goals as a staff and with the collaborative model we had built. We wanted a fourth team member to contribute to process-oriented thinking who would deepen the work of the program and our ability to tell important and useful stories about it. That was the beginning of what I consider an incredibly important and generative relationship for Art21 Educators and for my own growth. We spent the next two years working together and with the other program facilitators, teacher participants, and organizational staff to better understand the possibilities for this kind of professional development experience and content.

METHODS

Lois: Jess and I entered into this co-evaluation relationship through intuition, feeling trust for each other based on a very tenuous foundation. Jess was clear that she did not want a "judgment evaluation" but, rather, something that reflected the foundational ideas of co-development and all-directions-collaborative-learning among teachers, facilitators, evaluator, and Art21 leadership. There were the several audiences, and though they were not immediately apparent to me, they all had their own goals that would shape how we conducted the evaluation.

Jess: It was years later that Lois and I were able to look at the program with some objective distance and discuss and analyze our work together, and only then could we identify the different levels of simultaneous inquiry that happened in our work together. In the very beginning, program staff and educators loosely conceived of and facilitated the program as a form of participatory action research. We posed questions to each other and the participants, collected anecdotal evidence and advice, revised and refined specific program elements, then repeated the process to continue improving our collective experience and learning. Collaborating with Lois, we were able to more effectively facilitate informal inquiry through participatory observation among staff and participants. Based on what she noticed and her prompts and queries, we all collected and shared anecdotes, observations, and other data about program participation and experiences. This research was informed by the different kinds of sharing and interactions that the program required and helped us see if we were really doing what we said we were doing.

Secondly, we designed the evaluation to support more formal organizational needs. This data-driven evaluation used self-report surveys answered by the participating educators that attempted to formalize what the program achieved for external audiences.

The First Prow: Understanding the Program
Qualitatively

Lois: We began our work together by my attending the second summer institute as a participant observer for an on-the-ground view of what the program was and how it worked. I hoped to begin collecting data toward a thick, rich description of the facilitators' decisions and actions and of the teachers' experiences and responses at the institute and when they returned home, including presentations on practice at their schools, teacher-reports of student responses, and analysis of samples of student work.

In July of 2010, I checked into an NYU dorm on 12th Street in Manhattan with fantastic views uptown before making my way to a gallery in midtown Manhattan where the first institute session—a *Task Party* hosted by Art21 artist Oliver Herring—was about to begin. My schedule only allowed me to stay for two days, but I became so intrigued that I went home to Boston, rearranged things, and immediately returned to New York for the last three days of the institute.

I madly took notes on everything and asked questions non-stop of the participants; of the facilitators (Jess, Mark, and Joe); of the Executive Director, Susan Sollins; of Art21's Associate Curator, Wes Miller, who offered a session on curation; and of Jonathan Munar, Director of Digital Media and Strategy, who helped everyone figure out technical issues with cameras and websites. But most exciting—for me and for the educators, I think—were the meetings during the institute with Art21 artists. Oliver Herring hosted the initial *Task Party* and debrief; we visited Ursula von Rydingsvard's studio in Brooklyn and saw her 60th birthday present from her husband (a backhoe), and we talked with Allan McCollum, who visited with us at MoMA. It was such a thrill to speak personally with these artists, and that made the whole enterprise worthwhile, in my view.

But there was much more going on. I remember being impressed with the non-hierarchical relationships Jess, Joe, and Mark set up with the teachers, as well as their clever structural decisions. They had chosen, for example, to start mid-week, and the facilitators took the weekend off so teachers could see art in New York and let their ideas for curriculum percolate and take form gradually before one-on-one review sessions on Monday. These reviews were followed by more sessions, more individual work, and finally an inspired teacher-sharing session on the closing Wednesday. During these days, I held one-on-one interviews with several participants to find out why they elected to do this program and what they were getting out of it. They all loved it, but I wanted to get beyond the accolades to find out what the teachers thought the program was doing for them *as teachers*. What a week. I was breathless and walking several inches above the ground, and the teachers seemed to feel the same way. Though, technically, I "collected data during participation" and then had ongoing conversations with Jess to analyze it iteratively as the program unfolded, it felt much more personal than that.

After the week in New York, Jess and I discussed my interviews, my notes from the week, and her reflections. From these conversations, we began an iterative process of co-creating a post-institute survey to generate responses from participants about the Institute experience. Every educator responded. There was no control group, since we were simply looking at what this program was and what it wanted to be, and we asked about the extent to which it actually *was* that for these teachers. We began with a loose guiding question:

What happened during the Art21 Educators' institute that led to teachers reporting so many positive changes in their learning, attitudes, and behaviors and to so many perceived benefits by teachers for themselves, their students, and their organizations?

At this time, the intention of the program had not been formally stated—the program's goals were still implicit. Before articulating any program goals explicitly, however, we went back to our general question and refined it to focus the evaluation on our *process* more than on an explanation of participant *outcomes*:

How can we conduct a mentored self-evaluation that (1) names, guides, and mirrors the ongoing development of the Art21 Educators' program and (2) supports the program's improvement as it evolves?

In hindsight, we can see that providing data on program quality for the organization had slipped from our immediate view—we were focused on program development much more than any measures of value or quality.

In addition to ethnography around this somewhat vague question, we also had a wide array of evidence that could be tapped over the course of the following year. There were participants' applications; participants' contributions to the monthly online, real-time sessions that included comments, responses, and presentations; and participants' postings on the asynchronous site, called "The Ning." Archived on that site were ongoing conversations among teacher participants, Art21 facilitators, and myself as the evaluator; selections of student work; selected lesson plans; ongoing conversation threads around emerging topics; responses to assignments; written reflections; postings of photos and videos of teachers' classrooms; and teachers' videoed "confessionals." We tried to take it all in, without any formal analysis. As the program evolved, we saw video become a favorite and powerful learning tool that catalyzed teacher growth in a wide variety of ways, from self-reflection, to peer-sharing, to student learning when students took the cameras from the teachers and used them to demonstrate their own thinking, and to assessment of teacher learning by program staff.

Setting Goals

Lois: We had rich sources of qualitative information, but we also needed a way to quantify and compare experience across different participants and across different cohorts year to year, to assess the qualities of participants' experiences. Jess re-stated the need to develop better surveys, which she saw as a way to gather "objective" data needed to solicit funding and to build institutional support for the program among the Art21 Board and management. Data-driven results would help objectively describe and "prove" the value of what we were coming to understand intuitively from our participation in the program.

But before designing the survey, I pushed to articulate program goals. I was nervous about doing so, because Jess had told me she was interested in my ideas, and not my "Project Zero" self. Still, while explicit goals are somewhat counter-cultural to art practice, I believed in their importance based on my work, first as a teacher-participant and then as a researcher, on the Teaching for Understanding research at Harvard's Project Zero in the 1990s (Blythe, 1998; Wiske, 1998).

I thought that the program facilitators needed to articulate publicly— to themselves, the teachers, and the Art21 leadership—what participants were expected to gain from their experience in the program. Such clarity would, I felt, help the Art21 Educators' staff address a wide range of purposes. Goals would support their planning and working together to articulate questions that might lead to new purposes. They would also help participants focus their energies on developing understanding of particular intended purposes. In addition, goals would focus the Art21 leadership on accurately marketing and raising funds to support the program, and goals would help the Art21 Educators' staff and evaluator decide which data sources to mine, work efficiently to co-design surveys, and examine collaboratively the teachers' responses and reported actions relative to these explicitly stated program purposes.

But the development of goals was a lengthy, iterative process that continued even beyond my participation as evaluator. We developed our first stable set of goals in the fall of 2010, after designing the post-institute survey. By early 2011, the goals had evolved to those listed in the left-hand column of Table 13.1; by 2014, ongoing revisions had resulted in the goals in the right-hand column of Table 13.1.

The refinements focused on elements of the program needed by the two different audiences—Art21 Educators' staff and Art21 organizational leadership. The intent wasn't merely to deepen knowledge of contemporary art, artists, and ideas (a need for the program staff), but, rather, to *use Art21 resources* to achieve that (the organization's need). It wasn't just "improving" practice (program), but *supporting innovative practices by using Art21 resources (organization)*. The intention wasn't just reflection and documentation (program), but specifically *how those practices influenced professional practices, student learning, and classroom culture (organization)*. And it wasn't merely enhancing participation in the professional

Table 13.1 Art21 Educators program goals

Program goals, 2011	*Revised program goals, 2014*
1. Expand and *deepen teachers' knowledge and views* about contemporary art, artists, and ideas	Use Art21 and other resources to develop *greater knowledge of and expanded perspectives* about contemporary art, artists, and themes
2. Expand and improve teachers' *practices of curriculum development and teaching* with and about contemporary art and video	Support *innovative teaching and learning across disciplines* using Art21 and experiences with contemporary art, artists, and themes
3. *Improve teachers' approaches to documenting and reflecting* on changes in student learning and classroom culture	*Support documentation and reflection practices* that capture how Art21 and contemporary art, artists, and themes are influencing professional practices, student learning, and classroom culture
4. Enhance teachers' attitudes, approaches, and commitment to working in a *professional learning community* with other educators	Cultivate a dynamic and supportive *learning community of educators* engaged with contemporary art, artists, and themes, using Art21 resources and strategies to support their work

learning community (program), but, rather, *cultivating a community around Contemporary art, artists, and ideas that would model ways to use Art21 resources and strategies (organization).* The differences were subtle, but they clarified our thinking and the data we gathered.

The Second Prow: Understanding the Program Through Survey Data

Now, let's return to mid-fall of 2010. With draft goals in hand, we began our first task: designing a mid-year survey for participants' self-assessments to track change over time. The surveys served as a primary data source for final reports to inform the Art21 organization and management at the end of the program year, and participants filled them out three times: at mid-year, at end-of-year one, and at end-of-year two, for alumni who continued to participate beyond the single year. We asked several types of questions so that we could triangulate different kinds of information: short answer, anecdotal narrative, frequency data, and constrained choice.

Short answer and anecdotal narrative questions gave us rich, descriptive information to flesh out our qualitative understanding of the teachers' experiences. For example, "How has the Art21 Educators' program helped you develop new competencies and confidence with contemporary art?"

Sample answer 1: *The Art21 Educators' program has made me more confident teaching about contemporary art because now I can speak with experience. I have met some of these artists first-hand and been able to discuss their work. I have colleagues from all over the United States that I can get input from about my ideas for the classroom.*

Sample answer 2: *Coming from a very traditional artistic background (New Mexico Santero/a traditions) and having a strong art history background, I used to have a hard time connecting with contemporary art. A lot of times I did not understand it or thought it was too "out there" to connect. I also had a hard time judging contemporary art and its importance. Because it's so new, it's hard to tell if it will pass the test of time in its significance. When I began watching Art21 videos, hearing the artists talk about their ideas and work helped me to understand it better, and I found some amazing connections with these artists and their work. I was able to see how the work of contemporary artists relates to the history of art in general, but also tradition. I think I became more open to contemporary art.*

We used frequency questions to count how often teachers used various resources and platforms (e.g., Which resources: Art21 Web Exclusives, the PBS Videos, Educator Guides, Art21 Companion Books, Art21 Blog; Which Reasons for Use: Inspiration, Planning Curriculum, Teaching).

Constrained-choice questions helped us assess attitudes that teachers had about program elements and resources. Using a five-point Likert scale (1 [low], Strongly Disagree; 2, Disagree; 3, Somewhat Agree; 4, Agree; 5, Strongly Agree), we assessed such qualities as the following:

1. Teachers' feelings of confidence or inclination to teach in particular ways (e.g., planning curriculum based on a big idea or concept instead of being driven by a specific skill, foregrounding students as producers of content, using video and online resources in the classroom, making connections between contemporary artistic practice and teaching practice, filming and documenting classroom and teaching practice, reflecting on and changing the way I teach).
2. Teachers' satisfaction with Art21 Staff interactions (e.g., "are open and available to me"; "offer constructive and helpful feedback").
3. How well different program structures worked for them (i.e., online sessions, Ning, Office Hours). Other constrained-choice questions assessed teachers' satisfaction with the program, asking, for example, how well it was able to "Expose teachers to a wide range of artist/educator practices"; "Promote documentation of diverse teaching practices through video, photography, and written narratives"; "Establish useful connections between the artistic process and teaching process"; or "Encourage teachers to reflect on and share curriculum planning methods and implementation strategies that utilize Art21 resources."

The co-established goals were critical to keeping the surveys focused and allowed us to group questions around each goal within sections. The questions themselves grew out of our constant monitoring and discussions about how the program was working for participants, based on what they shared online and on staff reflections about interactions. Because we had focused the different goals on issues of relevance to both Art21 Educators staff and Art21 organizational leadership, sequencing the surveys around the goals better enabled us to gather both quantitative and qualitative data that addressed the multiple needs. However, the tensions between those purposes and expectations continued.

We were able to make qualitative comparisons over time based on responses that indexed the impact of the program on attitudes and practices. We made connections between the quickly sketched before- and post-institute surveys and the goals-organized design of the middle-, end-, and one-year post program surveys. As the third cohort entered in summer 2011, we administered the survey as a baseline about participants' attitudes and practices *before* beginning the program, allowing us to be more certain that changes were the result of experiences in the program.

Quantitative analysis centered on tabulating the Likert scale questions to uncover central tendencies (means and ranges) and change over time in different categories of interest (e.g., competency in using the video cameras, uses of different virtual and physical resources, working with local artists, teachers taking students to museums and/or visiting museums themselves). We represented the results in graphs to show changes from one wave of data collection to the next. Changes over time also appeared in the qualitative data (narrative answers) as patterns of responses that explained the quantitative responses. For the reports, we selected from the narrative comments linked to the quantitative data to flesh out stories told by measures of central tendency in the quantitative analysis. We also checked other data sources—online participation on the Ning, comments in the real-time monthly sessions, video posts from teachers' classrooms, and conversations with Art21 staff—to corroborate or refute the numerical ratings.

In addition to the surveys, I continued to act as a participant observer in the monthly online sessions and periodically reviewed content on the asynchronous site where teachers posted. Jess and I talked at least twice a month to discuss all the different elements of the program and the individual work of participants. I remember these conversations as the most significant element of the evaluation for me personally, even though they were the least planned part of our work together. Our extended conversations helped us understand all the moving parts of the program in relation to each other. We used the time not only to process and plan for each of the program components, but to further refine the evaluation tools, motivated as we were by wanting to develop our own understanding (the perspective of program developers) along with creating accurate descriptions of what was happening (the perspective of the organization).

Jess: In future years of the program, we continued to revise and implement the evaluation tools developed collaboratively with Lois, even after she was no longer our formal evaluator and had evolved into an informal critical friend of the program. She had given us the resources to conduct our own evaluation process and our findings continued to support the evolution of the program and contribute to official reporting and fundraising needs—fulfilling both the external and internal functions we needed from them. It was only through the difficult process of following the two different directions of our evaluative prows that we managed to develop a system that worked!

RESULTS

Lois: Three levels of outcomes emerged from the data as we analyzed it. The first level, which happened while "steering the boat," was for the Art21 Educators' program facilitators. They used the evolving trends and guidance to refine and improve the program "in the moment." The second level was for Art21's organization and leadership, including staff outside of education and the Executive Director. Art21 leaders used the final reports that synthesized quantitative data and narrative responses so that they themselves could understand the value of the educators' program and then use that understanding to educate the board, supporters, and funders. A third level arose from Lois's orientation toward the field of education—the likely readers of this chapter. By examining the qualities of *this* program and developing criteria for judging its quality and the impacts synthesized from the quantitative and qualitative data, we began to see a theory emerging that might generalize to the broader field of education, to support the creation and/or evaluation of other professional development programs.

Internal Applications: Results for Program Facilitators, Participants, and Evaluator

Jess: For the Art21 Educators program staff and participants, the lines between program evaluation and program facilitation blurred. Lois's contributions and her ongoing support for self-reflection and use of more formal evaluation tools helped us all understand what we were doing and make adjustments as we went along. Reflecting on our work together, ostensibly to design and analyze data from the survey, became an important opportunity to add new layers of understanding about the reciprocal influences of learning through the program and our participatory evaluation. We created the figure below as we wrote this chapter to better

Fig. 13.1 Diagram of roles, relationships, and fields of influence for Art21 Educators evaluation

describe to each other how we saw the key players in the Art21 Educators program influencing each other and, by extension, participating in the survey evaluation, the program development, and the collective understanding of the program as a whole within the field of professional development (Fig. 13.1).

The diagram illustrates the core collaborators (program staff, evaluator, program participants, and organizational leadership) having two-way dialogues, with the exception of program participants and organizational leadership, who did not communicate directly. Participants spread their learning to their students and colleagues; organizational leadership shared theirs with funders and the board. Over the course of the evaluation, we refined our intuitive appreciation of how all voices mattered in the design and outcomes of the evaluation and program and described our understanding in this model.

It was only over time that we recognized that everyone needed to talk and listen to everyone else to develop fully our collective understandings. Refining how and why this could happen and averting a cacophony of all voices all the time became the focus of our work together. This model of 360 degrees of listening also built productive understanding of our program goals. The web of interrelated communication, and by extension accountability, was central to the program's success. The Art21 Educators staff and the evaluator genuinely believed that everyone learned from everyone else. The participants came to understand this, too; as they worked together and with the program staff and evaluator over the year, they saw their ideas and opinions shaping the direction of the program.

One way this collaborative communication process was initiated was through questions that Lois posed to us as staff, and her ability to use our answers to help refine the language we used about our work deepened and clarified what we thought we were doing and what we wanted to be doing. Sometimes these questions were broad and probing such as, "What kinds of expertise do you want to support in participating teachers?" Other times her questions prodded us to confront uncomfortable issues we weren't addressing: "Is program diversity important to you, and why are there not more teachers of color participating?"

Inevitably, we would bring these questions back to the teachers through individual conversations or more public forums to generate a clearer, collective understanding. Transparency—our shared effort to be as honest and inclusive as possible with participants about how and why we were working the way we were, making the changes we did to improve, or trying the new approaches we explored—became a signature strategy we used as a staff to share our own learning from the evaluation process and involve participants in building the program with us. In this way we cultivated shared expectations for understanding and improving the program and also modeled a way that a culture of transparency and shared responsibility might transform classroom environments.

The difficult effect of this focus on transparency lay in exposing our own uncertainties as a staff. As a result of continually refining our program goals, they became clearer and stronger through the years, but we also felt some reservations when sharing those revised goals with participants in the midst of our work together. We worried that it might seem as if we didn't know what we were doing and that, by extension, the work was less professional or less valid than if we had started from the very beginning with one set of goals and stuck with them, regardless of their integrity. These were insecurities born of an understanding of traditional "objective" and "scientific" evaluation that, in the end, I am certain would have provided far less useful data than the messy, complex, dynamic, and ultimately productive process we all contributed to. In work as difficult as teaching, modeling the process of making a good effort and then refining that over and over seemed as important as anything else that might be learned, so we stayed the course and took the risks.

In addition to the impact of our ongoing dialogue and culture of transparency, the more formal surveys that we developed to solicit and measure the program against its stated goals yielded important insights for the program itself about a range of program components and about the satisfaction and clarity with which participants were able to engage with or access the information or resources they needed. Not only could we track, for example, how frequently teachers were utilizing *Art21 Educator Guides* in their curriculum planning, but we could also gauge their confidence in using Art21 films and contemporary artists in the classroom over time, and we could see the data at different points of the program and across several years of participation. We also gained insights about specific program components such as the summer institute, online sessions, and the Ning (the asynchronous, social networking site), where teachers posted their work. In the second and third years of the program, the evaluations made it clear that the online sessions were not as productive or robust as participants wanted them to be. None of the staff came with online facilitation skills, and we were learning by doing. After swallowing hard on the honest participant feedback from surveys, we were able to regroup and tether our planning back to our program goals while building better strategies to facilitate the online sessions with more relevant content and modes of engagement.

Multiple Applications: Teachers, Students, Colleagues, Art21 Leadership, Board, Funders, Program Staff, and Evaluator

Lois: The evaluation had to serve internal and external program functions simultaneously—directly influencing the facilitation of the program itself while also serving larger organizational expectations for validation and proof of achievement. While these divergent needs did create the opportunity to look closely and analytically at what was happening both within and as a result of the program, it was difficult to turn attention to the survey analysis when the dialogue was such a fulfilling use of our limited time. But we had to consider each of the stakeholders and what they needed from the evaluation. In the end, I produced an official report for each year; lengthy tomes that included basic descriptions of the program, quantitative data from the year, qualitative data from participant narratives, and a reflective analysis of the effects of the year-long experience not only for the 12–14 educator participants, but also for their students and teaching sites, for the staff facilitating the program at Art21 Educators, and for the evaluator. I worried that no one would read them, but was proved wrong!

Jess: Beyond supporting the ongoing facilitation of the program, Lois's final reports helped us identify larger trends and important "bigger picture" outcomes difficult to see at the granular level of program facilitation—and important in relation to the wider field of art education, and perhaps educational practice and professional development more broadly. The reports summarized the conversations and knowledge we as a staff had been looking at over the course of the year, but they also helped us look at the outcomes and learning in new ways, with the advantage of time and a little distance. Hidden trends and ideas surfaced that allowed us to talk about our work in new ways. These findings were useful to us as program staff, but they also served as the major headlines that the organization wanted to share with organizational supporters, including board members and funders.

Lois: In addition to affirming that the program effectively supported teachers in enhancing and building their teaching practices according to our program goals, the evaluation reports supported claims that participating teachers valued the changes that they experienced and were able to use what they learned to support their students in ways that they believed to be effective. The program had legs!

Teachers described a strong positive influence not only on their own practices, but also on student learning and classroom culture generally (one of our explicit program goals). The data also show the benefit to teachers in terms of reflexive learning in mutually supportive relationships with knowledgeable, trusted colleagues. Regardless of individual differences, all participating teachers made changes that they valued as important and attributed to the program. The Art21 Educators' Program worked effectively across the full spectrum of this group's interests and abilities.

Jess: With these larger thematic findings, Art21 leadership and board members were able to gain a deeper understanding of the program's impact and a fuller appreciation for the program, building important organizational buy-in. We as education staff developed clearer language and specific narratives to share with colleagues to help them understand the work we were doing. People with whom I had worked for years finally were able to say, "Oh that's what you're doing!" As a program staff, we could tell better stories about why the work mattered to us and should matter to the entire organization.

More broadly, the evaluation results and data helped the Executive Director and those tasked with fundraising to communicate the significance of the program to funders and other supporters outside the organization. The traditional evaluation outcomes of "objective" data and "proven" outcomes helped to underscore the value of the program and support the search of funding for its sustainability. In addition, the teachers' quotations gave the program evaluation a more personal validity and helped underscore our own organizational language about it. These quotations offered insight into the program's diverse personal impact on participating educators, as these two examples show:

I have reflected on my teaching practice more intensely than I have ever done before. I have a totally different viewpoint on what it means to be an art teacher than I had prior to Art21 Educators. I have learned a lot about technology and how to use it in meaningful ways not just some "gimmicky" art project, but how to truly integrate it into my teaching practice. I've also gained a lot of new resources (and friends!) where I can now turn to ask questions or get feedback.

I have more respect for Contemporary artists and my mind is more open to contemporary art and actions, objects, etc.... I am able to connect more easily with artists' ideas and experiences by hearing them talk about their work, seeing them working on it. Before it seemed like contemporary art and artists were out of touch to me. How do you know which contemporary artists are good? My familiarity with contemporary art and artists as a result of Art21 has given me my own criteria and ideas for considering all contemporary work.

In many ways, the evaluation suggested that the program was worth even more than any of us had claimed.

Conclusion: A Theory of Change

My head's still sort of spinning from this whole experience, and I'm still digesting a lot of the info, but I think this will fundamentally change the way I teach for the rest of my life, and to me—a year's worth of self doubt is a small price to pay if it makes me a better teacher.

Lois: What general processes cause change and make teachers more effective in ways that help their students learn better? The literature describes clear patterns that answer this question generically (Day and Sachs, 2004; McLaughlin and Talbert, 2006; Schön 1984, 1990; US Department of Education, 2010). While what happened in the Art21 Educators' program is unique to that program, we made connections to broader professional development practices to begin looking at our evaluation results as a potentially generalizable process that could be tested in other contexts. Intuitively, we began to feel that Jess's view of the program as a complex causal web of interactions linking reciprocal professional development among teachers, organizational and program staff, and a university evaluator had something important to contribute to the field at large. We began to see the specifics of this evaluation as a research project whose outcome was a theory—a theory of change that could be tested as a model for the field of teacher professional development more generally.

The theory was built from the specifics of the Art21 Educators' program, but it defines categories of inputs and outcomes that operate interactively and that might operate generally across diverse contexts and programs. The theory is a hypothesis that suggests how the program's system of elements and outcomes worked together to cause change, and these mechanisms might be useful in designing or refining programs of professional development in other contexts. We have illustrated the theory in the table below. There are nine elements in the matrix: three categorical rows representing phases of development (introductory program components, direct classroom outcomes, and indirect outcomes beyond classrooms of participating teachers), and three categorical columns of who/what is affected (teachers, students, and learning settings). We numbered the nine cells left to right and top to bottom to more readily describe their unique qualities. The table can be read across rows to reveal the phases of development, or by columns to reveal who/what is affected (Table 13.2).

The theory reveals general regularities in the stories told in the teachers' unique responses in the Art21 evaluation. Below, we select a few rich anecdotes in which teachers synthesize their thoughts about what the program did and how it did that. By inserting cell numbers into these texts that tie educators' comments to the theory's cells, we illustrate the theory of change in the teachers' own words and show connections among the cells that arise in the teachers' accounts. These connections begin to bridge the critical gap between changing teacher practice and impacting student learning.

The first quotation illustrates all three cells of Column 1, referencing qualitative changes in direct levels of growth in teacher practice over time. Over and over, the educators told similar stories to this one about how the program changed their practice: If they used the Art21 films before, they didn't use them well (cells 1, 4). They mostly did not use the Educator Guides or center their curriculum on big ideas or themes (cells 1, 7). Their participation in the program fundamentally changed their pedagogy around each of these elements (cells 4, 7).

Table 13.2   A theory of change for learning across roles and contexts, based on the Art21 Educators' program evaluation

	Changes in Teacher Learning	Changes in Student Learning	Changes in Learning Settings
A. Program Offerings	Cell 1. Staff of the professional development program transparently model uses of new and familiar resources, tools, and pedagogical practices. (Examples from Art21 include teaching with themes, using suggestions from the Educator Guides to facilitate discussions; ongoing self-reflection, looking strategies, public reviews of draft work.)	Cell 2. Teachers reported using the materials, tools, and practices introduced in the professional development program directly with their students (from the Art21 program, examples include using films of contemporary artists, video cameras in the classroom, discussion prompts).	Cell 3. Professional development program creates a professional community for educators within an intensive, face-to-face summer institute with peer experiences and public critiques, followed by regular, accountable work in an online, asynchronous social network-like site, and in real-time monthly online class sessions. This community models the practices and benefits of a supportive professional community.
B. Changes Evident in Participating Teachers' Classrooms	Cell 4. Teachers and program staff noted changes to teachers' baseline practices. These changes evolve from initial pedagogical explorations based on	Cell 5. Teachers reported changes in student learning of curricular content, as compared to observations and assessments from previous years (i.e., learning is more engaged, thoughtful,	Cell 6. Teachers noted changes in classroom culture that supported learning, as compared to their memories of previous years. They report less didactic, one-way teacher to student teaching; more

(*continued*)

Table 13.2 (Continued)

	and following an intensive summer institute, provoked and demonstrated through monthly assignments and meetings in a year-long, course-like structure.	and in-depth; more personal; more student-initiated)	curricular collaboration among teachers and students, and more student suggestions to teachers; more student-initiated peer teaching and support; more peer discussion, projects, and comfort in public critique.
C. Changes Evident Beyond the Participating Teacher's Classroom	Cell 7. Teachers report broad changes in their practice and philosophy as provoked by their engagement in the professional development (Art21 Educators') Program, demonstrated through teacher-initiated practices and projects.	Cell 8. Teachers report changes in student learning across and beyond disciplines. (Evidence from Art21: the few non-arts teachers in the program describe students bringing non-arts content into their artwork; using art ideas and themes in non-arts classes; initiating projects; and being drawn to interdisciplinary projects.)	Cell 9. Teachers report changes in organizational cultures. Teachers show more confidence as professionals, begin actively influencing school, community, and experiences around field-based issues (for Art21, these were around Contemporary art and art education), and begin to assume roles as educational leaders more generally.

Note: Cells 4–7 are shaded to represent the core evidence and main story of the Art21 evaluation

Last year I used two Art21 artists (and a few other Contemporary artists) for about half my units. Now I try to use a Contemporary artist for almost every unit when possible (cells 1, 4, 7). I have revamped several units to integrate new artists and ideas, but not all (cell 7). If I had more time I would revamp all of my units and throw some out and develop new ones (cell 7). For example, I have been doing the sand painting at the beach for years, but this year, in addition to Goldsworthy, I integrated most of the artists in the Ecology segments into the unit (cells 1, 2, 7) *and then developed a second project for the students so that they could delve further into the themes* (cell 7).

In this example, the theory helps us see a story of teacher change from her initial instruction within the program, through guided practice, to internalization and personal extensions. The theory also reveals connections between teacher change and changes in student learning and/or learning settings. Such relationships are illuminated by narratives that connect elements across rows and columns, linking changes in the teacher practice column to changes in the student learning and learning settings columns.

In this account, one participant begins to link far-reaching changes in her own practice (cell 7) with her participation in learning communities (cells 3, 9)—both in the Art21 Educators program and as a teacher leader in her school.

I think the biggest thing is the way that I feel comfortable applying all of the things I find and learn from all of my experiences (beyond Art21, too) into my classroom (cell 7). *We've done a lot of Professional Developments this year, and although we do address them later in the year, it's not on the consistent level that Art21 does* (cells 3, 4). *But because I have this Art21 experience, I am able to apply things from these PDs and experiences in a meaningful and lasting way* (cell 7). *I think the difference from previous years is that I now have this mindset of continual development of my teaching* (cells 4, 7). *I had it before but not on the deep level I do now. And because of this different mindset, all these new things are sticking for me in ways that they never have before.... [I want to] further develop my understanding of interdisciplinary teaching and apply it to my teaching* (cell 7) *but especially share it in an accessible fashion with other teachers at my school* (cell 9).

In this last anecdote, another participant suggests several indirect effects described in the bottom row of the theory—where practices extend beyond the contexts in which they are learned and begin to transfer broadly to new settings. Although complexity is not in itself a virtue, it is remarkable to see narratives such as this that depict complex interactions among six of the nine cells of the theory.

Transparency is a philosophy that I picked up at the Art21 Educators Institute (cell 1), *and it's now a philosophy that I live by in my classroom* (cell 7). *I reviewed each unit plan with students before we embarked on the unit* (cell 6). *Because I did this, I rarely had students ask me why they were learning a particular concept...* (cell 5). *The students' acceptance was surprising to many of my colleagues* (cell 9) *who complain of consistently being asked to justify what they teach. I think we should justify it; otherwise, education becomes about coercion instead of a need and want to know and do* (cell 7). ...*[The students] acknowledge their acquiring this knowledge and skill-set has value* (cell 5), *value that I explicitly communicate to them up front and later ask them to ponder* (cells 7, 8).

The theory of change helps us see beyond a strictly quantitative or qualitative perspective, synthesizing these different forms of knowing to generate a more expansive picture of the impacts of professional development programming. Like ripples in a pool, the theory of change shows the interactions among changes in teacher learning, student learning, and larger classroom culture. The results imply that learning through professional development can go beyond individual participant transformations to inform long-term, interactive, and participant-driven professional learning communities—which can be much more significant than we ever originally anticipated.

Although the Art21 Educators' program is small and focuses on a specialized area of curriculum and instruction with and about contemporary art, artists, and ideas, its influence could be quite broad. In addition to the teacher-leaders whose development it nurtures (and that is no small thing given the need for practical leadership in the field of art education), analysis of this carefully evolved and executed program also offers the field of educational reform this theory of change. This theory has implications for professional development within and beyond the field of art education.

Jess: Many organizations conduct institutes or intensives for educators— such programs occur in museums, community centers, schools, institutions of higher education, or independent collaborative initiatives that form professional learning communities across subjects and contexts. Cells 1, 2, and 3 could guide the planning and evaluation of effective programs. If such programs extend interactions or employ distance learning in collaborative and/or long-term relationships and resource development, the model could guide identification of evidence of change over time by looking at the categories in rows 2 and 3. And if communities of learning are situated within a larger context (a school, a museum, a community organization), then analyzing reflections periodically could serve as a spot-check for how individual teacher learning connects to student and/or group learning. Using this model, professional learning groups can work collectively and effectively toward identifiable goals, engaging in what Lois identified as "staying nimble but systematic" as an approach to collaborative and integrated modes of facilitation, learning, reflection, and evaluation.

Although we initially saw the data-driven assessment as only for the organization's branding and fundraising, and as peripheral to program development, we found that it complemented the more qualitative, lived experiences and understandings we were collecting through our own participation in the program and with each other. The theory of change lets us see these different modes of working in productive dialogue with one another. Often experienced as tension in our own evaluative process, the two prows actually lead to a stronger vessel for a longer journey.

REFERENCES

Blythe, T. (1998). *Teaching for understanding guide*. San Francisco: Jossey Bass.
Bruner, J. S. (1974). *Toward a theory of instruction*. Cambridge, MA: Belknap.
Bruner, J. S. (1977). *The process of education*. Cambridge: Harvard University.
Bruner, J. S. (1996). *The culture of education*. Cambridge: Harvard University.
Day, C., & Sachs, J. (2004). *International handbook on the continuing professional development of teachers*. London: Open University.
McLaughlin, M. W., & Talbert, J. E. (2006). *Building school-based teacher learning communities: Professional strategies to improve student achievement*. New York: Teachers College.
Newmann, F. M. (1996). *Authentic achievement: Restructuring schools for intellectual quality*. San Francisco: Jossey-Bass.
Newmann, F. M., & Wehlage, G. G. (1995). *Successful school restructuring: A report to the public and educators*. Madison, WI: Center on Organization and Restructuring of Schools.
Schön, D. (1984). *The reflective practitioner: How professionals think in action*. New York: Basic.
Schön, D. (1990). *Educating the reflective practitioner toward a new design for teaching and learning in the professions*. San Francisco: Jossey Bass.
U.S. Department of Education, Office of Planning, Evaluation, and Policy Development. (2010). *Evaluation of evidence-based practices in online learning: A meta-analysis and review of online learning studies*. Retrieved June 13, 2013, from http://www2.ed.gov/rschstat/eval/tech/evidence-based-practices/finalreport.pdf
Wiske, M. S. (Ed.). (1998). *Teaching for understanding: Linking research with practice*. San Francisco: Jossey-Bass.

CHAPTER 14

Arts Policy and the Creative Economy

Ivonne Chand O'Neal, Brian Kisida, Laura Smyth, and Rekha S. Rajan

The creative economy has been addressed by a number of chapters in this volume either as a direct topic of discussion or as a related outcome. As arts organizations determine their economic imprint, a number of considerations are raised. In this chapter, the authors bring varied perspectives that focus on the intersection of arts policy and economics through the public policy lens. We discuss the creative economy not just as a concept or outcome; but a process. We will discuss how policy has been influenced by arts evaluation and use two case studies to expound our ideas.

Consider, first, a historic moment in our nation's history: the recognition of the arts and creativity as a *contribution* to the GDP of the United States. July 31, 2013, marks the day that the US Bureau of Economic

I.C. O'Neal (✉)
MUSE Research, LLC, Kensington, MD, USA

B. Kisida
Department of Economics, Truman School of Public Affairs, University of Missouri, Columbia, MO, USA

L. Smyth
California Alliance for Arts Education, Washington, DC, USA

R.S. Rajan
PANCH RESEARCH, LLC, Chicago, IL, USA

© The Author(s) 2018
R.S. Rajan, I.C. O'Neal (eds.), *Arts Evaluation and Assessment*,
https://doi.org/10.1007/978-3-319-64116-4_14

Analysis (BEA) changed the way it measures the contribution of the arts and creativity to the gross domestic product (GDP) (U.S. Department of Commerce, Bureau of Economic Analysis, 2013). This new calculation includes research and development, entertainment, literary and artistic original works as *investment*; not as inputs to production. By including the cost of publishing a book, and producing a play as investment, the BEA now measures these activities' productivity and contribution to economic growth. Figure 14.1 identifies the results from the 2012 estimates of the production of arts and cultural goods, adding more than $698 billion to the US economy, or 4.32% of GDP. Most critical, however, is the message the BEA's plan sends to the public.

By including investment as an asset, not an expense, the Department of Commerce is saying that there is value in the artistic and creative work we do. In other words, it is not just the fruits of our labor that matter, it is also the time, energy, motivation, intellect, and creativity that it takes to create something—the process is just as important as the product.

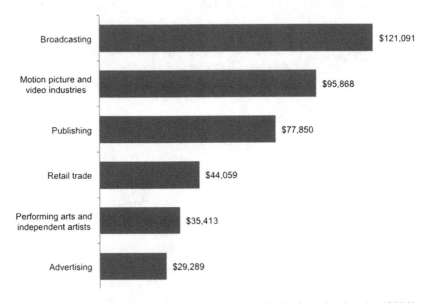

Fig. 14.1   Top contributors to arts and cultural GDP selected industries (2012) (in millions). Source: Arts and Cultural Production Satellite Account (ACPSA), U.S. Bureau of Economic Analysis (2015)

In a resolution to assign economic value to creative efforts, the BEA in collaboration with the National Endowment for the Arts (NEA) released its first-round estimates for a new Arts and Cultural Production Satellite Account in the Fall of 2013. These estimates serve to parse out production for selected arts and cultural industries. This, too, is a largely symbolic action by both agencies to assert that the arts and culture are critical components to consider as contributors to GDP. Surely, the estimates produced will provide arts advocates with ammunition for arguing for more public funding. However, the real value in this and the BEA's new method of valuing intellectual property is in illustrating with numbers, that creativity and the arts contribute to a healthy economy. Equipped with this information, industries can begin to incentivize creative workers and practices through public policies: *Where and how do we begin to increase the impact of the arts and creativity to boost the nation's economy?*

The question is not a trivial one for those involved in arts evaluation. Rather, it is the foundation for the work that we do. Evaluators in any field are certainly driven by a deep affinity for their subject, but such motivation seems especially true for arts evaluators. In fact, informal conversations with people involved in the field of arts evaluation often highlight individual's backgrounds as artists—not just consumers or advocates for the arts. The field of arts evaluation has no shortage of former actors, musicians, dancers, designers, and visual artists who have moved into the evaluation space. At the very least, those involved in arts evaluation typically have a deep love for the arts.

Although some arts industries, such as popular music and film, are under no threat of elimination, those involved with these disciplines feel the constant pressure of budget constraints and must continually make the case to patrons and government funding agencies. This puts arts evaluators in the difficult position of trying to do their best work for a field they love, all the while knowing that resources are scarce and difficult to allocate for evaluation.

As such, the stakes are high for arts evaluation projects to make an impact, especially projects that demonstrate the public value of the arts (Rajan, 2015). How can we continue to provide evidence-based data that shows how students learn and how our communities benefit from artistic experiences? Arts evaluation commonly takes one of three forms: formative evaluations that explore how arts interventions or activities can best be designed; process evaluations that determine the effectiveness of the implementation of an arts program; and impact evaluations that demonstrate the value of the arts, both in terms of the effects on individuals' cognitive functions, abilities, and changing attitudes and the positive outcomes that benefit the community. While the findings from any of these types of arts evaluations can have an effect on policy, impact evaluations are the most likely candidates because they employ the language and methodologies that have come to dominate policy decisions.

Observers have long noted that arts and cultural policy lack a strong presence in the United States (Bradburn, 2013) and that "cultural policy is seen and defined as the outcome of state-driven process" (Paquette & Redeaelli, 2015). Compared to mainstays like education policy, energy policy, health policy, and immigration policy, arts and cultural policy remains underdeveloped and underfunded. Consider that the annual budget for the National Endowment for the Arts, the closest thing the United States has to an agency that deals with arts and cultural policy, is under $150 million. In relative terms, the NEA budget makes up roughly 0.012% of federal discretionary spending and has seen significant cuts in recent years (National Assembly of State Arts Agencies, 2013). The National Endowment for the Humanities operates at a similar funding level. Yet, as a consequence of the 2016 presidential election, calls to truncate funding for the agencies (or the agencies themselves) have resurfaced under the guise of fiscal restraint (Bowley, 2017).

The reaction from arts advocates elicits a natural response: An abundance of testimonials about the values of the agencies and a parade of well-worn yet unsatisfying policy-relevant statistics—all of this with the hopes of demonstrating the value of the arts to an external audience. A board member for Americans for the Arts, the nation's leading arts advocacy organization, issued a letter highlighting the fact that the "arts are a $704 billion industry," account for "4.2% of the nation's annual GDP," and generate a "$24 billion annual trade surplus" (Gioia, 2017). A quick glance at Americans for the Arts' talking points shows more of the same, with additional claims such as "low-income students are 5X more likely to graduate when they receive arts instruction," and "Students with four years of arts education average 100 points better on their SATs."

Notably, these claims focus solely on the extrinsic and monetary benefits of the arts, having little to do with the intrinsic value of the arts. The arts, it seems, only have value if demonstrated in other policy areas, bringing back the argument presented in our first chapter and one that has dominated the arts for much too long. Are the arts important for their intrinsic value, or for how they contribute to other disciplines. Or, does it really matter at all? One of the largest analyses of arts evaluations conducted to date, the Wallace-commissioned *Gifts of the Muse*, concludes just that: The vast majority of arts research relies on justifying the value of the arts by looking for instrumental benefits (McCarthy, Ondaatje, Zakaras, & Brooks, 2004). That is, benefits important for reasons other than by demonstrating the intrinsic values of the arts. Perhaps this is simply a reality that must be dealt with. This presents a challenge to evaluators of the arts, as the arts don't naturally lend themselves to easily quantifiable forms of measurement on outcomes that traditionally drive policy discussions.

As many chapters in this volume demonstrate, the field has just begun to develop outcomes that quantify the intrinsic value of the arts and find ways to measure them in various settings. The case studies that follow highlight the relationships that exist between evaluation, research, and policy. First, at the national level through the example of current work being conducted by the NEA, and second, through the work at the state level conducted by the California Alliance.

The National Endowment for the Arts: A Case Study at the National Level

Given their relatively small budget, the NEA has taken some great strides to improve the state of arts research. The NEA monitors trends in arts education and provides informational support to federal and state government agencies through the Survey of Public Participation in the Arts and accompanying reports. They are also working with Americans for the Arts on the State Policy Pilot Program (ten states are currently participating), to provide technical assistance to states to advance state-level education in ways that support arts education.

The NEA also directly funds a number of research grants. The Research: ArtWorks grant opportunity, now in its fifth year, supports research that investigates the value and impact of the arts—a decidedly policy-oriented task. Evidence of this trend is seen in the projects that have been funded over the past few years, many of which consist of interdisciplinary teams of researchers in the arts, public health, medical, and statistical fields (see Rajan, Rajan, Manning & Evans, 2016 as a sample project funded from this grant). In 2016, they added larger awards to the ArtWorks: Research lineup by introducing a new track to specifically fund experimental and quasi-experimental research projects to demonstrate the causal impacts of the arts. This year also saw the launch of another new initiative to support

NEA Research Labs—partnerships grounded in social and behavioral science to produce empirical insights about the health benefits of the arts.

A similar example of ingenuity is the NEA's Task Force on the Arts and Human Development, an interagency task force of 20 federal agencies that explored how to strengthen research in the arts (e.g., stronger statistical methodology, longitudinal data sets) and demonstrate the impact of arts participation on the human condition, across the lifespan. In a particularly promising development, in 2016 the NEA's Task Force worked with the US Department of Education's National Center for Education Research to introduce "Arts in Education" as a funding category for the first time ever. For too long, evidence regarding the benefits of arts education has lagged behind that of other subjects, and funding has been a major hurdle for keeping the arts in our schools. This inclusion will provide long-needed research support to empirical investigations into how K-12 arts programs and policies improve educational outcomes. The US Department of Education's annual budget exceeds $100 billion, which makes partnerships with other agencies a natural way for arts research to have more of an impact.

Funding research is a wise strategy for the NEA to leverage their limited budget toward greater influence in the policy arena. If evaluation and research can demonstrate that the arts have certain benefits, the goal is that investments in the arts from government, nonprofit, and private entities could increase.

For those conducting evaluation with the hopes of moving policy, the task relies on adopting a long-term perspective, as well as a good amount of faith in the power of evidence. In a world which seems to increasingly hold truth as a relative construct and deals in alternative facts, the job of the evaluator is as important as ever, as we see in the following example.

The California Alliance for Arts Education: A Case Study at the State Level

As an advocacy organization, the job of the California Alliance for Arts Education (the Alliance) is to tell stories and connect people with resources that help them advance access to arts education. The Alliance cannot and should not be in the business of evaluating what works, as its primary purpose and expertise is in advocating for the arts through public policy, and the building of strategic partnerships. However, access to high quality impact evaluation and arts research is essential to making the case for new or better policies supporting arts in education.

In 2011, in the wake of a Los Angeles study that revealed a significant gap in access to arts education among low-income students, the Alliance learned that schools in Los Angeles County were not being permitted to use Title I funds—the federal funds designed to close the achievement gap for high-poverty schools—to support any arts-related activities. Despite ample evidence of the positive effects of arts education, and the existence of federal guidelines indicating the permissibility of using Title I funds to support effective arts programming, somehow the message— and the evidence—was not getting through at the state or local levels where decisions get made. At the state level, communication was hampered by both a lack of awareness of the evidence and competing priorities, and at the local level, there was a fear of change and reprisal that kept the information from reaching its target audience. Examining that policy paradox led us to an initiative that, five years on, is still teaching us a great deal about how advocacy, policy, evaluation, and partnership can lead to actual change in the education ecosystem.

Early meetings with the State Department of Education revealed that, in spite of federal guidance, many education leaders were unaware of the impact evaluations and research that showed the effectiveness of arts strategies in improving student achievement. Through the use of the website, ArtsEdSearch (developed by the Arts Education Partnership as a clearinghouse of evidence-driven research on the impact of the arts in education), we were able to find resources with the language and evidence that state officials needed. For example, we included how integrating the arts with other subjects increases student learning and achievement (Podlozny, 2000), that sustaining arts integration increases students' cognitive flexibility (Chand O'Neal, 2014), and that both integrated and non-integrated arts instruction can increase student engagement, improve school culture and climate, and increase parent and community involvement (Stevenson & Deasy, 2005).

Title I compliance language clearly states that funds can only be used for strategies that improve student achievement, either through direct instruction or addressing the factors that lead to student achievement. Being able to use the language of Title I specifically to talk about successful arts strategies, in addition to continued traditional advocacy pressure through phone calls and meetings, created a key moment in our conversation with state officials. It led to the issuing in June 2012 of a signed letter from the then-Deputy Secretary of Education, Deborah Sigman, outlining the case for the appropriate uses of Title I funding to support arts education. We then used our partnership with the Department of Education to create a roadmap for planning, developing, implementing, and evaluating programs utilizing arts strategies to achieve Title I goals.

In the wake of the passage of the Every Student Succeeds Act (ESSA) in 2016 and the rationalization of evidence-based evaluation and research requirements for all federal programs, we went back to the federal Department of Education for clarity and guidance. We wanted to be sure that the assistance we were offering to districts and schools was still in alignment with federal practice and interpretation of the law. The message we received was that the Department was encouraging more, not less, flexibility for Title I programs, with the stipulation that any program must still meet the rigorous evaluation requirements to justify expenditures. Coupled with the fact that the new law's definition of a "well-rounded education" that each state must provide its students now included the arts twice in its definition, we felt armed to go back to the California State Department of Education to request an update. We also worked closely with the department to identify and highlight the very best arts evaluation research examples to create sample school plans for Title I arts programming, publishing five examples of the school plans on our website in September 2016. In February 2017, the State Department of Education released an updated letter, signed by Deputy Superintendent Keric Ashley, that clarified and expanded the ways in which federal funds could be used to support research-based, effective arts education strategies.

A carefully constructed paper trail may not look like a policy revolution, but, in the end, our goal was to make arts education in the context of Title I commonplace. The cumulative evidence grounded in impact evaluation and research would give education leaders the flexibility to make a programmatic choice for their school that may naturally include the arts as an essential component of educational equity (Chand O'Neal, Walker, & Smyth, 2017).

WHERE DO WE GO FROM HERE?

Our perceptions of evaluation, especially arts evaluation, are still evolving. The current culture is impeded by fear, uncertainties, the hesitation to try something new, and to protect the arts as a vital part of our society. We are still questioning, arguing, and justifying how artistic experiences influence human development in every stage of life. However, the compelling evidence of program evaluations and recent policy changes, coupled with groundbreaking research, have given us the opportunity to change the conversation.

The varied contributions, perspectives, and evaluations presented in this volume hopefully challenged, engaged, and augmented your understanding of arts evaluation as a field of study and cemented the need for arts advocacy in our lives. While much of the discussion in the following years may continue to rest on the topic of including the arts for their intrinsic value, or debating whether they serve a greater purpose, our collaborative goal as authors, researchers, artists, and evaluators is really to establish a place for the arts in our schools and communities.

Those familiar with the musical *EVITA*, by Sir Andrew Lloyd Webber, will recognize the subtitle of this final section of our chapter (and volume) as taken from the opening line of a song he wrote for the film version of his successful Broadway musical. The question elicits many emotional and open-ended responses: What is the next step for evaluators in the arts? What is our role? Are we researchers, or advocates, or both?

Ultimately, the inclusion of the arts in our lives is our choice. And, it is important to acknowledge that *it is a choice*—regardless of funding, policy, or research and evaluation (Rajan, 2012). Certainly, the arts are a part of everyday experiences: we listen to music in the car, watch our favorite shows in the evening, dance with our loved ones, and enjoy new exhibits and performances within the community. The fact remains that the more evidence-based data we can provide to funders, stakeholders, leaders, and policy-makers, the more likely we are to be given an opportunity to evaluate the impact of the arts for what they are worth (for art's sake, or otherwise). And more importantly, we are then able to lift the burden we often bear as patrons and advocates of the arts, to leave behind a need to justify our field and to explore, experience, evaluate, assess, and simply love the work we do.

References

Arts and Cultural Production Satellite Account (ACPSA). (2015). U.S. Bureau of Economic Analysis. Retrieved from www.arts.gov/artistic-fields/research-analysis/arts-data-profiles/arts-data-profile-6

Bowley, G. (2017). Can programs that help the military save the federal arts agencies? *The New York Times*, March 27. Retrieved from https://www.nytimes.com/2017/03/27/arts/design/nea-walter-reed-military-art-therapy.html?_r=0

Bradburn, N. (2013). *An investigation into the feasibility of establishing an arts and culture research network*. National Endowment for the Arts. Retrieved from http://arts.gov/sites/default/files/Research-Art-Works-NORC.pdf

Chand O'Neal, I., Walker, E., & Smyth, L. (2017). *Arts research to policy pipeline: The impact of policy on arts education in title 1 schools*. For presentation at the 31st American Evaluation Association Meetings, Washington, DC.

Chand O'Neal, I. (2014). *Selected findings from the John F. Kennedy Center's Arts in Education Research Study: An impact evaluation of arts-integrated instruction through the Changing Education through the Arts (CETA) program*. Washington, DC: The John. F. Kennedy Center for the Performing Arts.

Gioia, M. (2017). Americans for the arts responds to possible national endowment for the arts cuts. *Playbill*, May 7. Retrieved from http://www.playbill.com/article/americans-for-the-arts-respond-to-possible-national-endowment-for-the-arts-cuts

McCarthy, K., Ondaatje, E., Zakaras, L., & Brooks, A. (2004). *Gifts of the Muse: Reframing the debate about the benefits of the arts*. The Wallace Foundation.

National Assembly of State Arts Agencies. (2013). Fast facts about the national endowment for the arts. Retrieved from http://www.nasaa-arts.org/Research/GrantMaking/NEAStateFactSheet_2016_ID.pdf

Paquette, J., & Redeaelli, E. (2015). *Arts management and cultural policy research*. New York: Springer.

Podlozny, A. (2000). Strengthening verbal skills through the use of classroom drama: A clear link. *Journal of Aesthetic Education, 34*(3–4), 239–276.

Rajan, R. S. (2012). Who needs the arts? *Focus on Teacher Education. ACEI, 11*(4), 6–8.

Rajan, R. S. (2015). Artistic assessment: Strategies for documenting learning in the arts. *Journal of the Grant Professionals Association, 13*(1), 31–37.

Rajan, K. B., Rajan, R. S., Manning, L. K., & Evans, D. (2016). Aging audiences: Association of live, performance attendance and cognitive decline in a biracial population study. *Journal of Aging and Health*, 1–13. https://doi.org/10.1177/0898264316682290

Stevenson, L., & Deasy, R. J. (2005). *Third space: When learning matters*. Washington, DC: Arts Education Partnership.

U.S. Department of Commerce, Bureau of Economic Analysis "2013 News Release Schedule". (2013, June 6). Retrieved from URL.

Index[1]

[1] Note: Page numbers followed by "n" refer to notes

© The Author(s) 2018
R.S. Rajan, I.C. O'Neal (eds.), *Arts Evaluation and Assessment*,
https://doi.org/10.1007/978-3-319-64116-4

333